MIND-REACH

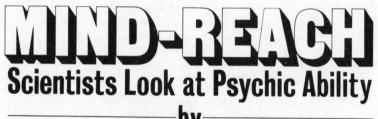

MIND-REACH
Scientists Look at Psychic Ability

by

RUSSELL TARG

and

HAROLD E. PUTHOFF

Introduction by MARGARET MEAD
Foreword by RICHARD BACH

DELACORTE PRESS / ELEANOR FRIEDE

ACKNOWLEDGMENTS

Excerpt from *Green Eggs and Ham* by Dr. Seuss used by permission of the publisher, Random House Inc.

Excerpt from "Prematurity and Uniqueness in Scientific Discovery" by Gunther Stent. Copyright © 1972 by Scientific American, Inc. All rights reserved.

Library of Congress Cataloging in Publication Data

Targ, Russell.
  Mind-reach.

  Includes bibliographical references.
    1. Psychical research—Case studies. I. Puthoff,
Harold E., joint author. II. Title.
BF1029.T37   133.8   76-26160
ISBN 0-440-05688-8

Manufactured in the United States of America
First printing

Without going outside,
  you may know the whole world.
Without looking through the window,
  you may see the ways of heaven.

TAO TE CHING
Lao Tsu, sixth century B.C.

For Devin, Nicholas, Alexander, and Elisabeth, whose energies will help to shape our emerging view of ourselves; and to Joan and Adrienne, who stood by us through it all, with love, encouragement, and uncommon good sense.

ACKNOWLEDGMENTS

The authors wish to express their appreciation to those who have provided financial support for their research. These include Mrs. Judith Skutch of the Parasensory Foundation, and Mr. George W. Church, Jr., of the Science Unlimited Research Foundation who have assisted us from the very beginning. Others who have helped us to make this work possible include Mr. Richard Bach, Dr. Edgar D. Mitchell of the Institute of Noetic Sciences, Mr. Werner Erhardt of the Foundation, Mrs. Eileen Coly of the Parapsychology Foundation, the National Aeronautics and Space Administration, and Dr. George Pezdirtz, who was right in insisting that there was a way.

We also wish to acknowledge the vision and the willingness to take risks in a new and controversial field that has been displayed by the management of Stanford Research Institute: Mr. Bonnar Cox, Director of the Division of Information Science and Engineering; and Mr. Earle Jones, Director of the Electronics and Bioengineering Laboratory; and Mr. Ronald Deutsch, SRI's public information officer, who was the first to propose that we write this book to describe our work to the public. Each of these men has at one time or another placed his personal and professional integrity on the line in support of our efforts to pursue this research.

Acknowledgments

In addition, the authors have benefited greatly from their many discussions with Dr. Robert Ornstein of the Langley-Porter Neuropsychiatric Institute in San Francisco, Dr. Ralph Kiernan of the Department of Neurology at the Stanford University Medical Center, Dr. Charles Tart of the Department of Psychology at the University of California, Davis, and SRI consultant Dr. Arthur Hastings.

Finally, our principal indebtedness is to our subjects and tireless companions Ingo Swann, Pat Price, Uri Geller, Hella Hammid, Duane Elgin, Phyllis Cole, and Marshall Pease, without whose patience and energy none of this work would have been possible.

PREFACE

Discoveries of any great moment in mathematics and other disciplines, once they are discovered, are seen to be extremely simple and obvious, and make everybody, including their discoverer, appear foolish for not having discovered them before.
—G. Spencer Brown, *Laws of Form*

Scientists have long attempted to determine the truth or falsity of claims for the existence of so-called psychic, or paranormal functioning; that is, the ability of certain individuals to perceive and describe data not discerned by any known sense. During a lengthy series of experiments conducted in the Electronics and Bioengineering Laboratory of Stanford Research Institute for the past three years, we have been investigating those facets of human perception that appear to fall outside the range of well-understood perceptual or processing capabilities.

The primary achievement of this research has been the demonstration of high-quality "remote viewing": the ability of experienced and inexperienced volunteers to view, by means of mental processes, remote geographical or technical targets such as roads, buildings, and laboratory apparatus.

Our accumulated data from over a hundred observations with

more than twenty subjects indicate the following:[1] The phenomenon is not limited to short distances; electrical shielding does not appear to degrade the quality or accuracy of perception; most of the correct information given by subjects is of a nonanalytical nature pertaining to shape, form, color, and material rather than to function or name, suggesting that information transmission under conditions of sensory shielding may depend primarily on functioning of the brain's right hemisphere; and finally, the principal difference between experienced and inexperienced volunteers is not that the inexperienced never exhibit the faculty, but rather that their results are simply less reliable. This indicates to us that remote viewing is probably a latent and widely distributed perceptual ability.

Although we do not yet understand the precise nature of the information channel that couples remote events with human perception, certain ideas in information theory, quantum theory, and neuropsychological research appear to bear directly on the issue. As a result, our assumption is that the phenomenon will be found consistent with modern scientific thought, and can therefore be expected to yield to the scientific method. We consider it important to continue data collection and to encourage others to do likewise; investigations such as those reported here need replication and extension under as wide a variety of rigorously controlled conditions as possible.

We have two principal reasons for writing this book: The first is our desire to put our research into perspective with regard to the publicity it has received over the past three years. For example, early in our program we carried out a six-week series of experiments with Uri Geller. We eventually published the results of these experiments along with those of two much more extensive studies in the British scientific journal *Nature*.[2] Since that time we have observed that although our work with Mr. Geller accounts for only 3 percent of our overall effort, it has received 97 percent of our publicity. Therefore, one of our purposes here is to present a more balanced view of our research.

Our second objective is to attempt to prevent psychic functioning from again becoming undiscovered. There is great resistance to accepting data indicating the existence of the paranormal. Its acceptance by society is limited to the degree it violates the main tenets of our shared conditioning with regard to the sensory limits that we have come to accept as absolute. Its acceptance by science is limited to the degree that the underlying laws governing the phenomena remain unidentified. With the success of modern science in organizing and explaining most of the (normal) observable phenomena and available experience, we have become accustomed to dismissing the merely unexplained as nonexistent.

Psychic functioning is simply a body of observational data whose scientific description is as yet very incomplete. Until the observations described in this book can be fit into niches that allow them to be perceived and experienced as the familiar, there will be a continuing desire to sweep them away, since they are annoying reminders of the incompleteness of our knowledge of the world around us. Our attempt here is to provide the beginning of a stable data base upon which an understanding of these phenomena can be constructed.

After we have presented this data in lectures, inevitably we've received a telephone call or letter within a couple of weeks from someone who had followed the procedure we outlined, exclaiming, "It really works!" Thus we go beyond just describing our work, detailing a procedure which can be followed by the reader should he desire to experience paranormal functioning for himself.

The authors have followed a procedure in their work of alternating the order of names on publication of mutual efforts, and therefore the order is not significant; they share equal responsibility for the material presented in this book.

Russell Targ
Harold E. Puthoff
Palo Alto, California

CONTENTS

Contents

INTRODUCTION
BY
MARGARET MEAD

This book is a clear, straightforward account of a set of successful experiments that demonstrate the existence of "remote viewing," a hitherto unvalidated human capacity. The conventional and time-honored canons of the laboratory have been observed, aided by our current repertoire of instrumentation, Faraday shielding, specifically generated sets of random numbers, and cathode rays. People—both inexperienced learners as well as those who have previously demonstrated psychic proficiency—have been used as subjects successfully. It is a perfectly regular and normal piece of scientific work, as is the study of communication among bees, the luminescence of fireflies, the way in which frogs discriminate between the sexes, or the scientific study of any new biological phenomena.

Contemporary quantum physics, specific qualities of electromagnetic fields, and advances in brain research not only have determined the experimental methods, but have contributed to the tentative explanations advanced in this book as to how this newly observed ability might operate. As all work following the canons of science must be, the experiments are presented in a form that can be inspected and replicated under the same conditions, and further tested by altering various experimental parameters.

The claimed results are narrow but clear. The particular set of human beings studied have been able to produce formal drawings on paper approximating some distant spatial target mediated only by the independent designation of the target and the concentration and attention of the subject.

In terms of the ordinary type of painstaking procedures of the scientific method, we should now be well launched into a new era of exploring aspects of the human mind, with which scientists previously have had difficulty in dealing. There have been other thoroughly creditable, conventionally structured experiments before. But these have not received the kind of acceptance normally given within what scientists feel is a wholly rational, totally trustworthy scientific community. In fact, I think it may be fair to say that as the experimental methods to investigate so-called psychic powers have improved, so have the violence of controversy, the proclamations of disbelief, and the accusations of either conscious or unconscious fraud.

These particular experiments do start with several advantages: they come out of physics, popularly believed to be the hardest of the hard sciences; they come out of a respected laboratory; and they do not appear to be the work of true believers who set out to use science to validate passionately held beliefs. Tremendous efforts have been used which far outstrip the normal procedures to guarantee scientific credibility. Perhaps this in itself may make them less easily accepted. For scientists on the whole take each other's word for most of their experiments, and only present their data in completely accessible form when others have failed to replicate their experiments, seldom distrusting the carefulness and honesty of their colleagues.

We may well ask why it is necessary, in studies of this kind, to have at least twice as many safeguards and artificial substitutes for integrity as those usually demanded. Why does the psychic research worker, following ordinary rules, have to anticipate more hurdles than research workers in other controversial fields—such as the study of the inheritance of acquired characters, the existence of eidetic imagery, mind/body relationships postulated for somatotypic studies, or the findings of psychoanalysis. In all of these fields, those who claimed new results have been subjected to enormous academic punishment. They have been tempted to distort or suppress their data. Many have become unscientifically dogmatic and stubborn advocates of their positions. And, occasionally, some have been driven into exile, or even into desperate situations involving suicide, misery, and death.

The scientific world and the literate public have been fully exposed to the intricacies of disputes involving scientific theories so dogmatic as to resemble religious beliefs. Among other topics, they have been treated to diatribes on the impossibility of transmitting acquired characters and to the inextricable associations made between some scientific claim and the sociological platforms of communism, capitalism, fascism, or racism. We have read *Double Helix*, the accounts of Lysenko, *Tempter* by Norbert Wiener, and most recently the story of Bill Summerlin in June Goodfield's *The Siege of Cancer*. We have even read of the early use of the microscope to find miniature horses in horse sperm.

Psychic researchers do, I think, sometimes forget that they are not the only research workers who are subjected to harassment, misquotation, and unfair attack when they challenge old theories and propose new ones. Yet when we examine the history of the last hundred years, in which careful experimentation has been continuously misrepresented and denied, we find many recognized scientists insisting that psychic research should be endlessly repeated because it is not a "recognized area of scientific research." As one person quoted in this manuscript said, "This is the kind of thing that I would not believe in even if it existed." We can easily conclude that this is indeed an area of scientific research more fraught with irrational opposition than most, although hardly more subject to attack than, for example, psychoanalysis.

There are, I think, a series of historical reasons for this. It would be valuable for the open-minded reader to explore some of the historical and cross-cultural backgrounds of psi capacity. It seems to be a very unevenly distributed ability, overtly manifested by only a few individuals. In most societies, no connection is made between these very special unique "sensitives" and the rest of the population. Sometimes, in other societies, the capabilities exhibited by the few individuals are generalized, but if there are a large number of individuals believed to be capable of some exercise of psi—like predicting the future, diagnosing illness, or healing the sick—then the individuals who would normally stand out are simply absorbed into a group of practitioners and their special abilities go unremarked. Other societies outlaw all such behavior as coming from the devil or involving fraud, and here again, both the uniquely gifted and the somewhat gifted will be discouraged.

Furthermore, there is good reason to believe that the practitioner of an uninstitutionalized art—such as a prophet or healer or diagnostician—may have limited understanding or control of his or her special capacities. There is therefore a tremendous temptation to include various kinds of tricks in the practitioner's repertoire, in case the little understood and unreliable power fails. This may be why the tricks of the healer who palms a "pain" by extracting a small crystal from the body of a patient go hand in hand with the demonstration of special healing abilities. The charismatic leader may also substitute oratorial tricks for the spontaneity which won him his original place. The medium who once could easily attain an altered state of consciousness may take along a glove filled with wet sand, in case the spirits fail to arrive. There seems to be a fluctuating, unpredictable quality about these special powers, which may be due to nothing more than the lack of a stable cultural understanding.

In any event, such abilities should probably be classified with all other statistically unusual abilities, such as the amazing aptitudes of some individuals to arouse awe or wonder.

As scientific exploration tells us more about how these capabilities can be disciplined and developed—as mathematical and musical ability have been fostered in the past—many conditions of uncertainty surrounding psi capacity can be removed. For example, the sophistication possessed by one of the subjects mentioned in this book in his describing the necessary conditions for "remote viewing" is particularly striking.

Psychic powers have historically been closely associated with powers of healing, an area where faith and hope and response to placebos means that many diagnoses and many cures remain problematical. Faith in the healer is essential to the ability of the healer to heal, so that both healer and patient are held in a tight circular system which is beneficial to both, and dangerous to break. The vested claims of other kinds of healers inevitably come in conflict with the claims for and by the psychic healer, further obscuring rational discussion. The reception accorded psychoanalysis and all attempts to trace symptoms or their relief to communicative activities is analogous to the reception given to reports of psychic healing —sometimes with amusing overtones such as when the psychoanalyst who holds to a carefully structured theory of what is happening is obliquely credited with "just having generalized therapeutic powers" as a way of explaining the theory away!

Through the ages, deliberate magical procedures have also taken on independent life, and guilds of conjurers and magicians naturally hold vested interests in their bags of tricks. It has become customary to include expert magicians among the groups testing the powers of sensitives, and to give critical comment on the conditions under which experimental proof for some psychic ability is sought. From this has arisen the curious type of criticism which will undoubtedly plague psychic research for a long time to come, that if a particular act could have been performed by a magician, then it could not have been genuinely psychic. But is this any more meaningful than the kinds of doubt which plague the study of the psychosomatic disorders of a single patient who displays a mixed set of symptoms which could be "caused" by several different sets of antecedent circumstances?

I think one of the worst complications arises when both sensitives themselves and their followers advocate psychic energies as being "extrasensory," as proof of life after death, or of the existence of supernatural or transcendent powers of some sort. When they attach such a belief system to something as little-known and undependable as psychic energy, fanaticism is often substituted for open-mindedness. The very tenuousness of the connection, the insistence upon a physical manifestation of a power claimed to be outside the physical universe, means that they must cling to their beliefs more strongly in the face of all evidence to the contrary. When scientific methods were applied to the study of psychic powers, the confrontations became increasingly dogmatic, the arguments became more farfetched, and paranoia on both sides arose.

It is often hard to tell the fanaticism of the true believer from the paranoia of the serious experimenter, as each side feeds upon the other's obstinate insistence. No researcher on psychic abilities can expect to be free of this situation, and certainly the authors of the present book were not immune to misrepresentations by both the credulous and the stubbornly unconvinced.

The SRI research not only displays the elegance characteristic of physical experimentation and theory, but the experimenters have also used an imaginative approach to the human aspects of their problem. Where too many experimenters have put their "subjects" through long, dull, repetitive performances—during which whatever psychic capacities they had first displayed eventually deteriorated— Targ and Puthoff have realized that boring experiments are unproductive for learners, and resented by sensitives with developed psychic powers. Furthermore, where much of existing research has treated the human participants as either "subjects" (usually thought of as human substitutes for rats persuaded to run a maze) or impostors or self-deluded oddities, Targ and Puthoff have treated both their apprentice learners and experienced sensitives as collaborators and persons whose views were to be respected. It is unique here that the subjects were considered as partners in research. And Puthoff and Targ have been richly rewarded and have gained new insights into the complicated and delicate processes involved in "remote viewing."

In addition to the "remote viewing," in which the participants were most successful in picturing by drawing rather than by verbally describing and interpreting the nature of the "target" areas, the authors present a few cases of precognition—correct viewing of the target area *before* it is known to the observer who is later to be directed there by randomly chosen instructions. These are the cases which raise the most interesting questions both for the contemporary state of theory in physics, and for the way in which precognition may be expected to function in everyday life. If there is precognition of a future event, such as a train wreck, can death in the wreck be avoided by not taking the train, even though the wreck still occurs? Stated succinctly, does precognition add up to greater freedom of the will, or to a new prescription for despair? There seems little reason to believe that human beings could live with the certain knowledge of disasters which they would have no power to prevent. This issue is not yet faced by the experimenters, but will, I understand, be on their future agenda.

A second issue, which will undoubtedly be picked up by the sensationalist press, and which flows from the accounts of Soviet interest in mind influencing from a distance, is the prevalence of fantasies surrounding spying and being spied upon. "Could the enemy read the President's mind?" as one newspaper account put it. But such fantasies of omnipotence or total vulnerability to inimical forces have been continuously fed and exaggerated for over a quarter century by the science fiction in which many dilemmas are solved not by science, but by ESP. These fictions represent easy solutions, most likely unreal and certainly regressive and unchallenging in nature.

Thirdly, these experiments are concerned with the ability of participants to penetrate shielding when both participants are willing to do so. But it may prove quite possible that this channel could be as successfully blocked as it can be successfully opened. Experiments which demonstrate that there is a counterpart to the cooperation between the observer at the target and the observer in the shielded laboratory, in which a trained observer at the target blocks the channel, would go a long way to avert all the suggestions that one's mind can be "read," creating the strange paranoia that, in this postwar world of nuclear threat, is inevitably exacerbated in the minds of the public, in the press, and even by fellow scientists.

Finally, I think it is important to realize that if a certain psi phenomenon can be studied by scientific methods and one or more of its mechanisms involved can be related to existing scientific theory, this does not necessarily lead to a reductionist demolition of the essence of the phenomenon. Explaining the behavior of great artists in terms of childhood trauma, order of birth, or congenital excess of a hormone may advance our knowledge of biological functions far more than it explains a great work of art. Those who wish to relate the human condition to some transcendent power in the universe should be better, not worse, off by an increased knowledge of electromagnetic mechanisms. Science is not simply a device for explaining away events and capacities hitherto thought to be God-given. Because science expands one type of knowledge, it need not denigrate another. All great scientists have understood this. But those who hold a slavish belief in "scientific facts" and who do not understand the glorious uncertainties of modern science are likely to come to small conclusions that are as trivializing as reducing "remote viewing" to repetitious "readings" of a pack of cards.

As I understand contemporary trends in physical science, there is increasing recognition of vast unknown areas which science may explore and assist in ordering, but to which it may never provide anything like complete answers. Such explorations, however, should greatly expand our present paradigms.

—M.M.

FOREWORD
BY
RICHARD BACH

It was comfortable, human . . . warm, soft-leather chairs in a quiet room away from the lasers and bevatrons and whatever else was going on at SRI's center in Menlo Park. Somehow I hadn't expected it to be human. I had expected to be plugged into a big steel machine with blinking lights, with white-smocked doctors watching dials and frowning over germ-masks at me, because that's what advanced paranormal research is in the movies.

I didn't even change from my civilian clothes. I sat there on the couch and Russell Targ said, "We don't care what you do outside this room, but while you're here, you have permission to be psychic."

He looked at the clock and reached for a miniature tape recorder. "Hal should be there in three minutes," he said, and switched the machine on.

"It is eleven o'clock on Tuesday, July 18, 1975. This is a remote viewing experiment with Richard Bach as the subject, Russell Targ and Hal Puthoff as experimenters."

He clicked it off and handed the machine to me. "You can start anytime. Press the button there on the microphone and tell me where Hal is."

My throat went dry. "You know, Russell, I've never been in Menlo Park before."

"That's okay," he said cheerfully.

He did not tell me to close my eyes or open them or to breathe or meditate or anything of the sort. He just asked me to describe where a man was who had been in this room half an hour before, who was now somewhere 300 square miles in some direction, across, roundabout. Describe where he is, please, in detail. I forced myself quiet. I did not remind him that what he asked was impossible, that psychic things are fun to talk about but to sit in this chair no matter how comfortable, and somehow leave my body—are you asking me to leave my body, Russell?

Hal's last words as he left to drive to his secret destination were not much help. "See you in the aether," he had said cheerily, and I had laughed. Now he was waiting for me in the aether and I somehow had to find him, no excuses accepted. I closed my eyes and pressed the switch on the microphone.

As soon as the dark fell behind my eyes, I saw city streets, gray watercolors of asphalt and concrete, as though I hovered on some noiseless gliding carpet a thousand feet over the ground.

My imagination, of course. There's no place Hal could be that wasn't on some city block, somewhere. I was just imagining the logical.

But my carpet stopped, and looking over the side I saw Hal's car pull to the curb just past an intersection. "Got him in sight," I said in total fake confidence. It was a surreal television picture that I watched in my mind, and all I had to do was to tell the machine what this other me was sending—no incense required, no dim lights, no magic words.

My other me sometimes sent me wrong pictures. What he showed as a tiny steep-roofed building was in fact a gigantic steep-roofed building, and what he showed as parks were tree-lined residential streets. But everything else he sent turned out to be a clear description of a place I had never been.

Mystics for years have smiled mysteriously and told us that we are limited by the world only because we believe that we are limited by it. That it is all illusion for our eyes to accept.

Today, the teachers who once chalked diagrams of matter in solid unsmashable protons and billiard-ball electrons tell us that matter

is energy, that space is time, that an electron is not so much a particle or a wave as it is a field of probabilities, not a thing as much as an
energy event. That behind solid matter is nothing touchable at all.
Modern physics, in short, is no longer physical, and the new scientific method shows up surrounded in adventure.

It is okay to be right, it is okay to be wrong. Let's pretend it is
possible and see what happens. Out of this method we begin to
meet aspects of our being that have powers next to which nuclear
violences are faint cat's-puffs in the air.

When I first realized the implications of the Targ/Puthoff research, I was afraid for their lives—these were established scientists
who had found a principle that has made secrets impossible. But it
is too late now to burn their files; what they've found is already
being duplicated and expanded in laboratories and private organiza-
tions around the world. As I am coming to know more of the powers
that I have, so are thousands of others, so will the readers of this
book.

This world-changing, I think, is going to be fun.

—R.B.

WHEN PARANORMAL BECOMES NORMAL
WHERE WILL YOU BE STANDING WHEN THE PARADIGM SHIFTS?

Many times in the history of human thought a belief once heretical has become a universally accepted truth ... the history of science is partly the history of paradoxes becoming commonplaces and heresies becoming orthodoxies ...

—Encyclopedia Britannica, 1959 edition, on "Heresy"

A New Concept of Psi

Date: May 29, 1973
Time: 4:34 P.M.
Location: Stanford Research Institute, Menlo Park, California
Subject: Ingo Swann
Project: SCANATE

We are about to attempt the first in a long series of experiments which, on the face, seem impossible. The man with whom we are working today is Ingo Swann, a New York artist who came to our laboratory preceded by a reputation for extraordinary psychic ability. We are about to ask him to close his eyes and try to experience and describe a faraway place he has never seen. He will be supplied with only the geographic latitude and longitude by which to guide himself.

Ingo sits comfortably on an orange imitation-leather sofa in our laboratory, puffing on a cigar. The blinds are drawn and the video recorder is running.

"Ingo," we begin, "a skeptical colleague of ours on the East Coast has heard of your ability to close your eyes and observe a scene miles away. He has furnished us with a set of coordinates, latitude and longitude, in degrees, minutes, and seconds, and has challenged us to describe what's there. We ourselves don't know what the answer is. Do you think you can do it, right off the top of your head?"

"I'll try," says Ingo, appearing unperturbed by a request that we, as physicists, can hardly believe we are making. For us, this is a crucial test. We are certain there is no possibility of collusion between the subject and the challenger. The coordinates indicate a site that is roughly 3,000 miles away, and we have been asked to obtain details beyond what would ever be shown on any map, such as small man-made structures, buildings, roads, etc.

Ingo closes his eyes and begins to describe what he is visualizing, opening his eyes from time to time to sketch a map. "This seems to be some sort of mounds or rolling hills. There is a city to the north; I can see taller buildings and some smog. This seems to be a strange place, somewhat like the lawns that one would find around a military base, but I get the impression that there are either some old bunkers around, or maybe this is a covered reservoir. There must be a flagpole, some highways to the west, possibly a river over to the far east, to the south more city."

He appears to zero in for a closer view, rapidly sketching a detailed map (see Figure 1) showing the location of several buildings, together with some roads and trees. He goes on: "Cliffs to the east, fence to the north. There's a circular building, perhaps a tower, buildings to the south. Is this a former Nike base or something like that?" He hands over a detailed map. "This is about as far as I can go without feedback, and perhaps guidance as to what is wanted. There is something strange about this area, but since I don't know what to look for within the scope of the cloudy ability, it is extremely difficult to make decisions on what is there and what is

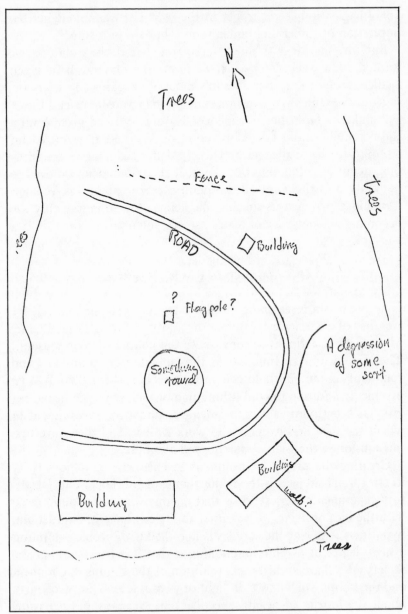

DRAWING BY SWANN OF EAST COAST TARGET SITE

Figure 1

not. Imagination seems to get in the way. For example, I get the impression of something underground, but I'm not sure."

But imagination was not a factor on that decisive day, as we learned a few weeks later when we received a phone call from our challenger. Not only was Swann's description correct in every detail, but even the relative distances on his map were to scale!

A fluke? A fantastic coincidence? Hardly. We had given Swann the coordinates and taken his response. We had transmitted his response to the challenger and received the challenger's confirmation, detail by detail, point by point. If the phenomenon proved to be stable in further controlled experimentation, physics as we knew it would experience its greatest challenge. And this was only the beginning of a new idea of man's psychic potential.

Our Approach to Psychic Research

As physicists researching so-called paranormal phenomena, we are, first of all, scientists. But by necessity we are also facilitators whose field of action is in some sense the politics of consciousness. Therefore, we often function in the laboratory as counselors and confidants in our efforts to convince subjects that it is "safe" to be psychic. In addition to establishing rigorous scientific protocols, our task has been to find a way to provide a supportive environment in which the men and women who work with us feel they have permission to use their latent paranormal abilities.

Creating the proper environment to encourage psychic activity in our several subjects is the major theme of this book. Our laboratory experiments suggest to us that anyone who feels comfortable with the idea of having paranormal ability can have it. At least one hypothesis as to why the country is not filled with people exhibiting a high degree of psychic functioning is that it is frowned upon by society. We share an historical tradition of the stoning of prophets and the burning of witches. In light of what is known in psychology about the impact of negative feedback in extinguishing behavior, there can be little doubt that negative reaction from society is sufficient to discourage many fledgling psychics. In sharing our experiences, our methodologies, and our results, we hope to provide the reader with an opportunity to examine the effects of conditioning, obvious or subtle, which may be limiting his own abilities.

Even worse, psychic functioning has had more than its share of charlatans. As a result, the issue of psychic functioning is avoided by a large segment of society who do not wish to chance being fooled, even at the cost of being wrong. It is acceptable to be wrong if you have company; it is painful to be right when alone.

Nonetheless, throughout history there have been those courageous enough to venture forth into the roughly charted land of the paranormal. The shelves of local bookstores are full of books describing the exploits of reputedly gifted sensitives such as D. D. Home, Eileen Garrett, and Gerald Croiset. Accounts of virtuoso psychic performers have not persuaded the majority that there is such a thing as psychic functioning, however. There are also shelves filled with "how to" books, which have been just as ineffective. Apparently, one reason for this is that those who reveal in good faith their favorite recipes, unfortunately, are describing only what works for them but may not be of help to anyone else. We have seen in our laboratory that psychic functioning is a very personal thing. One subject likes to begin with a few deep breaths, while another desires only a cigar and a cup of coffee. Some prefer lying down, while others prefer sitting up. One individual finds that ignoring the flash images and concentrating on the slower-emerging pictures produces better results, while for another the reverse is true. What works, works.

Another purpose of this book is to share with the reader those observations and experiences that might be useful to him in taking the first steps toward functioning as a psychic individual, should that be his desire. In our experience, anyone who decides for himself that it is safe to experience paranormal functioning can learn to do so. In our experiments, we have never found anyone who could not learn to perceive scenes, including buildings, roads, and people, even those at great distances and blocked from ordinary perception. The basic phenomenon appears to cover a range of subjective experience variously referred to in the literature as astral projection (occult); simple clairvoyance, traveling clairvoyance, or out-of-body experience (parapsychological); exteriorization or disassociation (psychological); or autoscopy (medical). We chose the term "remote viewing" as a neutral, descriptive term free of past prejudice and occult assumptions.

Our observation that apparently everyone can experience remote viewing was a particularly hard-won truth which emerged from our efforts to handle the following problem. A government visitor who heard that we were doing ESP experiments arrived wanting to "see something psychic" by way of a demonstration. Although this sounds like a reasonably simple request, one of the things we learned quickly in our new program was that no matter how miraculous the result of an ESP demonstration, an observer often tries to discount it as a lucky day, or is convinced later by a skeptical colleague that he was mistaken, or deceived, or both. Arthur Koestler considers this to be an important phenomenon in the observation of psychic functioning, and he calls it the Ink Fish (Octopus) Effect —i.e., a paranormal event clearly seen today is seen through ever darkening clouds as time moves on.

Fortunately, we evolved a simple way to remedy the mistake-or-deception problem: by a frontal assault. In a word, the only way to be sure that the observer has seen something psychic is to have him do it himself—close his eyes and describe what he sees. Of course, some people say only "It's dark" when they close their eyes, but with patience and encouragement that first step can lead to others.

Our skeptical government visitor agreed to be a subject in a series of three of our standard remote viewing experiments. A tape recorder was started and the subject and experimenters identified themselves. A couple of sentences giving the time and date were then spoken into the recorder, along with an announcement that the experimenter on whom the subject should target would be at a remote site in a half hour.

Then the outbound experimenter—in this case Hal (Harold Puthoff)—left for the Division Office where an SRI officer not otherwise associated with the experiment selected an envelope at random from a collection stored in his security safe. Each envelope contained a file card on which were traveling orders for a target location within thirty minutes' driving time from SRI. As the experimenter remaining with the subject, I (R.T.) was kept ignorant of the possibilities, so from my point of view, the target team could be going anywhere from the Golden Gate Bridge to the San Jose airport, an area covering several hundred square miles.

These preparations had to be accomplished in less than a half hour, at which time the subject would be asked to describe his impressions of where the target team was and what they were doing.

In the first experiment, Hal was sent to stand on a bridge over a stream in Burgess Park, not far from our laboratory. The subject in the lab described Hal standing on a wooden walkway with a railing in front of him, the ground falling away underneath. When finally taken to the target, the subject felt that there were many similarities between his internal images and the actual site.

He then proposed a second experiment, in which he would be left in the experimental room without an experimenter present. We agreed to this change in protocol and left the room. To prevent him from secretly leaving, we taped the door shut from the outside. (We don't trust them any more than they trust us!) In this case, Hal's sealed instructions took him to the Baylands Nature Preserve in Palo Alto, which consists of a nature museum with walkways over the marsh at the edge of San Francisco Bay. The subject, trying to view Hal and the environment around him, described a "kaleidoscope picture of triangles, squares, and more triangles," and "some kind of electrical shielding." As it turned out, this description was generated during the time that Hal was lying on his back, looking up at the inside of a seventy-five-foot transmission-line tower over a walkway, which corresponded quite well to the subject's description (see photo on page 8). He also described a building with a small movie theater, twenty by thirty feet, which was also correct!

After we played the tape made by the subject, and he learned of his accurate description, he told us why he had wanted us out of the room. In trying to explain the first success to himself, he had decided that perhaps he was being cued either by the body language of the experimenter remaining with him, or by means of subliminal audio coming through a loudspeaker in the wall behind his chair. To guard against these possibilities, he had carried out his second experiment alone, sitting on the floor in the corner of the room with his hands over his ears.

On learning that this experiment also had striking correlations with the target location, he thought for a moment and then offered us another explanation: Perhaps Hal had come back from the target site, listened to the tape recording, and then taken him to a place that matched his description, whether or not it was the place he actually visited.

UPWARD VIEW FROM BOTTOM OF HIGH-VOLTAGE TRANSMISSION TOWER AT BAYLANDS NATURE PRESERVE

This was of course an ingenious suggestion, and, from his standpoint, a legitimate possibility. Therefore, for the third experiment, again leaving the subject alone, we both went to the remote site and made a tape recording of our own. Then, when we came back we traded tapes and obtained the subject's drawings (see Figure 2) before anyone said anything. The subject then knew where *we* had been, and we had *his* description. Just as his second description was better than his first, his third was even more remarkable than the second.

In this case, the traveling orders had brought us to a merry-go-round at a playground, about four miles south of SRI. We immediately took our subject to the merry-go-round to decide for himself if his drawings bore any resemblance to the target location.

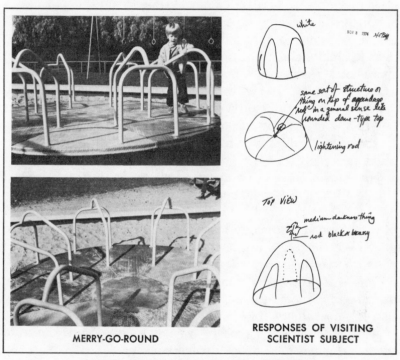

MERRY-GO-ROUND

RESPONSES OF VISITING SCIENTIST SUBJECT

SUBJECT V1'S DRAWING OF MERRY-GO-ROUND
Figure 2

As we crunched across the gravel outside a children's playground, the subject spotted the merry-go-round through the wire fence. "That's it, isn't it?" he asked as we walked into the little enclosed area. "My God, it really works!" was all he could say, as we stood watching children pushing and riding the merry-go-round. He had to admit that remote viewing must signify the existence of an astonishing hidden human potential.

We have carried out more than one hundred experiments of this type, most of them successful, as determined by independent judging. The majority of our subjects have not been "psychics"; at least they didn't think of themselves that way when they started.

The Discovery of Remote Viewing

For us, the discovery of remote viewing began with two men whom we found to have much more than the average ration of psychic ability, and who, furthermore, were extremely articulate about how it functioned. These men were Ingo Swann, a New York artist, and Pat Price, a former police commissioner and recent president of a coal company in West Virginia. They virtually taught us how to research psychic phenomena by giving us the insight to focus on those aspects of psychic functioning that people find natural to use in their daily lives.

This insight contained two important truths. First, we learned that to ask a subject to do our experiment rather than his is analogous to asking a pianist who shows up for an audition to play a piccolo. Second, the more difficult and challenging the task, the more likely the results will be good. Our subjects who can describe remote scenes in extraordinary detail when "the necessity level is up" often can't do better than anyone else in trying to see a picture on the wall in the next room, a task seen by them to be a trivialization of a great ability. If we had begun with targets in the next room yielding little success, it probably wouldn't have occurred to us to try the seemingly more difficult remote viewing.

As we have become known in the public mind as investigators of such phenomena, we have been the recipients of phone calls and letters, the volume of which indicates that the world is filled with individuals, many in high places, who have experienced this phenomenon, but would not readily admit it. This leads us to hypothesize that the ability is natural and innate.

In order to develop this ability in a disciplined fashion, it is useful to arrange for the selection of unknown targets by a second person to maximize the surprise element and to minimize "educated guessing." It is also helpful to arrange for feedback, for example, by a visit to the target site when the experiment is over so that false images of memory and imagination can be separated from the true images of the place or person one has tried to visit. Our contribution in the laboratory has been just this: to set up a random protocol for target selection, and to give our subjects feedback and reinforcement. One result of such a protocol is that, unlike the usual experience in card-guessing experiments, our subjects get better rather than worse as they continue to work.

From the beginning of parapsychological research, the hope has been that a repeatable experiment could be found, one that gave concrete evidence of psychic functioning. Along with this has been a need for psychic subjects who don't lose their ability as they continue to do experimental work. Charles Tart has written extensively about the so-called "decline effect" in which subjects engaged in repetitious tasks such as card guessing can be counted on to lose their high-scoring talents. He considers card-guessing experiments to be "a technique for extinguishing psychic functioning in the laboratory," that is, they bore subjects into a decline effect. Therefore, we avoid repetitious tasks whenever possible.

With regard to physical factors that might play a role in remote viewing, we found out early in our work that electrical shielding did not in any way seem to diminish the quality or accuracy of remote viewing. Our next task was to determine whether distance between the subject and the target site would be a significant factor. Hal Puthoff was to be the target as he traveled through Costa Rica. Two subjects in Los Angeles and Menlo Park who said they had never been to Costa Rica were asked to participate in the series.

Hal was to spend ten days traveling through Costa Rica on a combination business/pleasure trip. This was all the subjects knew about his itinerary. Hal was to keep a detailed record of his location and activities, including photographs, on each of seven target days at 1:30 P.M. California time. A total of twelve daily descriptions were collected before Hal's return: six responses from one subject, five from another, and one response from an SRI researcher, who filled in on a day when one subject was not available.

The single response submitted by the experimenter filling in as a subject was a drawing submitted for a day in the middle of the series (see Figure 3). Although Costa Rica is a mountainous country, the subject unexpectedly perceived Hal at a beach and ocean setting. With some misgivings, he described an airport on a sandy

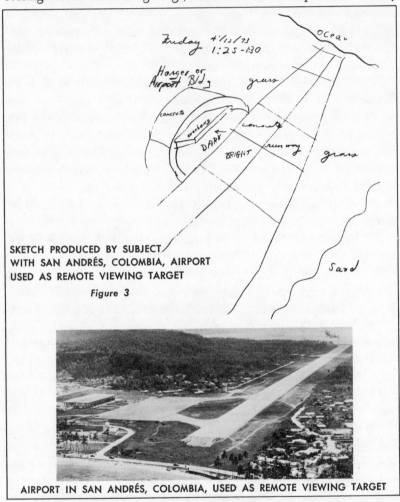

SKETCH PRODUCED BY SUBJECT
WITH SAN ANDRÉS, COLOMBIA, AIRPORT
USED AS REMOTE VIEWING TARGET

Figure 3

AIRPORT IN SAN ANDRÉS, COLOMBIA, USED AS REMOTE VIEWING TARGET

beach and an airstrip with the ocean at the end (correct). He also drew an airport building with a large rectangular overhang (correct). Hal had taken a one-day, unplanned side trip to an offshore island and at the time of the experiment had just disembarked from a plane at a small island airport as described by the subject. The sole discrepancy was that the subject's drawing showed a Quonset-hut type of building in place of the rectangular structure.

The above illustrates two major points observed a number of times throughout the program. First, contrary to what might be expected, a subject's description does not necessarily portray what might reasonably be expected to be correct (an educated or "safe" guess), but often runs counter even to the subject's own expectations. Second, it is a typical example of an individual with no claim to paranormal ability experiencing remote viewing.

The remaining submissions in the Costa Rica experiment provided further examples of excellent correspondences between target and response. A target period of poolside relaxation was identified; a drive through a tropical forest at the base of a truncated volcano was described as a drive through a jungle below a large bare table mountain; a hotel room target description, including such details as rug color, was correct; and so on. To determine whether such matches were simply fortuitous—that is, could reasonably be the result of chance alone—when Hal returned he was asked to blind match* the twelve descriptions to his seven target locations. On the basis of this evaluation procedure, which vastly underestimates the statistical significance of the individual descriptions, five correct matches were obtained, a result significant at odds of 50:1. As encouraging as such a statistic is, it still fails to convey the impact of reading the transcript of an excellent description, as some were.

Just as psychic functioning in general was not invented in the laboratory, but rather had its own existence in the field, so too did remote viewing thrive as an ability decades before we thought to investigate it.

Examples of remote viewing experiments are described in the four-volume 1927 *Outline of Science*, edited by J. Arthur Thomson. Among its sections on biology, chemistry, and physics is a section entitled "Psychic Science," nestled between Applied Science (Flying) and Natural History (Botany). The section on

---

* Blind matching is a procedure whereby an individual is asked to determine which targets go with which responses under conditions where he is ignorant of the true correspondences.

Psychic Science is written by Sir Oliver Lodge, who introduces his subject with the following ideas:

> The two branches of knowledge, the study of Mind and the study of Matter, have usually been dealt with separately; and the facts have been scrutinized by different investigators—the psychologists and the physicists. The time is coming when the study of these apparently separate entities must be combined. ... To ascertain the real nature of the connection—whether those possibilities are generally recognized or not—is the object of Psychic Science.

In a subsection entitled "Telepathy at a Distance," Lodge describes a series of experiments which sound like our own remote viewing studies. Lodge writes:

> In order to ascertain whether distance was any obstacle in telepathy, two ladies, members of the Society for Psychical Research [London] who knew that they were often in telepathic rapport, decided to keep a record of what one perceived, and what the other saw at a certain time each day, when they were hundreds of miles apart, their descriptions being sent to the office of the Society, there to be compared. ... The illustrations below must serve here as samples of a large number of recorded observations.

Those figures are reproduced here in Figure 4. These researchers, like us, did not observe any decrease of accuracy with increasing distance.

The Problem of Being Psychic

To return again to the problem of being psychic in an unpsychic world, it is difficult to stress enough the importance we place on the necessity of providing a climate in which subjects feel safe to use their remote viewing abilities. Our arguments in this direc-

HENBURY CHURCH—THIS IS WHAT MISS MILES, IN THE SOUTH, PHOTOGRAPHED AS A PLACE SHE HAD BEEN VISITING

THIS IS WHAT MISS RAMSDEN, IN SCOTLAND, DREW, ADDING, "SOMETHING IS WANTING, AS IT SEEMED BIGGER AND MORE IMPOSING"

PHOTOGRAPH BY MISS MILES OF SILK FACTORY AT MALMESBURY IN WILTSHIRE—THE PERCIPIENT, MISS RAMSDEN, HAD NEVER BEEN TO MALMESBURY, AND WAS AT THE TIME IN SCOTLAND WHEN SHE DREW AND DESCRIBED WHAT SHE THOUGHT WAS IN MISS MILES'S NEIGHBORHOOD AS FOLLOWS: "A WATERFALL; IT LOOKS ARTIFICIAL BECAUSE IT IS VERY BROAD AND REGULAR AND NOT MORE THAN TWO OR THREE FEET HIGH; IT MIGHT BE A MILLSTREAM. THEN I BEGIN TO SEE A HOUSE—A FARMHOUSE?—WITH A VERY TALL POPLAR NEAR IT. THERE IS RISING GROUND—NOT TO BE CALLED HILLS—AND YOUNG PLANTATIONS." THEN SHE DREW THIS DIAGRAM

Figure 4

tion unfortunately meet resistance from our subjects' daily interaction with a world that tells them that people shouldn't be able to do what they are being asked to do in the laboratory. Fortunately, this hostility toward psychic functioning is not worldwide. For example, if a Dutch or Icelandic child appears to have paranormal ability, his parents will usually be happy to help and encourage him, rather than take him in for therapy. This might account for the fact that these countries apparently produce more than their share of psychics.

One of the tactics of those hostile to the concept of paranormal functioning is to generate a polemic about believers and nonbelievers, which we consider a false dichotomy. In 1960 when we were both involved in early laser research, no one ever asked us if we *believed* in lasers. The closest question to that would be, "Have you ever seen a laser?" When we reported that we had indeed seen one, and could describe its properties, the question of its existence was quickly settled.

There is often a remarkable inversion of this logic when applied to psychical research. An oft-repeated suggestion is that people who have seen examples of psychic functioning are soft on ESP, that is, they are believers, so their observations cannot be trusted. This raises the following paradox: If observing an event disqualifies one as an observer, who then is qualified to observe?

It is the existence of this dilemma that has led us to ask visitors to our laboratory to personally generate a psychic event, rather than observe one. They are then faced with the decision of accepting what they have just done, or denying their own experience. This can often be very stressful because it can force a person to face a contradiction within his own belief structure. An individual likes to feel that all his ideas are logically consistent. If he finds that there is an internal contradiction, he either has to change one of his premises or admit that he is using some criterion other than reason for reaching decisions in this particular area.

By and large, the Western world has a materialistic world view. In its extreme case, this view holds that things that can't be touched, tasted, seen, smelled, etc., do not exist. Physicists, paradoxically, are in a certain sense not faced with this problem, since almost everything in their world is invisible anyway. The reality with which the contemporary physicist deals is by and large revealed to him by indirect means such as meters, chart recordings, and logical inference. So to physicists, the world is not necessarily shaken by data that indicate that people can learn to "see" locations that are not accessible to ordinary vision. We cannot explain these data at present, but we can suggest coherent models which can be tested.

The emergence of the theory of relativity necessitated new thinking in the scientific community in order to accommodate new data not taken into account by Newton. Likewise, the emergence of paranormal functioning doesn't require the abandonment of contemporary physics, but rather says that there is more to the world than meets the eye of twentieth-century science; after all, there will be a twenty-first-century science and a twenty-second-century science, and no physicist would presume to say that little change will occur.

The theoretical physicist can offer many ways to extend our conventional four-dimensional space-time model of the universe to accommodate psychic functioning. Many models have been put forward for consideration ranging from ELF (extremely low frequency electromagnetic radiation) theories to multidimensional (additional space-time dimensions) theories. Until these models are tested, they are not worth presenting here, but it is clear that physics is by no means without resources to attempt to describe and predict the phenomena.

The emergence of a new world view compatible with the new physics is going to be a problem only for people who maintain what is called the Naive Realist view. "If I can't hold it in my hand, it doesn't exist." For these people the new data from psychic research may signal the death of Naive Realism.

Kuhn has written about what happens to a society when its commonly held world view, or paradigm, is caused to change as the result of new information.[1] The change is not always a harmonious one. It may be time to start thinking where you want to be standing when the paradigm shifts.

17

2
WHAT IS AN EXPERIMENT?
INGO SWANN— THE ARMCHAIR TRAVELER

There will be those who accept it with joy because they knew it was true all along, and there will be those for whom it will bring pain, for it exposes the inadequacy of their world view.

—Paraphrase, Leon Festinger

"What's a nice physicist like you doing in a research area like this?" This question comes to mind whenever I (H.P.) see the latest spate of sensational publicity misrepresenting our research and misinterpreting and exaggerating our results. Fortunately for my sanity, I feel that the past three years' work has given me a good answer to that question.

Although I was casually interested in popular reports of ESP research, my professional involvement with research into paranormal phenomena did not begin until 1972. At that time, I had submitted a proposal to Research Corporation, which was handling a laser patent for me, to obtain funds for some basic research into quantum biology. In the introduction to that proposal, I had raised the issue whether physical theory as we now know it is capable of describing life processes.[1]

I then went on to suggest possible areas of investigation that might shed light on the issue. These included measurements

18

with both plants and lower organisms. This proposal was widely circulated, and a copy was sent to Cleve Backster in New York who was involved in measuring the electrical activity of plants with standard lie detector equipment.

When New York artist Ingo Swann visited Backster's lab, he chanced to see my proposal, and subsequently wrote to me (March 30, 1972). In his letter, Swann described his successful work in psychokinesis with Dr. Gertrude Schmeidler, Department of Psychology, City College of New York. Swann argued persuasively that experiments of the type he had been involved in might be appropriate for investigating the boundary between the physics of the animate and the inanimate.

Although my proposal, which was funded in April of that year by Science Unlimited Research Foundation of San Antonio, Texas, was not specifically directed toward parapsychological research, I nonetheless invited Swann to SRI for a week of experiments to see whether his abilities could provide a vehicle for investigating quantum biological effects.

In preparing for Swann's arrival in June, I discussed with various physicists at Stanford University the experimental setups in use which operated near absolute zero temperature. I hypothesized that this was the type of device which would be optimum for investigating mind-over-matter phenomena. Several superfluid and superconductivity experiments met this requirement in principle, but only one setup was running and available. This particular piece of equipment was a superconducting magnetometer, the electronic equivalent of a supersensitive magnetic compass needle which could register magnetic fields on the order of one millionth that of the earth's field. This setup was part of an apparatus built to detect quarks, particles hypothesized to be the basic building blocks of matter. I arranged with Dr. Arthur Hebard, whose experiments were in progress, for us to have occasional use of the equipment.

I met Ingo at the San Francisco airport, armed only with a verbal description of his looks and the information that he would be smoking a cigar. I was to find that the ubiquitous cigar would become a permanent part of my scenery over the next year.

It is hard to remember what I expected a "psychic" to be like, but I knew right away that Ingo did not fit my preconceived image. He was a large man, good-humored, and extremely thoughtful and articulate. In place of the bravado I thought I might have to contend with, I found an unexpected sensitivity. Our conversation quickly turned to the details of what does or does not constitute "proof" in an experiment, what safeguards had to be taken to ensure that false data due to artifacts or subliminal cueing were not entered into the already polluted stream of popularly believed psychic marvels, and so forth. I was to find out what has now been reported to me from other labs, that Ingo would often be the first to discount an apparent success, pointing out some potential loophole in a protocol or possible misinterpretation of the data.

Ingo asked me what was on the schedule for the day. Choosing my words carefully, I said that we were going to Stanford University's Varian Physics Building where a well-shielded apparatus known as a quark detector was situated. Launching into a discussion of nuclear particles such as protons, which until recently had been classified as elementary particles, I explained how these were now thought by some physicists to be composed of even smaller subunits called quarks, and that a number of laboratories were endeavoring to find free quarks in nature.

I carefully refrained from mentioning the apparatus in any more detail so that the experimental environment would be a surprise. This was in part so that I could judge his ability to obtain information from an environment which contained much that I thought would be a mystery to him. Also, everything I had read in my self-imposed instant education process over those past two months had indicated that fresh spontaneous situations often contribute to better performance, paralleling more closely the natural conditions under which high-quality paranormal functioning often occurs.

We arrived in the basement of the Varian Physics Building, ready to discover whether rapport between man and magnetometer was possible. Dr. Hebard greeted us, rather skeptical about the whole procedure, but willing to observe. Dr. Martin Lee, a physicist at the Stanford Linear Accelerator Center and an interested colleague, joined us.

INGO SWANN PHOTO BY JULIA TURCHUK

Ingo looked somewhat shocked and dismayed to find that he was supposed to affect a small magnetic probe located in a vault below the floor of the building and shielded by a mu-metal magnetic shield, an aluminum container, copper shielding, and most important, a superconducting shield, the best kind of shield known (see Figure 5). Ingo said later that perhaps it was his state of shock that propelled him into a sufficiently altered state of consciousness to permit him to obtain the good results that followed.

Before the experiment, a decaying magnetic field had been set up inside the magnetometer, and this provided a background calibration signal that registered as an oscillating signal on a chart recorder (see Figure 6). The system had been running for about an hour with no noise, and the oscillation was being traced out in a stable pattern by a chart recorder.

Ingo was shown the setup and told that if he were to affect the magnetic field in the magnetometer, it would show up as a change in the output recording. Then, according to his own description at the time, he "focused his attention" on the interior of the magnetometer, at which time—after about a five-second delay—the fre-

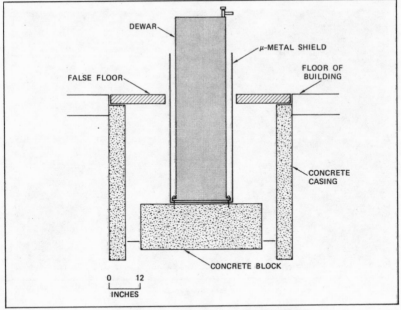

DEWAR

µ-METAL SHIELD

FALSE FLOOR

FLOOR OF
BUILDING

CONCRETE
CASING

CONCRETE BLOCK

0   12
INCHES

MAGNETOMETER HOUSING CONSTRUCTION
Figure 5

quency of the oscillation doubled for about thirty seconds, as indicated at A in Figure 6. Dr. Hebard looked startled; the main claim to fame of this device was its imperturbability by outside influences, and Hebard's work rested on the successful operation of this instrument.

The straightforward interpretation was that the magnetic field was decaying at twice the rate expected. In words that we have now become accustomed to whenever we get involved in psychokinetic, or PK, research with someone else's equipment, Hebard recovered by saying that "perhaps something was wrong with the equipment," and suggested that he would be more impressed if Ingo could stop the field change altogether.

(A constant complaint of subjects in psychokinesis experiments is that no matter what miracles they perform in the first experiment, the experimenter always responds by saying, "That was very interesting, but what I really would like to see you do is . . .")

Ingo said he would try, and in about five seconds he apparently

22

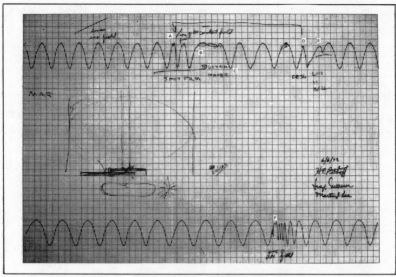

RAW DATA, MAGNETOMETER TEST RUN

Figure 6

proceeded to do just that, indicated at B in the graph, for a period of roughly forty-five seconds. At the end of the period, he said that he couldn't "hold it any longer," and immediately "let go," at which time the output returned to normal (C). We asked him what he had done, since as far as we knew, he could hardly be expected to know anything about the magnetic field distribution that had been set up, let alone know what to do to manipulate it inside a complex piece of instrumentation.

His answer set us back. He explained that he had direct vision of the apparatus inside and that apparently the act of looking at different parts resulted in producing the effects. In describing this, he sketched out on the graph a diagram of the interior as he "saw" it, even commenting on a gold alloy plate which indeed was there, and which had not been brought up in our earlier discussion. During his description of what he had done, further perturbations occurred, as shown at D and E in Figure 6.

I *had* to evaluate for myself whether the system was in fact noisy and what we were observing merely coincidence, so I asked Ingo to refrain from thinking about the apparatus and talked to him about other things. During this time, the normal pattern was traced out for several minutes (see lower trace of Figure 6). When we began discussing the magnetometer again, the tracing went into a high frequency pattern, shown at F.

Ingo said that he was tired, so we agreed to quit and have lunch. On our way out, I asked Dr. Hebard to continue monitoring and recording so that we could determine whether the apparatus was behaving erratically. He agreed, and the apparatus was run for over an hour with no trace of noise or nonuniform activity (see Figure 7). The top two traces show a continuing record following termi-

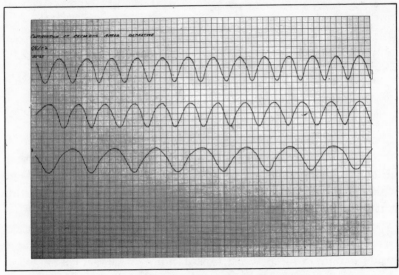

RAW DATA, MAGNETOMETER CONTROL RUN
Figure 7

nation of our experiment, and the third trace was taken a short while later.

I could not help but think back over a series of incidents involving sensitive laboratory equipment—a scenario every technologist is aware of. Some graduate students could make anything work, whereas for others there was clearly no hope. A "ghost in the machine"? Maybe there was more to that phrase than just a title for one of Arthur Koestler's works. However, that was speculation, not science, and my thoughts returned to the issue at hand.

What Is an Experiment?

In retrospect, I realize I must not have really expected excellent results with such a well-shielded instrument, for I had not arranged for multiple recording. Therefore, after the fact, I realized there was no objective way to tell whether the effect really occurred at the probe, or in the electronics, or in the recording device itself. Ingo's subjective description provided some circumstantial evidence that the effect occurred at the probe, but there was no way—after the fact—to validate it objectively.

We returned the next day, but the equipment was behaving erratically; it was not possible to obtain a stable background signal for calibration. Therefore, although Ingo tried, no positive conclusions could be drawn. This in no way cast doubt on the previous day's results, since at that time the perturbations occurred only in conjunction with Ingo's activity, the output remaining stable otherwise. It was nonetheless disappointing, and replication of these results had to wait another year before we obtained apparatus of our own for an extended study. Two years passed before independent replication was obtained in another laboratory.

I found myself torn between wanting to follow up on the physical perturbation effects on the one hand, and on the other hand being equally excited by Ingo's apparent ability to see shielded material. The physical effects would appear to provide an opportunity to examine under laboratory conditions what every quantum theorist knows: that observation of a system perturbs that system, and that consciousness might play an important part under certain conditions.[2] However, the description of hidden material seemingly opened Pandora's box to a whole host of possibilities, some of them quite practical. Since this second phenomenon was easier to research, that was the direction on which I settled.

To ensure that this apparent ability was stable enough to research, I carried out a short series of experiments before Ingo's return to New York. They were rather simpleminded tests: one researcher would place an object inside a snap-lock, thick-walled wooden case and leave the area. Then Ingo, accompanied by a second experimenter, would enter the room and describe what he thought was in the case. This approach worked so well that I invited potential sponsors to visit the lab and carry out the experiments themselves in order to determine whether they felt there was something worth investigating.

I recall one such visit during which Ingo was at his finest. Two visitors representing a potential sponsor ran Ingo through a series of ten hidden-object-in-a-box experiments. His descriptions were exceptionally good that day—motivation was high—but I was especially amazed in one of the series when Ingo said, "I see something small, brown and irregular, sort of like a leaf, or something that resembles it, except that it seems very much alive, like it's even moving!" The target chosen by one of the visitors turned out to be a small live moth he had captured, which indeed did look like a leaf.

Finally, after numerous similar observations, I invited Swann to work with us over an extended period of time. Swann agreed to return to SRI for an intensive eight-month study after clearing up some previous commitments in New York.

A few months passed during which time Russell Targ joined the SRI staff, proposals for additional funding were written, and an initial six-week investigation of Uri Geller's reported abilities was carried out (see Chapter 7). Swann then returned to begin a comprehensive series of experiments touching on many areas.

In retrospect, our first experiments were not much different from those done for years in parapsychological research, except for the modern twist added by our high-technology environment. Instead of Ingo identifying green and white cards picked at random at a remote location, he was to determine whether a red helium-neon laser or green argon laser was activated; instead of guessing which envelope contained a picture of a man and which a woman, he was to determine which canister contained a promethium-147 radioactive beta source and which contained a ruby laser rod, etc.

Although the statistics began to mount and the hypotheses began to emerge, all this work was to pale into insignificance on a day that began as any other. . . .

We were sitting around drinking our morning coffee and discussing experimental procedures when Ingo interrupted with, "I'm tired of these parapsychological experiments—they're so boring. Why don't we do something exciting? I did some experiments at the ASPR in which I moved my viewpoint to some remote location and described what was there. That was fun to do, and the studies were statistically significant.[3] I think I could look anywhere in the world if you just gave me some coordinates like latitude and longitude. Let's design an experiment around that!"

There was an awkward silence. In our experimentation, we had been trying to get a few bits of information from one lab to another via our unpredictable and noisy ESP channel, and now suddenly Ingo was proposing an experiment which sounded infinitely more difficult. Besides, we knew that latitude and longitude were completely arbitrary man-made constructs, adding one impossibility on top of another. Not knowing what to say, we said we would think about it. But we didn't.

A few days later, Ingo brought up the subject again. "These ESP experiments are a trivialization of my abilities. I want to look at something more interesting than what is in the next room." Sensing our reluctance to get involved in such experiments, he continued with, "Look . . . let's just do a few of them for a break. It'll take half an hour at most, and then we can return to our regular experimentation." Since an argument could hardly be made against such a reasonable request, Russell and I agreed to compile a list of ten coordinate pairs, latitude and longitude, and let Ingo attempt to give us a brief description of what he thought was there.

Since it was just a game—an interlude from our scientific experimentation—we simply consulted a map in an adjacent laboratory and picked out ten locations widely separated on the surface of the earth, and returned to the laboratory where Ingo was waiting. We read off each target location by latitude and longitude only; he had to immediately state what he perceived. Each response was checked for accuracy and the next coordinates were then given, until all ten pairs of coordinates were exhausted, a procedure which took roughly twenty minutes.

"Seventy-five degrees north, forty-five degrees west." "Ice." "Fifteen degrees north, one hundred twenty degrees east." "Land, jungles, mountains, peninsular mountains." "Thirty-eight degrees north, twenty-nine degrees west." "In my immediate vicinity, ocean. I see Spain off in the distance." And so it went. Not bad, not bad, but of course we couldn't overlook the possibility that perhaps Ingo knew well the geographical features of the earth and their approximate location by latitude and longitude. Or it was possible that we were inadvertently cueing the subject, since we as experimenters knew what the answers were.

On a later day, we ran through another series of ten pairs. This time, to be on the tricky side, I chose coordinates of small bits of land in the middle of large oceans, and small lakes in the midst of large land masses. As we ran through this series, it became clear that my trap wasn't working, for Ingo's descriptions continued to show high resolution as he ripped through the session telling us of islands and small lakes. But that still left the possibility that Russell or I had been cueing him inadvertently.

The next time we took a "break," we were ready for him. We had arranged with another SRI scientist, who was admittedly skeptical about the possibility of such an experiment being successful, to bring us a list of ten pairs of coordinates without telling us to what they corresponded. As Ingo breezed through the list with confidence, I could hardly wait to learn of the list of targets and to correlate Ingo's responses after the experiment was over.

Once again, even though the descriptions were perhaps a bit vague here, a little ambiguous there, they were accurate enough to make us begin to wonder whether we had on our hands a case of paranormal remote viewing or paranormal memory.

We knew, of course, that there was a phenomenon known as eidetic memory which enabled a person to close his eyes and reproduce complex pictures from memory. Julesz[4] described a case in which on successive days a subject was presented with what appeared to be random dot patterns, but which, when overlaid, actually constituted a recognizable picture. When presented the second pattern, while being asked to recall the first, the subject recognized the picture, a feat paranormal by mundane standards, but nonetheless observable in the laboratory.

In any case, the phenomenon we were observing with Ingo was interesting enough to take ten "breaks" altogether, yielding a total of one hundred descriptions—one for each coordinate pair. Details for the final run (Run 10) are shown in Table 1. The second pair

Table 1

Results of Global Targets Training—Run 10

Target	Response	Evaluation*
45°N, 150°W (ocean)	Ocean, beautiful blue-green waves, sun shining, ship toward north.	H
2°S, 34°E (eastern shore, Lake Victoria, Africa)	Sense of speeding over water, landing on land. Lake to west, high elevation.	H
55°N, 150°E (Sea of Okhotsk)	Not many trees, patches of snow, marsh?	M
64°N, 19°W (20 miles ENE of Mt. Hekla volcano, Iceland)	Volcano to southwest. I think I'm over ocean.	H
55°N, 130°E (Soviet Union)	Wind blowing there, night, telephone wires. Land, flat place with fields; cold.	N
60°N, 90°W (Hudson Bay)	Open water, stands of pine to north.	H
60°N, 91°E (Soviet Union)	City, snow on ground, city to northeast, factory to south.	N
30°S, 0° (ocean)	Ocean, Atlantic, deep blue water.	H
42°N, 105°E (Gobi)	Mountains.	H
28°S, 137°E (Lake Eyre, Australia)	Islands, land mass to east, west. An open sea, night.	H

* H—Hit; good description of area in near vicinity of target.
  N—Neutral; some possibility of correspondence.
  M—Miss; clear lack of correspondence.

of coordinates in Run 10 affords an example of the surprising precision that sometimes occurred. I had chosen the coordinates from a world map to correspond to the middle of Lake Victoria, Africa. However, when he was given the coordinates, Swann insisted that they triggered a picture of land to the right of a large lake. Subsequent checking with a detailed map of the region showed that his perception had been correct. Similarly, the fourth target of the day was a point twenty miles ENE of Mt. Hekla, a volcano in Iceland. His immediate response was "I see a volcano to the southwest."

At this point, we had circumstantial evidence we were indeed observing a peculiar and highly specific skill. Something was happening, but it was not clear what.

Ingo's successes on these map coordinate tasks caused us hours of consternation and days of questioning. As scientists, we had to repeatedly review the possibilities and draft various hypotheses. An individual could—in principle—obtain good results on the basis of eidetic memory. In certain cases, an individual also could—in principle—obtain the data subliminally from an experimenter who knew the target locations.

As far as that goes, if we are prepared to consider paranormal hypotheses, we may as well toss in the possibility that the data were obtained paranormally from whomever chose the target, whether that person was present or not.

Fortunately, such questions can be tested by the application of proper protocols, provided one is seriously motivated to ask the questions and then to establish the procedures with a dedication to rigorous scientific method. It is at this juncture, however, that the matter is usually dropped with the statement: "If it *could* have been done by ordinary means, it probably *was* done by ordinary means." Once again, Occam's now blunted razor* has been used to slice away another potentially valid part of reality, as those viewing a phenomenon decide which of the "ordinary" means or available hypotheses most fits their existing belief structures.

---

* Occam's razor is the philosophical injunction to accept the simplest hypothesis among alternatives.

From the scientific standpoint, however, possible circumstantial evidence *against* an apparent demonstration of paranormal functioning under relatively good conditions has no better footing than circumstantial evidence *for* paranormal functioning; either can only indicate hypotheses for further testing under rigorously controlled conditions, since only in the latter case can a scientific statement be made.

Intrigued by what we had seen, we set up a pilot study in which a series of targets from around the globe were supplied by SRI personnel and by interested scientists in other laboratories. Countermeasures against the subliminal cueing hypothesis were taken, keeping ourselves as experimenters ignorant of the target until after the experiment. The eidetic memory hypothesis was countered by requiring detail beyond that available on maps, such as the locations and structural detail of buildings, the shapes of structures such as towers and bridges. Thus was born Project Scanate (*scanning by coordinate*).

It was under the Scanate protocol that we received the coordinates 49°20′ S, 70°14′ E, telephoned to us by a scientist challenging our work. No maps were permitted and Swann was asked to reply immediately.

> My initial response is that it's an island, maybe a mountain sticking up through a cloud cover. Terrain seems rocky. Must be some sort of small plants growing there. Cloud bank to the west. Very cold. I see some buildings rather mathematically laid out. One of them is orange. There is something like a radar antenna, a round disc. [He draws a map.] Two white cylindrical tanks, quite large. To the northwest, a small airstrip. Wind is blowing. Must be two or three trucks in front of building. Behind, is that an outhouse? There's not much there.

Swann also described the coastline of the island, drawing segments on 8½ × 11″ pieces of paper as he went. See Figure 8.

> It's not completely dark there, sort of orangish light. If I look to the west, hills; to the north, flatlands, and I think, airstrip

31

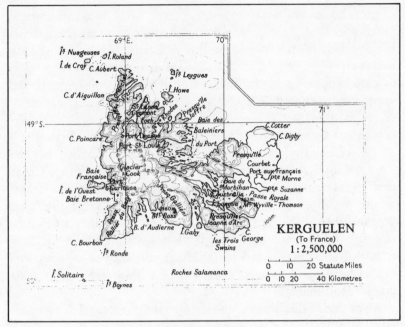

KERGUELEN ISLAND

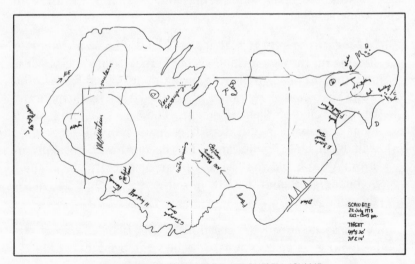

DRAWING BY SWANN OF KERGUELEN ISLAND

Figure 8

and ocean in the distance to the east; can't see anything to the south. I move to the coastline and follow it around. That's point A [begins to draw map]. Point B, rocks sticking up out of the ocean, breakers on them. Point C, little cluster of buildings with wharf, boats. Point D, jetty of land sticking out. Point F [sic] is sand basin, river coming through, lots of birds. Point E, brush of small trees. This is fun [laughs]; first time I've done this … [following E] almost a straight coastline, cuts in rocks, beach, then curves back. I see to northwest—a mountain rising, snow on top. Area G is irregular. Point H is a high cliff; point I is a promontory. Point J has big breakers; K is a bay; L is area I drew in detail [circles area, draws airstrip and buildings for orientation to previous map]. That will do for today. May be a lighthouse. I lacked courage going around point G.

The coordinates were of an island in the southern Indian Ocean, administered as part of the French Southern and Antarctic lands, called Kerguelen. Kerguelen now serves primarily as a base for a joint French-Soviet research facility for conducting upper atmosphere meteorological studies.

From a scientific standpoint, we were forced to consider every alternative hypothesis conceivable for the generation of the result, for the scientific game is as prescribed as a game of chess. Looked at through the glasses of science, carefully polished for hundreds of years, the experiment was certainly not definitive, since there was always the possibility that Kerguelen might have been at one time or another the focus of a magazine study, or a TV special, or some other information source available to the subject.

No such criticism could be leveled at the following type of experiment, however, of which we did many. A target site somewhere on the East Coast, again designated only by coordinates, was given to us by a scientist outside SRI challenging our work. From the record of that experiment:

Date: May 29, 1973; Time: 1634, SRI, Menlo Park, Ca.
PROTOCOL: Coordinates given by Dr. H. E. Puthoff to sub-

ject I. Swann to initiate experiment. No maps were permitted and the subject was asked to give an immediate response. The session was recorded on video tape.

SWANN: This seems to be some sort of mounds or rolling hills. There is a city to the north; I can see taller buildings and some smog. This seems to be a strange place, somewhat like the lawns that one would find around a military base, but I get the impression that there are either some old bunkers around, or maybe ...

And thus was generated the transcript that began Chapter 1. As indicated there, the result was excellent. For us, this type of experiment was definitive: There was no question of collusion between the challenger and the subject, and the target site was small and characterized by controlled access.

It was clear that several steps would have to be taken before this phenomenon was demonstrable under an easily replicable protocol. Nonetheless, Swann's ability to describe correctly details of buildings, roads, bridges, and the like forced us to accept the possibility that a subject, by mental means, could locate and describe randomly chosen, remote geographical sites.

The observation of such unexpectedly high-quality descriptions early in our program is what provided the motivation for the large-scale three-year SRI study of remote viewing under secure double-blind conditions (i.e., target unknown to experimenters as well as subjects).

Thus began a journey rich with unexpected findings. I have often mused that it was probably fortunate that we did not have to confront, all at once, all we were to learn about this phenomenon over the course of the following years.

These early experiments were useful in establishing the existence of remote viewing as a real phenomenon, but were unsatisfactory as a vehicle for investigating the phenomenon from a scientific standpoint. What was needed was a protocol involving local targets that could be visited by many judges for independent documentation and evaluation.

Furthermore, some procedure had to be devised to eliminate the possibility of target acquisition by ordinary means, such as the subject memorizing coordinates. Finally, a random target selection procedure and a blind judging (matching) of results would have to be handled independent of the researchers carrying out the experiments. Such procedures would have to be meticulously developed and rigorously followed to safeguard against charges of naïveté in protocol which might permit cueing or, worse, charges of fraud and collusion which were bound to be raised should the experiments continue to be successful.

The constant incredulity—although not universal—we faced for even being involved in such experimentation made it clear that positive results would not be welcomed by everyone. Scientists and nonscientists alike often find it difficult to confront data that appear to be greatly at odds with their world view. Entrenched belief structures die hard, even in the face of data.

Therefore, in carrying out our proposed program, we would have to concentrate on what we considered to be our primary responsibility: to resolve under unambiguous conditions the basic issue of whether or not this class of paranormal perception phenomenon exists. At all times, we and others responsible for the overall program would take measures to prevent sensory leakage and subliminal cueing and to prevent deception, whether intentional or unintentional.

After considerable discussion within SRI and consultation with interested scientists outside SRI, we designed an experimental protocol that promised to be foolproof and which could not be influenced by the belief structures of either the experimenters or the judges. No loose thread could be permitted, for in the study of the paranormal, if an avenue can be found whereby the outcome *could* have been influenced by subjective interpretation or, worse, chicanery, then there would be those who would assume that such *was* involved even if there were no evidence to support the charge. Following is a brief description of the program that emerged.

The study was to consist of a series of double-blind tests with local targets in the San Francisco Bay Area so that several independent judges could visit the sites to establish documentation.

The subject, closeted with an experimenter at SRI, was to describe an undisclosed remote site being visited by a target team. The purpose of the target team was to eliminate any possibility of a subject with an eidetic memory making use of knowledge of coordinates, because in this experiment coordinates would not be used. The site was selected at random to ensure that the subject had no prior knowledge of it, and no cueing by the experimenter remaining with the subject was possible, since both were kept ignorant of the particular target and the contents of the target pool.

In detail, to begin the experiment, the subject was closeted with an experimenter at SRI and was instructed to wait thirty minutes before beginning a narrative description of the remote location. A target location from a set of traveling orders, previously prepared and randomized by the director of the Information Science and Engineering Division, was obtained by the target demarcation team consisting of two to four SRI experimenters. The team, watching each other (paranoia can run high in an experiment such as this), went directly by automobile to the target without any communication with the subject or with the experimenter remaining behind.

The demarcation team remained at the target site for an agreed-upon fifteen-minute period following the thirty minutes that were allowed for travel. During this time, the subject described his impressions into a tape recorder. He also made drawings he thought appropriate.

When the team returned, the subject was taken to the site. This afforded him a firsthand opportunity to compare his paranormal perceptions with the target area.

Of course, no matter how we felt about the results of this informal comparison, the final determination of the success or failure of the experiment was made on the basis of independent blind matching by a research analyst not otherwise associated with the research. Following a series of several experiments, all of the subject's unlabeled response packets, which contained the typed, unedited transcripts of the tape-recorded narratives along with any associated drawings, were presented to the judge in random order. The judge then proceeded to each of the target locations alone.

While at each location, he was required to rank each of the subject's response packets, according to which best described the site (best to worst match). An exact statistical procedure developed by psychologist Robert L. Morris at the University of California, Santa Barbara,[5] for just such a matching procedure was then applied to determine whether the matches were significantly better than that expected by chance.

As an added precaution, SRI management sometimes arranged for those who had been most skeptical to judge the results, and often, much to their chagrin, their target matching generated some of the best statistical results we obtained.

Under this extremely tight protocol, which has not been faulted by even our worst detractors, the results with several subjects were excellent, and were eventually published in a leading engineering journal, the *Proceedings of the IEEE* (Institute of Electrical and Electronics Engineers).[6] Chapter 4 is a summary of these results.

The following experiment with Swann as the subject demonstrates the level of proficiency that can be attained with practice. The target chosen by the double-blind protocol was the Palo Alto City Hall. Swann described a tall building with vertical columns and "set-in" windows. His sketch, drawn during the experiment, together with the photograph of the sites, is shown in Figure 9.

Swann said there was a fountain, "but I don't hear it." (In fact, at the time the target team was at the City Hall, the fountain was not running.) He also made an effort to draw a replica of the designs in the pavement in front of the building, and correctly indicated the number of trees (four) in his sketch. The judge had no difficulty matching Ingo's response to the target, and this contributed to an overall scoring for a series of eight individual remote viewing experiments significant at odds of 2,500:1.

In the four years we have worked periodically with Swann, he has been studying the problem of separating the signal—those perceptions which are accurate—from the internal noise. It was Swann's idea to dictate two lists for us to record. One list contains objects that he "sees," but does not think are located at the remote scene. A second list contains objects that he thinks *are* at the scene, and are labeled as such. In our evaluation, he has made much

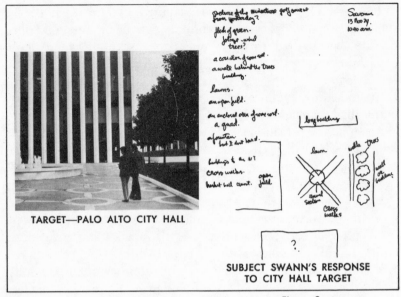

TARGET—PALO ALTO CITY HALL

SUBJECT SWANN'S RESPONSE
TO CITY HALL TARGET

Figure 9

progress in this most essential ability to separate memory and imagination from paranormal inputs, a key to developing the usefulness of the remote viewing channel.

A second example shows clearly the patience and forbearance accorded to us by our subjects, who unfortunately are treated at times more like guinea pigs than like responsible contributing participants. As a demonstration for a group of interested scientists outside SRI, we were challenged to arrive unannounced in New York City and to invite Swann over to our hotel room. Our challengers had chosen as the target to be used an abacus/clock toy of the type that is used to teach children how to count and tell time (see Figure 10).

While awaiting Swann's arrival, we made a tape-recorded statement to be played when he entered the hotel room. In this case, we knew what the target was—an exception to the double-blind rule followed in all our other work—and, therefore, we needed to be extremely cautious. A preamble for the experiment was prerecorded by Russell and then carefully checked to ensure against verbal cueing:

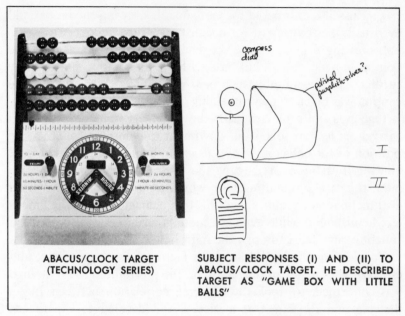

ABACUS/CLOCK TARGET (TECHNOLOGY SERIES)	SUBJECT RESPONSES (I) AND (II) TO ABACUS/CLOCK TARGET. HE DESCRIBED TARGET AS "GAME BOX WITH LITTLE BALLS"

Figure 10

Hal and I have brought a present for you. We wandered around New York this morning and we bought an object. This object is of the type that one interacts with, and Hal will use it for its normal purpose. Today is Friday, September 26, 1974. As in all our remote viewing experiments, we'd like to ask you to describe the object as you see it rather than attempting to give the object a name.

When Ingo entered the hotel room, Russell played the instruction tape while I took a large, locked suitcase containing the target object into an adjacent room. I locked the door and removed the abacus (we had earlier verified that such movement was inaudible from the other room). Thus the only available clue was that the target object could be no larger than the suitcase which I had carried with me into the adjacent room.

In response, Ingo produced the outline drawing (I) of Figure 10 in approximately one minute. (The large "purplish-silver" object corresponds to the suitcase lining, and may or may not be evidential.) Russell tersely asked for more detail, knowing the tape would eventually be scrutinized for cueing. Ingo then produced the second drawing (II) in Figure 10, describing the object as a "game box with little balls," but not wishing to commit himself any further. The five-minute experiment was tape-recorded and extreme caution was taken to prevent cueing of any kind.

Ingo was quite pleased with the result, as were we. We then carried out a short follow-up experiment to determine whether the position of the balls on the abacus could be determined by remote viewing, but this proved to be too difficult. As we were to learn later, this type of counting task, which requires functioning in an arithmetic mode, requires specialization characteristic of the brain's left hemisphere, while evidence mounts that remote viewing is a function channeled through the right hemisphere (see Chapter 6).

Considering the high-strangeness factor of the target item, and essentially total lack of restriction on the possibilities as far as Ingo was concerned, we took the observed correlation between Ingo's drawing and the target as a success and decided to experiment further at a later date with small-scale targets. For now, we decided Ingo had earned himself a steak dinner on us for his willingness alone, notwithstanding the clarity of his result, and we headed off for his favorite steak house.

This experimental effort was characteristic of Ingo's professional approach, his enthusiasm for and involvement in research. As others who have worked with Swann know, however, his contributions to paranormal research are not confined to his role as subject. He also is very articulate about his subjective experience, and slips easily into the role of a co-researcher investigating the underlying laws of the phenomena.

As an example, his analysis of why man-made coordinates work in remote viewing—although still leaving something to be desired by the rational mind—has a ring of authenticity about it. He argues that remote viewing, which is a task in mental space, is directed toward the description of a location in the physical universe and, therefore, requires in true engineering fashion an "impedance-matching" bridge which partakes of both the mental and the physical realms. The coordinate system of latitude and longitude, being an arbitrary man-made mental construct—but nonetheless having significance in the physical universe—is just what is required to fulfill the bridging requirement, according to Swann. This, of course, raises all kinds of questions with regard to the use of other coordinate systems, several of which are in use around the globe, but the answers will have to wait for further experimentation.

With regard to the problems in remote viewing, Swann submitted a lengthy report to us in which he likened the difficulties in remote viewing to those occurring in subliminal (low-level) or tachistoscopic (high-speed) viewing by ordinary sensory channels. The following are excerpts from his report:

> Experimentation in viewing of remote targets conducted at SRI has provided data confirming the existence of a paranormal remote viewing ability.
>
> Several breakthroughs were needed to uncover the remote viewing possibilities. . . . If breakthroughs have tended to expose such ability, subsequent quantitative analysis has also established the existence of certain qualitative problems that need to be resolved. . . . For various reasons as described below, the emergence of erroneous data in subjects' responses to given targets has been given the working name of "analytical overlay. . . ."
>
> Accumulated responses from subjects' attempts to view distant targets indicates that the target often is actually viewed, but in some way the target also acts as a prompter for the spontaneous appearance of seemingly irrelevant data. This is especially obvious when the subject's drawing of the target is by observation specifically applicable to the target, but his interpretation, either verbally or in the form of mental image pictures, is far from the mark. Since verbalization or imagery presupposes mental analysis, it seems reasonable to assume that we are dealing with automatic analytical functions of some sort, and that, hypothetically, these are the source of the diluted or erroneous response. . . .
>
> This is analogous to what occurs when a person has been presented with something he has never seen before. The ana-

lytical functions of the mind spontaneously output data-rich memories that assist in identification. . . . It seems relevant to hypothesize, then, that the subject is perceiving the target at some level of awareness sufficient to prompt logical mental processing in the subject. The subject's response therefore usually includes not only descriptors relevant to the target, but also other details coming out of the logical analytical comparison doubtlessly going on as he tries to "recognize" the target. This kind of situation is exactly one that might be expected were a person to be treated to only a momentary glance at an unfamiliar object and then asked to determine what it was. A series of analytical statements such as "looks like this," or "it is similar to" will probably be volunteered by the experient deprived of a continuing sensory information inflow about the object. The sensory and parasensory situations thus hold in common certain structures that can be studied either in the sensory or parasensory function.

More of Swann's subjective impressions can be found in his recent autobiography, *To Kiss Earth Goodbye*.[7]

A further view of Swann the researcher, as opposed to Swann the subject, was provided by the First International Congress on Psychotronic Research, held in Prague, Czechoslovakia, which Ingo and I (H. P.) attended together in July, 1973. I was there to present a summary of the SRI work, while Ingo was there to present a paper on the Scientology paradigm as a model for developing and exploring paranormal abilities.[8] We both were intrigued by the prospect of meeting Soviet and Eastern European researchers.

It was fitting that Czechoslovakia should be the home of a major international conference on parapsychology, inasmuch as one of the most important experiments ever to be done in parapsychology was conducted there. Dr. Milan Ryzl, a chemist with the Institute of Biology of the Czechoslovakian Academy of Science, had shown that, as imperfect a channel as it is, ESP could be used to transmit a message without error provided one called the sequence over and over. The final choice for each element of the sequence was the one that came up most often.

Ryzl's self-imposed challenge was to transmit a fifteen-digit number without error (each digit was in the range of o to 9). Ryzl had an assistant select at random five groups of three digits each. These fifteen digits were then translated into a binary sequence of green and white cards in sealed envelopes. By means of repetitive calling and a majority vote protocol, Ryzl was able after 19,350 calls by his star subject Pavel Stepanek to identify correctly all fifteen numbers, a result significant at odds of a million billion to one.[9] The task of collecting the 19,350 calls took roughly fifty hours. Although the hit rate for individual calls was only 62 percent, the signal was extracted from the noise by a procedure not unlike that used in the space program to process the weak signals sent back by far-flung interplanetary probes.

Many laboratories in the USSR have long been engaged in paranormal research. Since the 1930's, for example, in the laboratory of L. L. Vasiliev (Leningrad Institute for Brain Research), there has been an interest in the use of telepathy as a method of influencing the behavior of a person at a distance. Vasiliev's book, *Experiments in Distant Influence*, reveals that the bulk of his experiments were aimed at long-distance communication and what we would today call behavior modification, for example, using long-distance hypnosis to put people to sleep.[10]

The behavior modification type of experiment has been discussed in recent times by I. M. Kogan, chairman of the Bioinformation Section of the Moscow Board of the Popov Society. He is a Soviet engineer who, until 1969, published extensively on the theory of telepathic communication.[11] Kogan was concerned with three principal kinds of experiments: (1) mental suggestion without hypnosis over short distances, in which the percipient attempts to identify an object; (2) mental awakening over short distances, in which a subject is awakened from a hypnotic sleep at the "beamed" suggestion from the hypnotist; and (3) long-range (intercity) telepathic communication. Kogan's main interest has been to quantify the capacity of the paranormal channel. He finds that the information rate decreases from 0.1 bits per second for laboratory experiments to 0.005 bits per second for his 1,000-kilometer intercity experiments. One bit is the amount of information needed to determine the answer to a yes/no question when either answer is equally likely.

In the USSR, serious consideration is given to the hypothesis that telepathy functions on the basis of extremely low-frequency (ELF) electromagnetic propagation. In general, the entire field of paranormal research in the USSR is part of a larger effort concerned with the interaction between electromagnetic fields and living organisms.[12]

While at the conference, for example, we heard Kholodov speak at length about the susceptibility of living organisms to extremely low-level AC and DC fields. He described how fish reacted to 10 to 100 microwatts of radio-frequency energy (a small amount) introduced into their tank.[13] The USSR takes these data seriously in that the Soviet safety requirements for steady-state microwave exposure set limits at 10 microwatts per square centimeter, whereas the United States has set a steady state limit 1,000 times higher.[14] Kholodov also spoke about the effects of microwaves on animals' nervous systems. His experiments were very carefully carried out and are characteristic of a new dimension in paranormal research.

While at the Prague conference, Ingo and I both had ample opportunity to discuss these matters with our Soviet counterparts. I found it interesting that whenever a discussion of the SRI work came up, the questions centered not on whether we felt we had proof of paranormal functioning, or even what the protocols, equipment, or results were, but rather on what we did to stabilize our subjects to overcome psychological stress. In comparing notes, Ingo and I found that we were both asked the same questions in the same order.

After a series of such interchanges, we came to the conclusion that the emphasis on subject stability indicated that the Soviets were most certainly beyond the stage of trying to decide whether paranormal functioning was a real phenomenon.

This conclusion was buttressed recently when the Soviet Psychological Association issued an unprecedented position paper calling on the Soviet Academy of Sciences to step up efforts in this area.[15] They recommended that the newly formed Psychological Institute within the Soviet Academy of Pedagogical Sciences review the area and consider the creation of a new laboratory within one of the institutes to study persons with unusual abilities. Also recommended was a comprehensive evaluation of experiments and theory by the Academy of Sciences' Institute of Biophysics and Institute for the Problems of Information Transmission.

A postscript to the Prague conference occurred a month after I returned to the United States. I received a letter from Dr. Rejdak, the Czechoslovakian host of the conference, requesting the loan of an SRI film on paranormal research with Geller which I had shown at the conference. The loan was to be for about a month during which time it was to be shown to the Czechoslovakian Academy of Sciences and the Polish Academy of Sciences. I responded to the request, only to find, after a three-month delay in its return, that it had also toured several laboratories in the Soviet Union.

The end of summer 1973 also brought to an end our eight-month program with Ingo Swann. He had not only introduced us to paranormal functioning of a caliber we had not expected, but also defined the role of subject as co-worker and contributor, in place of the stereotype of subject to be run through the maze. He left with us an unmistakable sense of the breadth and the scope of the human side of the research to which we were now committed.

3
PARAPSYCHOLOGY IN EVERYDAY LIFE
PAT PRICE–
A MAN FOR ALL SEASONS

Do you know why Einstein said the most original and profound things about space and time that have been said in our generation? Because he had learned nothing about all the philosophy and mathematics of time and space.

—Mathematician David Hilbert

Some individuals could be said to *have* paranormal abilities; for others, the only appropriate description is to say that they *are* paranormal. Such an individual was Patrick H. Price, an ex-police commissioner and vice-mayor of Burbank, a maverick president of a West Virginia coal company, and an Irishman, with all the toughness and tenderness that the stereotype implies.

The route by which Pat became associated with the SRI program was typical of the flair and drama that seemed to surround his activities. It began with a phone call from Lake Tahoe which started off similar to many of the dozens of others that we receive every month. "I've been following what you fellows are doing, so I thought I would call to let you know that I have similar abilities, and they are under pretty good control, enough so that I use them in my everyday life." Ordinarily, at about this point, I would begin to think about how to interrupt the conversation and thank the

46

PATRICK H. PRICE

person for calling. We try to explain that since we have found that everyone seems to have some latent ability, we are not in a position to experiment with everyone who calls. At the same time, we try to avoid giving the caller the impression that we don't believe him.

In this case, however, the caller was a businessman and a former police commissioner of Burbank I (H.P.) had met briefly a few years earlier. "In fact, as police commissioner I used my abilities to track down suspects, although at the time I couldn't confront the fact that I had these abilities, and laid my good fortune to intuition and luck. One day, though, I got a very clear picture in my mind of something going down that I couldn't possibly know about by ordinary means, and when I checked it out, it turned out to be true. After that incident, I began to wonder if all this psychic stuff I had put down for years might not have something to it."

On an impulse, I read off to him the coordinates of the East Coast site that Swann was targeting on at the time, and suggested that he try to see what was there. He said that he had not done anything quite like that before, but agreed to give it a whirl. That was on June 1, 1973, at 5 P.M.

On the morning of June 4, I received in the mail Pat's written response, dated June 2. It was a five-page running commentary beginning with a description of the area from an altitude of 1,500 feet and ending with a tour through building interiors. The tour was complete with descriptions of equipment, names from desks, and—just to show he was serious—a list of a dozen labelings on file folders locked in a file cabinet. I dutifully passed the information along to our East Coast challenger, confident that there was no way that such detailed information could be true.

I was stunned to hear some weeks later that Pat's description was essentially correct, and that the challenger was certain Pat could not have obtained the information by normal means. Furthermore, while we were awaiting confirmation of his first effort, he sent in additional data concerning various situations around the globe that he picked up during his nightly "scans," much of which involved tense political or military issues which could not be verified until later investigation brought the information to the surface.

As the confirmations began to come in, we decided to invite Price to SRI to participate in a rigorous investigation of his abilities. Although in semiretirement in Lake Tahoe, California, he agreed to relocate in the Bay Area to be a part of our program.

Upon his arrival at SRI, our anticipation mounted as we readied ourselves for our first experiments. With our now well-defined protocol for remote viewing of local targets, we felt prepared to carry out a definitive series of experiments, the results of which would be unambiguous. With his rough-and-ready attitude and a merry demeanor, Pat approached his first experiment with "Let's do it!"

Thus began the series with Pat Price, who participated as a subject in nine remote viewing experiments with local targets, a series which would eventually become known to the public via publication in a British scientific journal, Nature.[1]

In our standard protocol, an experimenter, usually Russell, was closeted with Price at SRI for thirty minutes before the subject began to describe the randomly chosen remote location being visited by the target demarcation team, consisting usually of one to three other experimenters and myself (H.P.). As discussed in the previous chapter, we picked up our traveling orders from the division director, who chose one at random from his safe, and departed for the target, in this case, Hoover Tower, a landmark on the Stanford

HOOVER TOWER ON STANFORD UNIVERSITY CAMPUS

University campus (see photos on page 49). Needless to say, we did not communicate with Russell and Pat. Since Russell never knew what the target was, he could encourage Pat to clarify his descriptions without fear of cueing.

As we were returning to SRI a half hour after looking over the mid-peninsula area from the observation deck atop Hoover Tower, I could hardly wait to hear the tape to see if Pat's apparent ability held up under our protocol. As the tape was played, we heard a somewhat rambling description about a general view of the area which became tighter and more coherent, gradually zeroing in on a description of a tower-like structure until finally we heard "seems like it would be Hoover Tower."

We sat there finding it difficult to believe that he had actually identified the target by name. Although the feat was no more spectacular than his original experiment, this one had to be confronted at much closer range. It may sound strange, but we still find ourselves burdened to a large degree by the collective conditioning of our society, wondering before every experiment how it could possibly work, and surprised every time it does. We have, however, satisfied ourselves by exhaustive investigation that the result is genuine, and not an artifact of a flawed protocol.

The fourth target in the series gave me a chance to experience the "fraud-and-collusion" paranoia that others sometimes express about us. For this particular experiment, our division director, Bonnar Cox, feeling the need to determine for himself personally if there was possibly a flaw in our protocol, decided to take us to the target location himself rather than giving us traveling orders. Cox deliberately drove in a random manner, turning left or right according to the flow of traffic. By this process, we ended up at the Redwood City Marina (see photos on page 51), a harbor for local boating enthusiasts. After our required stay, we returned to hear Pat's tape-recorded description made in the shielded room at SRI.

Pat's first taped words were "What I'm looking at is a little boat jetty or little boat dock along the bay. It is in a direction about like that from here [points in the correct direction]. Yeah, I see the little boats, some motor launches, some little sailing ships, sails all furled, some with the masts stepped and others are up. Little jetty

REDWOOD CITY MARINA

or little dock there." He went on to say, "Funny thing—this flashed in—kinda looks like a Chinese or Japanese pagoda effect. It's a definite feeling of Oriental architecture that seems to be fairly adjacent to where they are." He was describing quite accurately what in reality is a restaurant located on the dock. His voice on the tape continued, correctly describing the granite slabs leading down to the water's edge, indicating our location as being four miles northeast of SRI, and so on. As the narrative progressed, the excellent quality of the transcript began to raise a paranoid fear in me that perhaps Price and the division director were in collusion on this experiment to see if *I* could detect chicanery! Only the concern shown by our director as he tried to figure out how *we* could have fooled *him* brought me back to equilibrium.

The target for Experiment 7 was an arts and crafts garden plaza known as Allied Arts (see photo on page 53) which resembles a California mission. There are craft shops around the perimeter of the plaza, and in the plaza area itself are many gardens, flowers, ceramic pots, fountains, and paths; overhead are vines on arbors of redwood. Pat's description was accurate in almost every detail and he omitted little of importance. As an example of his output, we include the unedited transcript of this experiment at the end of this chapter.

In general, Pat's ability to correctly describe buildings, docks, roads, gardens, and the like, including structural materials, color, ambience, and activity—sometimes in great detail—indicated an exceptional remote perceptual ability. Nonetheless, in general, the descriptions contained inaccuracies as well as correct statements. A typical example is provided by the results of Experiment 9. Pat's drawing is shown in Figure 11 in which he correctly described a parklike area containing two pools of water: one rectangular, 60 × 89 feet (actual dimensions 75 × 100 feet); the other circular, diameter 120 feet (actual diameter 110 feet). He was incorrect, however, in saying the facility was used for water filtration rather than swimming. With further experimentation, we began to realize that the occurrence of essentially correct descriptions of basic elements and patterns coupled with incomplete or erroneous analysis of function was to be a continuing thread throughout the remote viewing

ALLIED ARTS GARDEN PLAZA

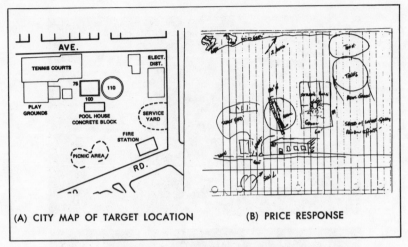

(A) CITY MAP OF TARGET LOCATION   (B) PRICE RESPONSE

SWIMMING POOL COMPLEX (PRICE)
Figure 11

work. This observation eventually led to a major breakthrough with regard to understanding the connection between remote viewing and brain functioning.

As can be seen from his drawing (see Figure 11), Pat also included some elements, such as the tanks shown in the upper right, which were not present at the target site. The left-right reversal of elements—often observed in paranormal perception experiments—is likewise apparent.

An SRI research analyst not otherwise associated with the research was called in to provide independent evaluation of the experiment. Pat's response packets, which contained the nine typed, unedited transcripts of the tape-recorded narratives and associated drawings, were unlabeled and presented in random order. Working alone, the analyst visited each target location and in a blind fashion rated Pat's answers on a scale of 1 to 9 (best to worst match). The results of the judging, shown in Table 2, included seven direct hits out of the nine. The overall result was statistically significant at odds of 35,000:1.

The SRI locations from which Pat viewed the remote targets were an outdoor park (Experiments 1, 2), a double-walled, copper-screen Faraday cage which eliminates much of the electromagnetic spectrum (Experiments 3, 4, and 6–9), and an office (Experiment 5). Judging from the matches indicated in Table 2, the use of Faraday cage electrical shielding does not prevent high-quality descriptions from being obtained.

Table 2

Distribution of Rankings Assigned to Transcripts Associated with Each Target Location for Experienced Subject Price (S1)

Target Location	Distance (km)	Rank of Associated Transcript
Hoover Tower, Stanford	3.4	1
Baylands Nature Preserve, Palo Alto	6.4	1
Radio telescope, Portola Valley	6.4	1
Marina, Redwood City	6.8	1
Bridge toll plaza, Fremont	14.5	6
Drive-in theater, Palo Alto	5.1	1
Arts and Crafts Plaza, Menlo Park	1.9	1
Catholic Church, Portola Valley	8.5	3
Swimming pool complex, Palo Alto	3.4	1
Total sum of ranks		16 $(p = 2.9 \times 10^{-5})$

As a backup judging procedure, a panel of five additional SRI scientists, not otherwise associated with the research and chosen by SRI management to check our work, were asked to blind match the unedited, typed transcripts (with associated drawings) generated by Pat against the nine target locations which they independently visited in turn. The transcripts were unlabeled and presented in random order. A correct match consisted of a transcript of a given date being matched to the target of that date. Instead of the expected chance results of one match per judge, the numbers of correct matches obtained by the five judges were 7, 6, 5, 3 and 3.* Thus, rather than the expected total number of five correct matches from the judges, twenty-four such matches were obtained.

Although the judging procedure is the final arbiter with regard to evaluating whether an experiment is successful or not, it was clear to us as we went along that the results being generated by Pat were of superior quality. To have found two individuals—Swann was the first—capable of such a high degree of remote viewing certainly exceeded our expectations for our first year's research. Furthermore, Price was not a professional psychic, which opened up the prospect that perhaps there were many individuals potentially capable of remote viewing.

What of Price's view of himself as he turned in success after success? In a word, Price was absolutely convinced that what he was doing was very ordinary. In a November 20, 1974, interview in the Huntington, West Virginia, *Herald-Dispatch* he expressed it this way:

> There is absolutely nothing mysterious about it: Just decide. There is nothing specific to do. If a person has convinced himself he can't, with certainty, he cannot. If a person is willing even to concede a slight possibility he can, then that's a point where he starts doing it.... If one observes that it could be useful to him, let that be so; if not let that also be so.

He was impish about his abilities. In talking with the secretaries at SRI, he loved to answer the hidden question that never got asked with, "If I can see anywhere in the universe, why would I want to follow you to the bathroom?" His impishness showed up in more forceful ways, too, as when, apropos of nothing, he casually began to describe to a visitor how he would build a certain type of airplane, a description we were told later corresponded precisely

---

* For example, should a judge elect to match all transcripts to a single target, he would perforce get exactly one correct match. Should he adopt other strategies, it can be shown that still one match can be expected on the average.

with what the visitor had been exposed to at a closed briefing two days prior to his visit to SRI.

Price's rough-and-ready approach made him ideally suited to the demonstration type of experiment that we were continually tasked with early in our program. In one demonstration for a potential sponsor, our standard protocol sent us to a building in the hills behind the Stanford campus which houses an Artificial Intelligence Laboratory. The building, originally designed to be circular, was only one-third completed, forming an arc. Pat's description began, appropriately enough, with a description of a banana-shaped building. Halfway through the allotted time at the site, our visitor, desiring to "test the system," insisted that we jump into the car and quickly drive to another place he had seen on the way, a beer garden housed in a century-old building that had once served as a relay station for the pony express. Accordingly, Pat's description changed in midstream to that of a small building with double-hung doors, and having some kind of historical significance (we found the bronze plaque later).

On another occasion, he was asked to reproduce, while flying overhead in a glider, a drawing being made on the ground by a visitor. Pat faithfully reproduced a moon and stars target chosen from a label found by the visitor as he searched randomly through a garbage dump on the ground below during the flight. There appeared to be one error, however. Pat had also included in his drawing a third symbol, a stylized ankh, or ansate cross. Our visitor chuckled, and pulled out from beneath his shirt, below the pocket carrying his drawing, just such a cross on a chain, which was never visible from the outside.

A man for all seasons, Price was also drawn to our equipment being set up for psychokinesis experiments. Experimentation along these lines was being undertaken to investigate the possibility that the remote sensing channel may permit energy to flow from an individual to a remote location as well as in reverse. There are reasons for thinking this might be so in certain of the quantum theories proposed to explain paranormal functioning.

Pat participated in a long series of experiments in which the goal was to register counts on a Geiger counter, but these proved to be unsuccessful. In a second series of experiments, we examined the possibility that a subject may be able to exert a physical influence on a remotely located mechanical system. The target was a torsion pendulum suspended by a metal fiber inside a sealed glass bell jar in a laboratory some distance from the subject. The position of the pendulum was monitored by a laser beam reflected from a small mirror on the pendulum onto a position-sensing detector. The output from the detector was monitored by a chart recorder. The subject was provided feedback at the remote location either by closed circuit video or by a second chart recorder connected to the recorder in the enclosed target laboratory. Pat was to try to increase or decrease the oscillation of the pendulum during one-minute intervals determined by a random number table. Although there appeared to be some evidence in pilot studies that Pat could, by concentration, influence the motion of the pendulum, data taken in controlled experiments, although showing a trend in the desired direction, did not reach statistical significance.

Such was not the case with the following experimental series, however. As discussed in the previous chapter, Swann was apparently able to affect the output of a sensitive magnetometer. The conditions of that observation, involving as it did the brief use of an instrument committed to other research, prevented a proper investigation, however. The number of data samples was too few to permit meaningful statistical analysis, and the lack of readily available multiple recording equipment prevented investigation of possible "recorder only" effects.

By the time Pat had joined our program, however, we had arranged for extended use of a similar instrument in our lab (see photo on page 59). The device is ordinarily used to measure magnetic fields originating from processes within the human body, such as currents in the heart that produce magnetocardiograms. The sensitive tip of the instrument is placed near the body area of interest. In our experiment, however, Pat was located in an adjoining laboratory four meters from the probe. As a result, he was located in a zone of relative insensitivity; for example, standing up, sitting down, leaning forward, and arm and leg movements produced no signals. We asked Pat, as a mental task, to affect the probe from

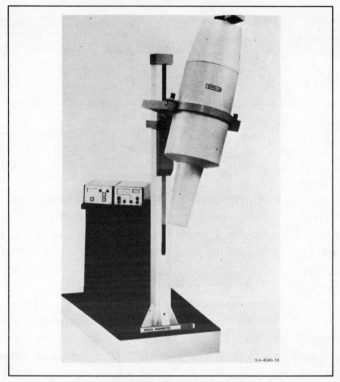

SUPERCONDUCTING DIFFERENTIAL MAGNETOMETER (GRADIOMETER)

where he was. The results of his efforts were monitored at different stages of the system by three separate recording devices: an oscilloscope, a panel meter, and a chart recorder, the latter providing a permanent record.

Pat was required to remove all metal objects from his clothing and body, and the effects of body movements were checked at the start of each experimental period. A random number table was used to generate a sequence of ten ON (subject activity) and OFF (subject no activity) periods of equal length, for example, twenty-five seconds each. We asked Pat to make an effort to affect the magnetometer during the ON periods, and to refrain from doing so during the OFF periods. The trace from the chart recording of a sample run is shown in Figure 12. The randomly generated ON trials occurred in periods 2, 8, and 9. As shown, signals appeared

Mind-Reach

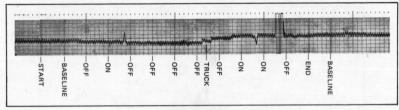

GRADIOMETER DATA
Figure 12

in each of these periods. A false signal due to the passage of a truck in the parking lot adjacent to the laboratory (under continuous surveillance) was noted in period 6.

A long series of experiments was carried out, and the observed activity was found to correlate with Pat's efforts to a statistically significant degree (odds of 250:1). Thus the experiment was a success. Eventually, the results were presented at an international conference on quantum physics and parapsychology held in Geneva that Russell and I attended in the summer of 1974.[2]

Pat was, of course, pleased with the success. He felt that by working with such sensitive equipment under good conditions he had increased his own knowledge of how the physical universe operates. After working with us on this particular experiment, he expressed the opinion he could write a whole book on physics from a subjective viewpoint, although as far as he was concerned, it didn't matter if anyone ever heard about what he did—he had gotten his reward from the activity itself.

We were also pleased with the results. This was our first statistically significant long-term study of psychokinesis, and the outcome indicated that the remote sensing channel might sustain energy transfer in either direction.

The above concept has a rigorous basis in quantum theory in the so-called "observer problem," the effect of an observer on experimental measurement. Detailed analysis leads inescapably to the conclusion that to the degree that consciousness is involved in observation and measurement (and it always is), to that degree consciousness must also be seen to interact with the physical environment.[3] Dr. Evan Harris Walker of the U.S. Army's Aberdeen Proving Ground and Professor O. Costa de Beauregard of the Poin-

60

care Institute in France have independently proposed theories of paranormal functioning based on these rather esoteric concepts.[4]

Based on our own observations of Pat and others, we developed a few working hypotheses which we intend to examine in future work. They are: (1) Researchers in the area of psychokinesis always appear to be plagued by the fact that observed effects are never much larger than the background noise always present. Rather than being perverse, Nature may simply be showing us that psychokinesis involves control over noise signals always present, rather than the generation of new energies—a "bringing-order-out-of-chaos" concept familiar in Eastern traditions; (2) Even when observed, psychokinetic effects often appear to be the result of "coincidence." This may indicate that such effects may be the result of a goal-oriented synchronicity that works at a very subtle level beyond the more obvious cause-effect mechanisms; (3) Psychokinetic effects often appear to be random or spontaneous. This may indicate a connection with weak quantum effects, which similarly appear to be random or spontaneous; (4) The more closely one attempts to observe psychokinetic effects, the less likely one is to see them, a factor considered by many to indicate poor observation, fraud, and the like. However, simple dismissal does not stand up under scrutiny. It may be, instead, that there are interfering observer effects of the type known to occur at the microscopic level. (For those prejudiced against the possibility of psychokinesis, the above principles would be labeled rationalizations or Catch-22. However, as scientists responsible for investigating the area, we are not permitted the luxury of dismissing the above possibilities without cause.)

Finally, we find it useful as a guiding principle to remind ourselves that all of the phenomena we deal with in psychokinesis are totally permissible at the microscopic level within the framework of physics as presently understood (tunneling through barriers, time reversibility, etc.). Therefore, there is hope that the bridge between the microscopic and macroscopic can be found, at which point psychokinesis will take its place alongside other phenomena now understood, but equally mysterious when first observed.

With the completion of the magnetometer study, Pat Price ended his stay at SRI to accept a new challenge, a position as president of a West Virginia coal company. We nonetheless carried on further experimentation with him from time to time when his busy schedule would permit.

Unfortunately, we must bring this chapter to a close by noting with sadness the death of Pat Price due to a heart attack in July, 1975. He will always be remembered by the authors for his willingness to place on the line for public scrutiny his very private abilities, a willingness stemming from a stated desire to bring to others, by whatever route, the realization that an individual is inherently capable of greatness infinitely beyond the ordinary world view. We have lost a friend and co-worker—the world has lost a courageous and talented explorer.

Remote Viewing Transcript of Experiment 7 with Pat Price

Following is the unedited transcript of a remote viewing experiment where the target was an arts and crafts garden plaza resembling a California mission. There are craft shops around the perimeter of the plaza. In the plaza area are many gardens, flowers, ceramic pots, fountains, and paths. Overhead are vines on arbors of redwood. Price's description is accurate in almost every detail and he omitted little of importance (see photo on page 53). The experimenter's statements and questions are indicated by capitalized text.

ONE FORTY. THIS IS A REMOTE VIEWING EXPERIMENT WITH PAT PRICE, DEAN BROWN, AND RUSSELL TARG IN THE SHIELDED ROOM IN BUILDING THIRTY. THE TRAVELERS TO THE REMOTE LOCATION ARE BART COX, HAL PUTHOFF, JUDY SCHMICKLEY, AND PHYLLIS COLE. WE EXPECT THE TRAVELERS TO BE AT THEIR PLACE IN ABOUT TEN MINUTES.

IT'S ONE FIFTY-EIGHT. OUR TRAVELERS SHOULD BE NEAR TO ARRIVING AT THE PLACE.

OK. Why don't I start scanning by quadrant using this as a center point. Twelve to three, six to nine. . . .

I'll go from twelve to three first. Seems to me right now that I'm picking them up in the twelve to three quadrant, but I'll go on in the rest and look. I haven't actually identified them, I just feel that they're there.

Nope, I don't get them there.

Now I'll go from six to nine. While I was looking at six to nine, it looks to me like I'm looking at an iris, a flower of some kind. I'll come back and identify that later. Just wanted to get it down as having a flash of an iris flower—purplish. I'll continue to scan that quadrant. Nope, don't get them there.

I'll go from nine to twelve. Don't get them there.

I'll go back twelve to three. Yeah, I get them in that quadrant.

Now I'll see if I can locate them physically and identify the area.

I'm looking at something that looks like an arbor, trellis-work arbor. Seems to be cool, shaded. Doesn't seem to me that they're out in the direct sunlight. Be more like there's lots of trees, in an arbor area. The arbor appears to be made of wood, possibly redwood.

They're just . . . looks like it's a dirt path, quite wide, I'd say maybe twelve feet. I can see some grass. Looks like possibly a fountain of some kind.

Yeah, I can see Bart in his red shirt and what looks like kind of a gray paisley tie—I didn't really look at that when he was down there. The red shirt, I did. Looks like he has on a gray paisley tie.

It appears they're walking along quite leisurely.

Looks like there's some red brick laid into a walkway. They don't seem to be on it, they just seem to pass over that.

I get—it seems like a little ways away from them there are quite a few people but right where they're walking it doesn't appear to be many right in there.

This is an arbor area. Back of that arbor, back here I'd say fifty feet from that arbor to here, seems to be a lot of people in here. They were walking along here on what looks like about a twelve-foot dirt path. [All correct.]

WHAT KIND OF PLACE IS THE ARBOR IN? IS IT A FIELD OUT IN THE OPEN?

No, I want to say park, but it doesn't exactly feel like a park. If you took a—the feeling I'm getting—it's not the specific place—but like the Town and Country Market. That type of an atmosphere, with quite a section of it into a little outdoor park, but basically I'm getting a very strong feeling of flowers.

Like the first one I saw was an iris.

TELL ME ABOUT THE TOWN AND COUNTRY ASPECT. IN WHAT WAY DOES IT REMIND YOU OF TOWN AND COUNTRY?

The buildings, not right where they're at but very close to them, have that same kind of architecture and look. The parking lot looks similar, grand, sweeping, not cluttered, it's a more expansive area. You take a place like Sears Mall—it seems cluttered. This seems more leisurely paced.

People are moving about slower—there's not the hustle and bustle —more or less meandering.

TOWN AND COUNTRY MEANS TO ME A COVERED WALKWAY.

Yeah, the back of them it seems to be—where they are seems to be a very large arbor like vines growing over it and things, and there possibly—I haven't looked in there yet to see if there's any displays like pottery and things—I get the feeling that there is right close to it.

ALSO, OUTDOORS?

Yeah, it seems like fairly high shade trees—kinda bordering. The center part doesn't seem to have it—this part in here. The trees seem to be way up in here along like this over here. This seems to be shaded in here, but it's sunny out here.

I just saw something that looked like a windmill—not a farm-type windmill—a Dutch-type windmill. It's smaller—it's not a huge thing, but I'm getting a definite feeling that it's like a windmill.

The area in there feels damp—not wet—they're not walking in water, but it's very moist.

The temperature in there . . . it's secluded. Feels very comfortable. A little on the shady side.

WHAT DO YOU FIND AS THE BOUNDARIES OF THE PLACE THEY'RE AT?

Outside of this little parklike affair that they seem to be in, there's a street. One side of it seems to be a kind of a residential . . . the other seems to be a little bit more heavily traveled.

Let me pick up a little bit more.

I can see one very large oak tree—exceptionally large.

Right now Bart is trying to point something out that is basically the significance of the whole place. It's like that key thing, well, if you'd have mentioned a salt pile I'd have blown my lid. Well, this has a significance that's just about comparable to that. I'm screening it out.

Thing that just flashed in was kind of like a stadium structure—like looking down into a stadium.

Just when I did that I—I'll have to reorient to make sure I'm looking in the same area now.

Seems like they're—I still get them in the same quadrant I had them in originally. Seems like some decorative brick walls.

THE QUADRANT YOU HAD THEM IN IS BASICALLY THE NORTHEAST QUADRANT?

Yeah, I got them out about this far—it's not far away—I'd say in this direction over here about—feels like a mile to a mile and a half. They don't feel as far away, and I'm not looking at the time continuum. They actually don't feel as far away. I'd say that it is about—not half the distance they were to the marina, and it seems to be on a line just about in that direction but just a hair more—rather than a direct line from here to the marina—they seem to be just slightly more to the left of that line.

I was looking back to where he had the car parked and it seems like it's on asphalt, then a curb in front, and then it's like a dirt walkway and then a sidewalk. But I can see eucalyptus buds on the ground and some branches of eucalyptus there.

One of the most dominant things to me in the way of unusualness is the size of the oak tree that I'm looking at. Looks like an arboretum, or I get the definite feeling of flowers.

Almost get the feeling like it's commercial flowers.

In fact, the most predominant feeling that I'm getting right now is flowers.

Don't know why iris particularly.

There's something about the windmill that I was going to look at. Wasn't that what you were . . . ?

Be like one you'd almost see in a miniature golf course . . . the windmill.

Has all the construction and detail but not as large—it's fairly small. Seems to be made out of dark redwood and it's kind of aged.

I'm going to try to look more directly to them. Let's see, there's Bart and Hal, and behind Bart is Judy and behind Hal is Phyllis, kinda staggered there.

Looks like a possible small pool of water—like a garden pond.

Looks like a little bridge.

I was trying to get the feeling of what type of an area it was.

Let me elevate a bit. I'm looking at much too small an area. There's some greater significance there that I feel I'm definitely not looking at—let's jack up a bit . . . maybe five hundred feet.

I see a lot of trees.

I see Judy's red hair and her brown eyes and her flashing teeth—she has beautiful teeth. Hadn't really looked at them before.

Phyllis and her are talking about something and Hal and Bart are talking about something and he's pointing at something and it seems to me that he's pointing over to what I'd call a windmill or something that looks like a windmill.

The water I see looks more like a pool or a pond than it does—you know, it's not big like a lake—not very large, but it looks like a definite pool.

Right where they're at I don't hear too much traffic noise—it seems to be fairly quiet.

Looks like a little wooden walkway.

Feels a little early, but it kinda seems like they're retracing their steps heading back toward the car, but they're still moving quite leisurely.

IF YOU LOOK DOWN ON THE PLACE FROM ABOVE, CAN YOU GET ANY FEELING FOR THE—IS THERE ANY OVERALL LAYOUT OR PLAN?

When I went up, I could see trees and stuff, and I kind of got the feeling of like in a corner of a golf course, you know—where there would be a lot of trees overhanging the green and some things in there —that seemed to be out of context, but when I elevated, that's what I got. It kind of looked like an overlap to me, so I didn't talk about it, but I will.

When I elevated, it kind of felt like it was right over the corner of a golf course of some kind, with a street running down one side, and they are fairly close to that.

In fact, the bricked area that I looked at or like a patio thing kinda looks like a walkway. Seems like there's small building—small meaning not tall—looks like a single-story building. Looks like it has a flat roof —slightly pitched. Looks like four by four poles supporting it—has a canopy out over it. They're painted white, place looks like very possible light yellow or cream color.

They're walking not too far from that. Still seems to me that they're on a dirt pathway.

In the area that they're in now, I get flowers again—where before they kinda fell out of the flowers.

Looks like maybe eighty to one hundred yards from where they are —looks like two guys on a motor scooter. They can see them.

WHAT WOULD YOU SAY IS THE INTEREST TO THIS PLACE? WHAT'S
SPECIAL ABOUT THIS PLACE?

It seems to be a kind of a recreational, relaxed . . . not energetic—
looks more relaxed. I'd say it's kind of combination recreational and
relaxation area that I'm getting out of it.

That would be the general character of it.

Two aspects—one is aesthetics and the other is a kind of a mild
recreational area.

There seem to be some unique features—I don't have it totally into
context as yet. There's a number of things that I've rejected—looked
at and rejected saying.

First, I got the impression that it was kind of like a miniature golf
course—I rejected that. Merely from saying it—I didn't reject the
principle—I just rejected saying it.

Then I kind of got the idea of a standard golf course—I also rejected
that on the same principle, so I'm just trying to describe the terrain.

Seems expansive—doesn't seem cluttered.

Just got a flash of something that reminded me of the gyroscope—
gimbals on the gyroscope.

Drinking fountain—looks like it's made out of kinda like fieldstone
built up into a fountain . . . bowl.

I'm going to elevate again and go through a search quadrant again.

I still get them in that general location, so that seems to set all right.

Distance—maybe a mile, mile and a half. Doesn't seem much farther—seems fairly close.

The area has an awful lot of grass, lot of trees—looks like dirt walkways, well trimmed. I can see the arbor, and the arbor could be a place
to sit and be out of the direct sun.

May be a few little tables and benches and chairs in there.

That outlooks over quite a grassy area—there are quite a few trees.
I see basically an oak.

Right after they got out of the car, I could see some eucalyptus buds
and branches on the ground, and it seemed like the trees were there.

Looked like they got out of the car, stepped upon a curb, dirt park-
way, a sidewalk, and then they went into this area.

I get the feeling this windmill-type thing—that all seems fairly real.

The feeling is still that it's relaxing and has some recreational aspects—I just haven't put it totally together as to giving it a name.

Right now I get a very strong impression of flowers again.

It seems like right now they're back to right where I originally
spotted them only they're going in the opposite direction—like they're
moving toward the direction they originally went.

While they were there, they walked on several pathways—walked
out quite a ways, then swung over and come over and worked around
and looked at . . .

One peculiar thing I might note—so far I haven't sensed, seen, nor heard an airplane.

Cars seem quite distant—outside of that little motor scooter affair with the two guys on it. That's about the only vehicular traffic I've seen—except out in the parking lot.

It seems like to me that they've got most of their attention off what they were looking at and they've got their attention more on the car now.

I want to look and find out what the significant thing was that Bart was talking about.

There's something quite unusual there and I ... damned if I can pick it up.

WAS HAL DOING ANYTHING BESIDES WALKING ALONG—WAS THERE ANY ACTIVITY FOR HAL TO DO?

Most of the time I was looking at Hal, he was kind of listening to Bart and Bart was pointing out a number of things.

Part of the time Bart was walking with Hal; part of the time he was back by Judy.

When I first saw them, it was Bart in the front on the left side, Hal was on his right, Judy was slightly behind—almost between Bart and Hal but behind, and Phyllis to her right.

They wandered around but the first time I picked up—they were that way.

When they were coming back, they just about reversed. Bart would be in front. When they were coming back, it looked like Bart was in front with Phyllis, and Judy was walking more behind Bart and Hal on her right when they were coming back out of there.

They're actually at the car.

TWO THIRTY. SHALL WE GO DOWNSTAIRS AND SEE HOW THEY'RE DOING?

4
LOOKING FOR
GIFTED SUBJECTS
IT TURNS OUT
THEY'RE ALL GIFTED!

I can do it on a plane;
I can do it on a train;
I can do it here or there;
I can do it anywhere.

—Dr. Seuss, *Green Eggs and Ham*

By the end of 1973, we had carried out more than twenty remote viewing experiments with Pat and Ingo, and it was increasingly evident that their unique window on the world was not limited by the conventional barriers to perception. Neither copper-walled rooms nor long distances in any way inhibited their ability to see places and events hundreds or thousands of miles away, or even to describe the interior of distant buildings thought to be secure against any sort of snooping.

Eighteen months had gone by since the first experiment with Ingo. No longer doubting the existence of paranormal functioning, we had come to expect our experiments to be successful, and were beginning to look for some physical laws that might be governing the phenomenon we were observing. Thus far, however, we had had no success in finding any such physical parameters. So we set aside our distance and shielding experiments, and decided to concentrate on finding out what personality factors or physiological characteristics might separate psychics from nonpsychics (a dichotomy, as it turned out, that may not exist).

To fulfill this requirement we put together two groups of subjects. One group was designated "experienced" because they had already participated in successful ESP experiments. The other group was called "learners," reflecting our interest in determining whether ESP skills could be learned. Three people were assigned to each group. The two groups were similarly constituted with respect to age and general interests to achieve as balanced an experiment as possible with so small a sample. We chose to work with only six subjects in this study so that we could carry out extensive medical, neuropsychological, and psychiatric tests on each of the participants. Lists of the tests carried out at the Stanford University Medical Center and at the Palo Alto Medical Clinic are given in Tables 3–5. Our subjects had a degree of scrutiny probably second only to that endured by the astronauts.

This experiment constituted a first step toward finding out how widely distributed psychic functioning is in the general population. Since we could not pretest our subjects without violating the intention of the experiments, our criterion for selection of inexperienced participants was simply to choose intelligent, cheery, agreeable people with whom we would enjoy working. That was satisfactory for the "learners."

We had a more difficult problem finding a third experienced subject to go with Pat and Ingo. Finally, Duane Elgin, an SRI research analyst, was prevailed upon to be our third experienced subject. He had obtained his experience, not in remote viewing, but rather with an ESP teaching machine with which he had worked successfully during the previous year. The teaching machine experiments are described in Chapter 6.

The stage was set for our experiments: Pat Price, Ingo Swann, and Duane Elgin comprised the experienced group. They were matched against our three other subjects, two of whom were SRI mathematicians, the other a professional photographer. We have already discussed the work with Pat and Ingo, so we will go on to the experiments with our first "learner."

Table 3

Medical Profile
(Department of Environmental Medicine,
Palo Alto Medical Clinic)

1. GENERAL PHYSICAL EXAMINATION
Complete Medical
Family History

2. LABORATORY EXAMINATIONS
SMA-12 Panel Blood Chemistries
Protein Electrophoresis
Blood Lipid Profile
Urinalysis
Serology
Blood Type and Factor
Pulmonary Function Screening
Electrocardiogram 12-Lead

3. NEUROLOGICAL EXAMINATION
Comprehensive Electroencephalogram, Sleeping and Routine

4. AUDIOMETRIC EXAMINATIONS
Comprehensive
Bekesy Bone Conduction
Speech Discrimination
Impedance Bridge Test

5. OPHTHALMOLOGIST EXAMINATIONS
Comprehensive
Card Testing
Peripheral Field Test
Muscle Test
Dilation Funduscope
Indirect Ophthalmoscopic and Fundus Examination

6. SPECIAL VISUAL EXAMINATION
Visual Contrast Sensitivity (SRI)

7. EMI BRAIN SCAN

Table 4

Neuropsychological Profile
(Department of Neurology,
Stanford Hospital)

Halstead Category Test
Tactile Performance Test
Speech Perception Test
Seashore Rhythm Test
Trail Making Test
Knox Cube Test
Halstead-Wepman Aphasia Screening Test
Raven Progressive Matrices
Verbal Concept Attainment Test
Buschke Memory Test
Finger-Tapping Test
Dynamometer Grip Strength
Groove Pegboard Test

Table 5

Psychological Profile
(Department of Psychiatry,
Palo Alto Medical Clinic)

W.A.I.S. (Wechsler Adult Intelligence Scale)
Bender Gestalt Visual Motor Test
Benton Visual Memory Test
Wechsler Memory Scale
Luscher Color Test
Strong Vocational Interest Blank
M.M.P.I. (Minnesota Multiphasic Personality Inventory)
E.P.P.S. (Edwards Personality Preference Schedule)
Rorschach Inkblot
T.A.T. (Thematic Apperception Test)
In-depth Interview

Experiments with Hella Hammid

I (R.T.) had known Hella for more than a dozen years, and we all agreed that we would enjoy working together.

HELLA HAMMID—SELF-PORTRAIT

Hella is an engaging, sensitive, friendly woman in her early fifties. She is a gifted professional photographer, working independently now, though in the past she free-lanced for *Life* and other magazines. Born in Germany, she came to the U.S. as a teenager. She speaks English flawlessly, although it is actually her third language, after German and French.

Prior to this series, Hella had participated as a volunteer in an ESP brain wave experiment to be described later. Outside of that encounter, she had no previous experience with the paranormal.

At the time we began working with Hella, she had no strong feelings about whether she would be successful. This was in contrast to both Ingo Swann, who had come to our laboratory fresh from a lengthy and apparently successful series of experiments with Dr. Gertrude Schmeidler at City College of New York, and Pat Price, who felt that he used his remote viewing ability in everyday life.

In contrast to Pat and Ingo, many people are reluctant to publicly attempt activities that are generally considered to be impossible.

Society often provides negative feedback and inhibits the individual who might otherwise have explored his capabilities. As already indicated, in addition to maintaining scientific rigor, one of our primary tasks as researchers is to provide an environment in which the subject feels safe to explore the possibility of paranormal perception. With a new subject, we also try to stress the *non*uniqueness of the ability; in our research, paranormal functioning appears to be a latent ability that all subjects can experience to some degree.

Before beginning a formal experiment with Hella, we set up an orientation series of mock experiments using a walkie-talkie link as a method of providing a comfortable transition into the type of experiment we wished to conduct. Since Hella was inexperienced with remote viewing, the walkie-talkie was to provide a familiar channel for immediate feedback during exploration of the unconventional channel. (Here we must emphasize that we *never* use such a link during an actual experiment because of the obvious danger of cueing.)

In these mock experiments, which are not considered demonstration-of-ability tests, the subject is asked to describe simultaneously what the remote experimenter is looking at.

We are often asked how we prepare a subject for a remote viewing experience. All we provide is a quiet, relaxing place to work, an assurance to the subject that the ability is natural and not unique, and finally we give them the assurance that it is possible to be successful, permissible to fail, and fun to try at any rate.

In this particular experiment, Hella made her maiden voyage into remote viewing while standing in the rain on the roof of our engineering building. Our walkie-talkie, unlike remote viewing, doesn't operate through walls, but the use of such devices helps to convey the idea that it is possible to communicate with a distant location, even though it can't be seen.

The tape recording of Hella's first mock experiment begins:

OUTBOUND EXPERIMENTER: I am at my first target location; what do you see?

HELLA: I see a little house covered with red, overlapping

boards. It has a white trim and a very tall, pointed roof. But the whole thing feels fake, like a movie set.

Her description turned out to be correct. The actual target building was a fifteen-foot-high model of a little red schoolhouse at a local miniature golf course (see photo on page 75). This is an ex-

"SCHOOLHOUSE" ON MINIATURE GOLF COURSE
USED AS REMOTE VIEWING TARGET

ample of the "first-time effect" which has been carefully explored and is well-known to experimenters in the field.[1] A half-dozen mock experiments with surprisingly good results completed the orientation series.

With the orientation at an end, we carried out a nine-experiment series which replicated the Price work with only two changes. As it had apparently made no difference whether or not shielding was used in the original nine-experiment series, this time we worked in an ordinary unshielded laboratory which was a more comfortable and convenient location. Second, the remote viewing periods were reduced from thirty to fifteen minutes, since in the mock-experiment orientation series the subject was observed to tire when viewing was extended beyond the shorter period. Otherwise, the procedures were identical.

As we proceeded through the series, we found that Hella, because of her artistic background, was able to draw and describe visual images that she could not identify in any cognitive or analytic sense. For example, when the target team went to a pedestrian overpass, Hella said that she saw a "kind of trough up in the air," which she indicated in the upper part of her drawing in Figure 13. She went

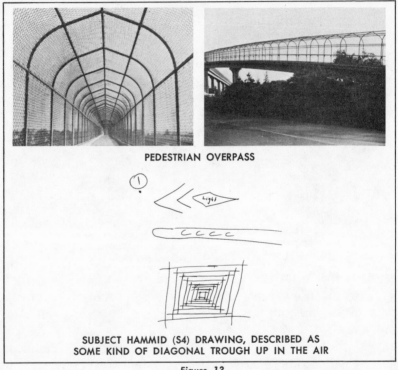

PEDESTRIAN OVERPASS

SUBJECT HAMMID (S4) DRAWING, DESCRIBED AS
SOME KIND OF DIAGONAL TROUGH UP IN THE AIR

Figure 13

on to explain that, "If you stand where they are standing, you will see something like this," indicating the nestled squares at the bottom of Figure 13. As it turned out, a judge standing where she indicated would have a view closely resembling what she had drawn, as can be seen from the accompanying photographs of the target location. (It needs to be emphasized, by the way, that judges did not have access to our photographs of the site, used here for illustrative purposes only, but were directed to each of the locations by written instructions.)

In another experiment, she described seeing "an open barnlike structure with a pitched roof." She also saw a "kind of slatted side to the structure making light and dark bars on the wall." Her drawing and a photograph of the actual bicycle shed are shown in Figure 14.

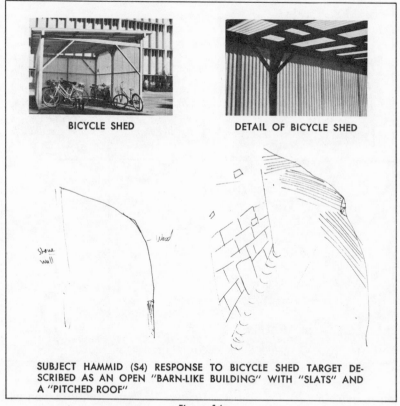

BICYCLE SHED   DETAIL OF BICYCLE SHED

SUBJECT HAMMID (S4) RESPONSE TO BICYCLE SHED TARGET DE-SCRIBED AS AN OPEN "BARN-LIKE BUILDING" WITH "SLATS" AND A "PITCHED ROOF"

Figure 14

In recent work, we have encouraged all subjects to make drawings of anything they visualize and associate with the remote location. We have found, as we will describe later, that the subjects' drawings are in general more accurate than their verbal descriptions.

Mind-Reach

As with the original Price series, the results of this nine-experiment series were submitted for independent blind judging by an SRI research analyst not otherwise associated with the research. While at each target location, visited in turn, the judge was required to rank—on a scale of 1 to 9 (best to worst match)—the nine unedited typed manuscripts of the tape-recorded narratives, along with any associated drawings made by the subject. The result, in this case, was statistically significant at odds of better than 500,000:1, and included five direct hits and four second ranks (see Table 6).

Table 6

**Distribution of Rankings Assigned to Transcripts Associated
with Each Target Location for Learner Subject Hammid (S4)**

Target Location	Distance (km)	Rank of Associated Transcript
Methodist Church, Palo Alto	1.9	1
Ness Auditorium, Menlo Park	0.2	1
Merry-go-round, Palo Alto	3.4	1
Parking garage, Mountain View	8.1	2
SRI International Courtyard, Menlo Park	0.2	1
Bicycle shed, Menlo Park	0.1	2
Railroad trestle bridge, Palo Alto	1.3	2
Pumpkin patch, Menlo Park	1.3	1
Pedestrian overpass, Palo Alto	5.0	2
Total sum of ranks		13 $(p = 1.8 \times 10^{-6})$

Again, as a backup judging procedure, a panel of five additional judges not otherwise associated with the research was asked simply to blind match the unedited, typed transcripts and associated drawings generated by the remote viewer against the nine target locations which they independently visited in turn. A correct match consisted of a transcript of a given date being matched to the target of that date. Instead of the expected number of one match each per judge, the number of correct matches obtained by the five judges was 5, 3, 3, 2, and 2. Thus, rather than the expected total number of five correct matches from the judges, fifteen such matches were obtained.

More than a year has passed since we stood on the rain-swept roof at SRI trying to convince Hella that it is okay to demonstrate psychic ability. In looking back on her past six months' work with us, we find that with only one or two exceptions every experiment conducted under standard conditions showed good correlations between her descriptions and the actual target location.

In comparing Hella's results with Pat's, we observe a difference in style which evidently affected the pattern of results. Pat's descriptions were in general more detailed than Hella's, leading to more first place matches, that is, direct hits in the rank order judging, but he also got two clear misses where the striving for detail resulted in erroneous analytical interpretations. Hella, on the other hand, preferring to be more cautious, got fewer first place matches but did not find any of her descriptions falling into less than second place. Such a comparison does not, of course, indicate that one is more psychic than the other. It merely shows a difference in style.

Experiments with Experienced Subjects

If Hella was to be considered a "learner" in our experiments, what should we expect from the "experienced" subjects?

Duane Elgin, one of the experienced subjects, is a senior social scientist at SRI who is in his early thirties and who does "futures" research—he anticipates alternative future patterns of social evolution and helps people to think and plan more creatively with respect to those emerging patterns. Duane credits much of his success in his "second life" as a psychic subject to simply paying attention to subtle and delicate changes within his "body-awareness" which, he feels, are oftentimes among the most useful indicators of the occurrence of psychic functioning.

PHOTO BY HELLA HAMMID

DUANE ELGIN

Having completed twenty-two remote viewing experiments on local Bay Area targets—nine each with Pat and Hella, and four with Ingo—we realized that it would take more than a year if we insisted on doing nine experiments with each of our six subjects. We therefore decided to do four experiments with each of the remaining three subjects, and, to put the shorter series on a similar footing with regard to judging, combine the results from the other two "learners" into a group of eight, and similarly combine the four transcripts each from Duane and Ingo into a group of eight.

Out of the combined group of Duane's and Ingo's experiments, one of Duane's transcripts was correctly matched in first place and three were put into second place (see Table 7). In Duane's first try, the outbound experimenters were sent by the standard random protocol to the Bay Area Rapid Transit (BART) station across the bay from SRI (see photo on page 82). Duane described ". . . a simple, heavy, solid building with unique function. It is in relatively natural surroundings." Duane then said (correctly), "They are standing at a metal railing looking out over a scene. They are up high enough that they can see some buildings down below."

He expressed some confusion whether the experiments were inside or outside the building. "I have the sense that they're outside, though, but they're near a building. There is a larger building-like structure. Feels like it has sort of one function. One primary func-

Table 7

**Distribution of Rankings Assigned to Transcripts Associated
with Each Target Location for Experienced Subjects
Elgin (S2) and Swann (S3)**

Subject	Target Location	Distance (km)	Rank of Associated Transcript
S2	BART station (Transit System), Union City	16.1	1
S2	Shielded room, SRI, Menlo Park	0.1	2
S2	Tennis courts, Palo Alto	3.4	2
S2	Golf course bridge, Stanford	3.4	2
S3	City Hall, Palo Alto	2.0	1
S3	Miniature golf course, Menlo Park	3.0	1
S3	Kiosk in park, Menlo Park	0.3	3
S3	Baylands Nature Preserve, Palo Alto	6.4	3
	Total sum of ranks		15 ($p = 3.8 \times 10^{-4}$)

tion. And although they're outside, they're relating to the building and its function." In fact, the experimenters were on the open station platform waiting for a train. At eleven twenty-two Duane said, "I have the impression that Russell is feeling a smooth metal surface. Sort of large plates. Large metal plates. Somewhat rectangular." The timing and description corresponded to just such an event. The photograph on page 82 illustrates my (R.T.) looking at the BART route map just before the train's arrival. I did have my hand on the map to find out if it was plastic or enameled. At exactly eleven twenty-five Duane said, "Everything changes" and "I don't

(A) SEEN FROM PARKING LOT

(B) CENTRAL PORTION OF BUILDING

(C) TRAIN PLATFORM ON UPPER LEVEL

(D) MR. TARG AT BART SYSTEM MAP

BART STATION AT UNION CITY, CALIFORNIA, USED AS REMOTE VIEWING TARGET

see them anymore." That is the precise time that we boarded the BART train and left the station. As seen in Table 7, in later judging this response was correctly matched to the target.

The third experiment with Elgin provided a further example of the dichotomy between verbal and drawing responses. (As with medical literature, case histories often are more illuminating than the summary of results.) This was a demonstration experiment for a visitor who had heard of our work and wanted to evaluate our experimental protocol. The target location in this case was a tennis court 3.4 km south of SRI.

In the laboratory, Duane held a bearing compass at arm's length, and began the experiment by indicating the direction of the target demarcation team correctly to within five degrees. (In all four experiments with Elgin, he was always within ten degrees of the correct direction.) He then gave a fifteen-minute tape-recorded description and made the drawings shown in Figure 15.

In discussing the drawings, Duane indicated that he was uncertain what the team was doing, but had the impression that they were

TENNIS COURTS

SUBJECT ELGIN (S2) DRAWINGS IN RESPONSE TO TENNIS COURT TARGET

Figure 15

at a museum (known to him) in a particular park. In fact, the tennis-court target was located in that park about 90 meters from the museum. A now familiar characteristic was noted. Although certain elements of the subject's response (especially the drawings) resembled the target site, the analytic interpretations were incomplete or erroneous. Nonetheless, when rank ordering transcripts 1 through 8 at the site, the judge ranked this transcript as 2. It was repeatedly observed throughout the experiments that most of the correct information related to us by subjects was of a nonanalytic nature pertaining to shape, form, color, and material rather than to function or name.

For the entire series of eight (four each) from our experienced subjects Elgin and Swann, the numerical evaluation based on blind rank ordering of transcripts at each site was statistically significant at odds of 2,500:1, and as shown in Table 7, included three direct hits and three second ranks for the target-associated transcripts.

Experiments with Learners

To complete the series, four experiments were carried out with each of the two learner subjects, a man and woman on the SRI professional staff, Marshall Pease and Phyllis Cole. The overall results in this case, taken as a group, were not statistically significant. (For the series of eight, judged as a group of seven since one target came up twice, once for each subject, the numerical evaluation based on blind rank ordering of transcripts at each site indicated odds of only 12.5:1, too low to be taken as evidential for the group as a whole.) However, there were two direct hits and two second ranks out of the seven (see Table 8).

Table 8

Distribution of Rankings Assigned to Transcripts Associated with Each Target Location for Learner Subjects Pease (S_5) and Cole (S_6)

Subject	Target Location	Distance (km)	Rank of Associated Transcript
S_5	Pedestrian overpass, Palo Alto	5.0	3
S_5	Railroad trestle bridge, Palo Alto	1.3	6
S_5	Windmill, Portola Valley	8.5	2
S_5, S_6	White Plaza, Stanford	3.8	1
S_6	Airport, Palo Alto	5.5	2
S_6	Kiosk in park, Menlo Park	0.3	5
S_6	Boathouse, Stanford	4.0	1
	Total sum of ranks		20 (p=0.08, non-significant)

Looking for Gifted Subjects

WHITE PLAZA AT STANFORD UNIVERSITY

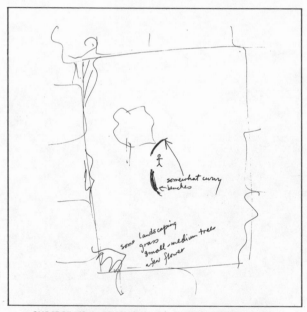

SUBJECT (S6) DRAWING OF WHITE PLAZA, STAN-
FORD UNIVERSITY. SUBJECT DREW WHAT SHE
CALLED "CURVY BENCHES" AND THEN AN-
NOUNCED CORRECTLY THAT THE PLACE WAS
"WHITE PLAZA AT STANFORD"

Figure 16

85

One of the direct hits, which occurred with Phyllis Cole in her first experiment, provides another example of the "first-time effect." The outbound experimenter obtained a target by random selection from the pool which was as always unknown to the experimenter staying with the subject. Phyllis Cole, a mathematician in the computer science laboratory, had no previous experience in remote viewing. She began to describe a large square with a fountain. Four minutes into the experiment she recognized the location as White Plaza on the Stanford University campus, and correctly identified it by name (see Figure 16). It should be noted that in the area from which the target locations were drawn there are several other fountains as well, some of which were in the target group. (As an example of the style of narrative given by a learner subject, and of the part played by the experimenter remaining with the subject in this

WINDMILL TARGET. SUBJECT CORRECTLY DESCRIBED "RED A-FRAME BUILDING WITH DECK, YELLOW TREE, A-FRAME SWING SET, AND GRAY TRANSFORMER," ALL SHOWN IN PICTURE. HE ALSO DESCRIBED "MASTER TYPE LOCK OF LAMINATED STEEL," WHICH IS ON FRONT DOOR OF WINDMILL (NOT SHOWN)

case, we include the entire unedited text of this experiment at the end of this chapter.)

One of Pease's results shows again the dichotomy between a likeness in pattern with regard to drawings, coupled with misinterpretation. The target was a windmill (see photo on page 86). Pease's drawings, shown in Figure 17, indicated a tapering tower, forty to fifty feet high (correct), but the windmill-like pattern was interpreted as a symbol mounted on a wall.

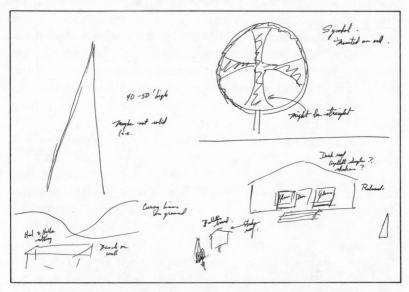

SUBJECT (S5) DRAWING IN RESPONSE TO WINDMILL TARGET

Figure 17

Experiments with Unselected Subjects

After more than a year of following the experimental protocol described above and observing that even inexperienced subjects got better than expected results, we began a series of experiments to explore further whether individuals other than so-called "psychics" could demonstrate the remote viewing ability. To test this idea, we have a continuing program to carry out additional experiments using local targets in the Bay Area with subjects who we have no particular reason to believe have paranormal perception.

The motivation for these particular experiments was two-fold. First, the experiments provide data that indicate the level of proficiency which can be expected from unselected volunteers. Second, when an individual observes a successful demonstration experiment involving another person as subject, it inevitably occurs to him that perhaps chicanery is involved. We have found that the most effective way to settle this issue is to have the individual himself act as a subject. This provides him with personal experience against which our experimental protocols and reported results can be evaluated.

Many scientists from the government and elsewhere have visited our lab to decide whether psychic research is something that their particular department should be involved with. Generally their requests, now as well as then, focus on their desire to "see something psychic." And for the previous year, we had been willing to demonstrate with one of our subjects the remote viewing protocol.

However, even though our visitor was generally satisfied, it was difficult when he returned home to describe to others what he had seen. This was especially true in the face of strong assertions to the effect that all reasonable men know that such a thing is impossible, and therefore it must have been a trick, in which we (or our subject) deceived the visitor.

Therefore, we no longer have demonstration experiments. Instead, we ask the visitor to become a subject, and thereby determine for himself what he experiences and sees. He is taken to the target after the experiment so he can determine firsthand if it corresponds to what he had visualized during the experiment. We have found that the experience of having participated in a successful remote viewing experiment oneself cannot be brushed aside as easily as the memory of having watched someone else do it.

These new rules were inaugurated during a five-experiment series with two government scientists interested in observing our experimental protocols. The first visitor's responses were excellent—well beyond our expectations (see Chapter 1).

Our second visitor gave one of the best results we have ever observed in his first experiment. He began his narrative, "There is a red A-frame building and next to it is a large yellow thing [a yellow tree]. Now further left there is another A-shape. It looks like a swing set, but it is pushed down in a gully so I can't see the swings." (Correct.) He went on to describe a lock on the front door that he said "looks like it's made of laminated steel, so it must be a Master lock." (Also correct.) (See photo on page 86.)

For the series of five experiments—three from the first subject and two from the second—the numerical evaluation based on blind rank ordering of the transcripts at each site was significant at odds of 60:1 and included three direct hits and one second rank for the target-associated transcripts (see Table 9).

Table 9

Distribution of Rankings Assigned to Transcripts Associated
with Each Target Location for Visitor Subjects V1 and V2

Subject	Target Location	Distance (km)	Rank of Associated Transcript
V1	Bridge over stream, Menlo Park	0.3	1
V1	Baylands Nature Preserve, Palo Alto	6.4	2
V1	Merry-go-round, Palo Alto	3.4	1
V2	Windmill, Portola Valley	8.5	1
V2	Apartment swimming pool, Mountain View	9.1	3
	Total sum of ranks		8 (p=0.017)

Observing such unselected subjects has led us to conclude that remote viewing may be a latent and widely distributed perceptual ability. We have, as of this writing, carried out successful remote viewing experiments with about twenty participants, almost all of whom came to us without any prior experience, and in some cases, with little interest in psychic functioning. So far, we cannot identify a single individual who has not succeeded in a remote viewing task to his own satisfaction.

Jonathan Livingston Seagull at SRI

In the fall of 1974, we had already concluded most of the experiments described thus far. Our work was going well. Other laboratories were beginning to replicate our remote viewing experiments. There remained, however, the seemingly perpetual problem of contract research, that of obtaining sufficient funding for further research.

Desperate times call for desperate measures. I had read *Jonathan Livingston Seagull*, and also the interview with its author, Richard Bach, which was published in *Psychic* magazine.[2] In that interview, Richard described how he was walking alone on the beach one day when he suddenly heard a clear, deep voice behind him call out, "JONATHAN LIVINGSTON SEAGULL." Since he was alone, and didn't know anyone of that name, he felt that he had experienced something of some special significance. He returned immediately to his home and wrote in a single sitting the first part of his now famous book. The second part came to him in a similar fashion six years later.

It is clear to any psychical researcher that when Jonathan Seagull crashed into the cliff, he experienced what Dr. Charles Tart would call a "classical out of the body experience." Therefore, propelled by Bach's idea that "the seagull that flies the highest sees the furthest," we called Richard Bach himself to see if he could pump new blood into our project.

That call led to a lasting and harmonious relationship. Richard turned out to be a warm and very subtle fellow. He is extraordinarily quick to catch on to new ideas, even the intricacies of modern

PHOTO BY RUSSELL MUNSON

RICHARD BACH

physics. He loves to travel and is most comfortable moving through space and time guided by only the spur of the moment.

Richard had read our paper in *Nature* and thought it would be interesting to try remote viewing. We suspected from reading his book that he, like many others we have come across, may have been doing it already, for years. We were happy, though, to share with him whatever we knew about the process and how it can be learned.

Finally, one sunny day in April, 1975, Richard flew his small plane into San Francisco airport and called to say that he was ready to visit our lab and see what we were up to.

The mechanics of remote viewing is still a mystery, but this does not prevent us from continuing to seek answers. It does, however, make us apprehensive each time we find ourselves in the position of possibly having to carry out a "demonstration" experiment.

We decided to use our newfound successful protocol and asked our visitor to be the subject. Richard and I stayed in the laboratory and waited the half hour until Hal reached his target.

Richard's first words were about a gray building with a pointed roof. At that point, he seemed to feel that he was done. (We have observed that new subjects have a tendency to say much less than they could about what they see. This is because they generally assume that their mental pictures probably do not in fact correspond to the targets. They will often pepper their narrative with disclaimers such as "I know this is just my imagination," or "This just came to mind, but I don't think it means anything." Our task is to convince subjects that "In order to be right, you have to be willing to be wrong." If all they say is "The grass is green and the sky is blue," then they will surely be right, but no judge will be able to separate one description from another.)

I asked Richard for more details. He said that the building was "some sort of fantasy house." I asked him what he saw that made him call it a fantasy house. He replied that "the roof is all scalloped in different colors."

Many times a subject is able to come up with more data if another point of view is suggested. With this in mind, I asked Richard to drift into the building and tell me what he could see inside. I also suggested to him that there would be enough light to see by. We have found that this form of leading is helpful, and since the experimenter remaining with the subject has no idea of the target, there is no possibility of cueing.

Richard replied that he found himself inside an airline ticket office with the counter on the right.

Since this was a very analytic statement, rather than a description of a perception, I asked him what he saw that made it look like an airline office. He described a "white block about three by three by eight" that "looked like it was covered with white formica." And "behind the counter attached to the wall was the logo of the company. . . . It looks like a big gold fleur-de-lis."

In fact, the target was a church (see photo on page 93), and "the logo of the company" was a large gold cross attached to the wall, just behind the white marble altar of just the dimensions that he described.

He also correctly indicated that the ceiling of the building was "pointed on the inside, just as it was on the outside," and that there was "light in the building coming through a hole in the roof." The unique feature of this church is that the roof has many trapezoidal cutouts framing stained glass pieces that fill the whole building with diffuse bands of colored light.

The next afternoon, Richard provided another, equally fine, re-

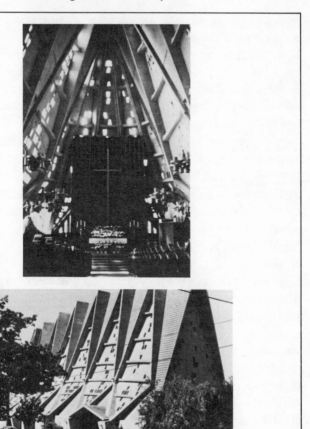

INTERIOR AND EXTERIOR VIEWS OF METHODIST CHURCH
USED AS REMOTE VIEWING TARGET

mote viewing description. He felt well satisfied with the work under way, was interested in contributing to our research, bade us farewell, and flew off for a speaking engagement in Hawaii.

Technology Series: Short-Range Viewing

Because remote viewing is a perceptual ability, it is important to find out how much detail can be discerned: in technical terms, its resolution capability. To accomplish this, we decided to use indoor, detailed targets.

Twelve experiments were carried out with five different subjects, two of whom were visiting scientists. They were told that one of the experimenters would be sent by random protocol to a laboratory within the SRI complex and that he would use equipment or apparatus at that location. It was further explained that the experimenter remaining with the subject was to be, as usual, kept ignorant of the target pool to prevent cueing. Unknown to subjects, targets in the pool could be used more than once. One of the goals of these particular experiments was to obtain multiple responses to a given target. This was in order to find out whether combining a number of responses would yield overlapping similarities, thus providing better results. Each subject was asked to describe the target verbally (tape-recorded) and by means of drawings during a synchronized fifteen-minute interval in which the outbound experimenter used the equipment in the target area; that is, he drilled holes with the drill press, typed on the typewriter, etc.

In the twelve experiments, seven different pieces of equipment were used: a drill press, Xerox machine, video computer terminal, chart recorder, four-state random number generator, typewriter and, in one case, an entire machine shop. Three of these were used twice (drill press, video terminal, and typewriter), and one (Xerox machine) came up three times in our random selection procedure.

Comparisons of the equipment at the target sites and subject drawings for three of the multiple-response cases (the typewriter, Xerox machine, and video terminal) are shown in Figures 18–20. As is apparent from the illustrations, certain of the experiments provide circumstantial evidence for the existence of a useful information channel. This includes experiments in which visiting government scientists participated as subjects (Xerox machine and video terminal) to observe the protocol. In general, it appears that use of multiple-subject responses to a single target provides better results than target identification by a single individual. This conclusion is borne out by the judging described below.

Given that in general the drawings constitute the most accurate portion of a subject's description, in the first judging procedure a

TECHNOLOGY SERIES TYPEWRITER TARGET

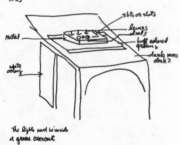

SUBJECT SWANN (S3) RESPONSE

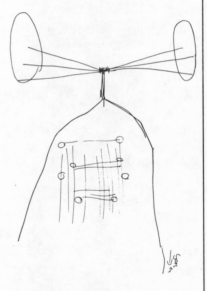

SUBJECT HAMMID (S4) RESPONSE

DRAWINGS OF A TYPEWRITER TARGET BY TWO SUBJECTS

Figure 18

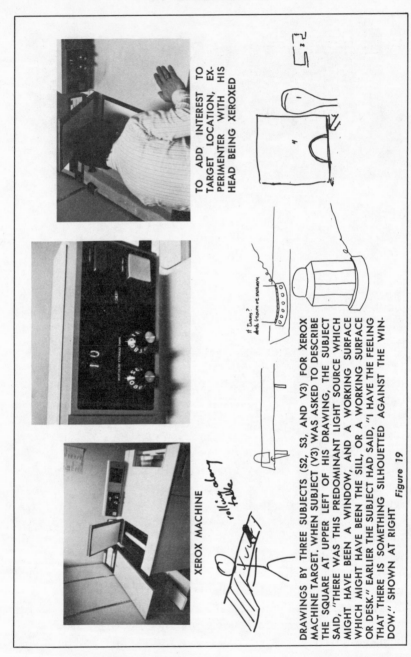

TO ADD INTEREST TO TARGET LOCATION, EXPERIMENTER WITH HIS HEAD BEING XEROXED

XEROX MACHINE

rolling along table

If Tauss? does (cream or maroon)

DRAWINGS BY THREE SUBJECTS (S2, S3, AND V3) FOR XEROX MACHINE TARGET. WHEN SUBJECT (V3) WAS ASKED TO DESCRIBE THE SQUARE AT UPPER LEFT OF HIS DRAWING, THE SUBJECT SAID, "THERE WAS THIS PREDOMINANT LIGHT SOURCE WHICH MIGHT HAVE BEEN A WINDOW, AND A WORKING SURFACE WHICH MIGHT HAVE BEEN THE SILL, OR A WORKING SURFACE OR DESK." EARLIER THE SUBJECT HAD SAID, "I HAVE THE FEELING THAT THERE IS SOMETHING SILHOUETTED AGAINST THE WINDOW." SHOWN AT RIGHT   Figure 19

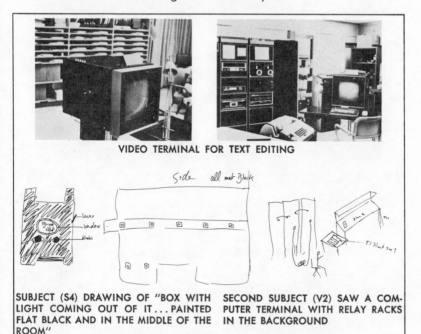

VIDEO TERMINAL FOR TEXT EDITING

SUBJECT (S4) DRAWING OF "BOX WITH LIGHT COMING OUT OF IT ... PAINTED FLAT BLACK AND IN THE MIDDLE OF THE ROOM"

SECOND SUBJECT (V2) SAW A COMPUTER TERMINAL WITH RELAY RACKS IN THE BACKGROUND

DRAWING BY TWO SUBJECTS OF A VIDEO TERMINAL TARGET
Figure 20

judge was asked simply to blind match only the drawings (i.e., without tape transcripts) to the targets. Multiple subject responses on a given target were stapled together, and thus seven subject-drawing response packets were to be matched to the seven different targets for which drawings were made. As in all of our other experiments, the judge did *not* have access to our photographs of the target locations, which are used here for illustration purposes only, but was sent by written instructions to each of the target locations.

The response packets (judged on a scale of 1 to 7—best to worst match) included one direct hit and four second ranks out of the seven (see Table 10). The result was significant at odds of 28:1.

In the second, more detailed effort at evaluation, a visiting scientist selected at random one of the twelve data packages (a drill press experiment) and submitted it for independent analysis to an engineer at his own laboratory requesting an estimate as to what was being described. The engineer, blind as to the target and given only

Table 10

**Distribution of Rankings Assigned to Subject Drawings
Associated with Each Target Location**

Subject	Target Location	Rank of Associated Drawings
S_3, S_4	Drill press	2
S_2, S_3, V_3	Xerox machine	2
S_4, V_2	Video terminal	1
S_3	Chart recorder	2
S_4	Random number generator	6
S_4	Machine shop	3
S_3, S_4	Typewriter	2
	Total sum of ranks	18 ($p = 0.036$)

the subject's taped narrative and drawings (see Figure 21), was able, from the subject's description alone, to correctly classify the target as a "man-sized vertical boring machine."

Summary of Remote Viewing Results

These experiments involved remote viewing of outdoor scenes or laboratory apparatus. Although containing inaccuracies, the subjects' descriptions were sufficiently accurate to permit the judges to significantly differentiate among various targets. A summary tabulation of the statistical evaluations of these fifty-one experiments with nine subjects is presented in Table 11. The results were evaluated conservatively on the basis of a procedure which ignores transcript quality beyond that necessary to rank the data packets as to how well they matched the target site. Such a conservative proce-

**DRILL PRESS
(TECHNOLOGY SERIES)**

**BELT DRIVE FOR DRILL PRESS
(CAN BE SEEN ONLY FROM ABOVE MACHINE)**

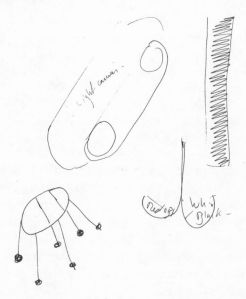

SUBJECT (S4) DRAWING OF DRILL PRESS SHOWING BELT DRIVE, STOOL, AND "VERTICAL GRAPH THAT GOES UP AND DOWN"

Figure 21

Table 11

Summary: Remote Viewing

Subject	Number of Experiments	p-Value, Rank Order Judging
With natural targets		
S1 (experienced)	9	2.9×10^{-5}
S2 and S3 (experienced)	8	3.8×10^{-4}
S4 (learner)	9	1.8×10^{-6}
S5 and S6 (learners)	8	0.08 (nonsignificant)
V1 and V2 (learners/visitors)	5	0.017
With technology targets		
S2, S3, S4, V2, V3	12	0.036

dure vastly underestimates the statistical significance of specific individual descriptions. Even so, the overall result clearly indicates the presence of a potentially useful information channel.

Furthermore, it appears that the principal difference between experienced and inexperienced subjects is *not* that the inexperienced never exhibit the faculty, but rather that their results are less reliable, more sporadic. Although the results may have been boosted by the "first-time effect" mentioned earlier, individual transcripts from the inexperienced are among some of the best obtained. Such observations support a hypothesis that remote viewing is probably a latent and widely distributed perceptual ability.

Thus, the primary achievement of our research has been the elicitation of high-quality remote viewing from individuals who agreed to act as subjects. Criticism of this claim could in principle be put forward on the basis of three potential flaws: (1) the study could involve naïveté in protocol that permits various forms of cueing, intentional or unintentional; (2) the experiments discussed could be selected out of a larger pool of experiments of which many are of poorer quality; and (3) data for the reported experiments could be edited to show only the matching elements, the nonmatching elements being discarded.

All three criticisms, however, are invalid. First, with regard to cueing, the use of double-blind protocols ensures that no one in contact with the subject can know what the target is. Second, selection of experiments for reporting did not take place; every experiment was entered on a master log and is included in the statistical evaluations. Third, data associated with a given experiment remain unedited; all experiments are tape-recorded and all data are included unedited in the data package to be judged, evaluated, and so on.

In the process of judging—attempting to match transcripts against targets on the basis of the information in the transcripts— some patterns and regularities in the transcript descriptions became evident. Our consultant, Dr. Arthur Hastings, pointed out to us that each person tended to focus on certain aspects of the remote target complex and to exclude others, so that each had an individual pattern of response, like a signature.

Swann, for example, frequently responded with topographical descriptions, maps, and architectural features of the target locations. Elgin often focused on the behavior of the remote experimenter and the sequence of actions he carried out at the target. Hammid, more than any other subject, gave the feel of the location, and experiential or sensory gestalts—for example, light/dark elements in the scene; indoor/outdoor and enclosed/open distinctions. Prominent features of Price's transcripts were detailed descriptions of what the outside experimenters were concretely experiencing, seeing, or doing—for example, standing on asphalt, or blacktop, overlooking water; looking at a purple iris.

The range of any individual subject's responses was wide. Anyone might draw a map or describe the mood of the remote experimenter, but the consistency of each subject's overall approach suggests that just as individual descriptions of a *directly* viewed scene would differ, so do those in *remote* viewing processes.

In summary, we do not yet have an understanding of the nature of the information-bearing signal that a subject perceives. We know only that the subjects commonly report that they perceive the signal visually as though they were looking at the object or place from a position in its immediate neighborhood. Furthermore, a subject's perceptual viewpoint has mobility in that he can shift his point of view to describe elements of a scene that would not be visible to an observer standing at ground level. Finally, motion is in general not perceived; in fact, moving objects often are unseen even when nearby static objects are correctly identified.

Finally, we observe that most of the correct information that subjects relate to us is of a nonanalytic nature pertaining to shape, form, color, and material rather than to function or name. In consultation with Dr. Robert Ornstein of the Langley-Porter Neuropsychiatric Institute, San Francisco, and with Dr. Ralph Kiernan of the Department of Neurology, Stanford University Medical Center, Stanford, California, we have formed the tentative hypothesis that paranormal functioning may involve specialization characteristic of the brain's right hemisphere. This possibility is derived from a variety of evidence from clinical and neurosurgical sources which indicate that the two hemispheres of the human brain specialize in different cognitive functions (see Chapter 6). The left hemisphere is predominantly active in verbal and other analytical functioning and the right hemisphere predominates in spatial and other holistic processing.[3] Although further research is necessary, it is clear that remote viewing has characteristics in common with other performances that require right hemispheric function.

As a result of the above considerations, we have learned to urge our subjects simply to describe what they see as opposed to what they think they are looking at. We have learned that their unanalyzed perceptions are almost always a better guide to the true target than their interpretations of the perceived data.

REMOTE VIEWING: A RECIPE

Telling someone how to do remote viewing is a little like trying to explain how to learn to see. There is little to tell, and we are the first to acknowledge that there is no secret. You learn to remote view by trial and error, getting feedback from the environment, in much the same way you learn to ride a bicycle. If you are interested in making use of your own, perhaps latent, psychic ability, here are a few pointers based on our experience with others in the past.

1. Ask yourself: "Is it okay with me if the world should be constructed in such a way that psychic functioning does exist?" If that is all right with you, then ask yourself: "Is it okay with me if I have ESP ability?" In an experimental vein say to yourself: "I can view a remote location."

How does that feel? If you feel any resistance to the idea of your describing a scene beyond your normal senses, then sort out the various reasons that might account for such a feeling. Has someone in authority said it was impossible, or nonsense? Do you find it difficult to explain? Repeat the questions in Step #1 until you feel comfortable with each statement, even though you may suspect that the suspension of disbelief is only temporary.

To carry out the experiment, it is useful to have the cooperation of a friend.

2. Ask your friend to pick a location—preferably unknown to you, to prevent educated guessing—and agree to be there at a particular time, and to remain there for fifteen minutes. The only requirement for the person at the target site is to pay attention to where he is, to observe. It is not necessary to try to "send" you any information.

3. At the appointed time, you, the subject, should be located in a quiet, perhaps dimly lit place where you are comfortable. Sit up and remain alert. About one minute before the time the experiment is to begin, relax and calm your thoughts, quieting the internal dialogue. It is not necessary to do more than this; no special routine or meditation is needed.

4. Now is the time for you to describe the target location—to yourself or, preferably, to a second friend who does not know what the target is and is free to ask you questions as you go along. Describe the mental images that seem to be associated with where the outbound friend has gone. What do you see? What are the colors? What kinds of shapes come to mind?

It is essential to avoid trying to figure it out by analysis, or trying to name the place. Just relate the basic images and feelings. The extent to which you are able to capture basic impressions is the extent to which you will probably be correct in your description of the remote place. It is important to remember that analysis appears to be antagonistic to the functioning of remote viewing, at least at first.

5. Try sketching the various aspects of the scene that come to mind. Even when erroneous interpretations creep in, drawings often remain true to the basic patterns of the remote scene. Be willing to draw what pops into your mind, even though you don't know what it is that the drawings represent. When you see the remote target in person, the significance of the drawings may become clear.

6. You, the subject, should visit the remote target as soon as possible after the end of the fifteen-minute interval allotted for remote viewing. In this way, feedback takes place while the images are still fresh in your mind, and you can make an internal comparison that will be useful in future experiments.

It will help to keep in mind that so far we have not found a single person who could not do remote viewing to satisfaction. Of course, there are differences in each person's ability—as there are in the ability to sing or play the piano: some subjects are more consistently reliable, others get better faster. The indications are that this is a widespread human talent, and chances are that you will be amazed at your own psychic ability.

Remote Viewing Transcript of Phyllis Cole

Following is the unedited transcript of the *first* experiment with an SRI volunteer, Phyllis Cole, a mathematician in the computer science laboratory, with no previous experience in remote viewing. The target, determined by random procedure, was White Plaza, a plaza with fountain at Stanford University (shown in Figure 16). Following our standard protocol, the experimenter with the subject was kept ignorant of the specific target visited as well as of the contents of the target pool.

TODAY IS MONDAY, OCTOBER SEVENTH. IT IS ELEVEN O'CLOCK AND THIS IS A REMOTE VIEWING EXPERIMENT WITH RUSS TARG, PHYLLIS COLE, AND HAL PUTHOFF. IN THIS EXPERIMENT HAL WILL DRIVE TO A REMOTE SITE CHOSEN BY A RANDOM PROCESS. PHYLLIS COLE WILL BE THE REMOTE VIEWER, AND RUSS TARG IS THE MONITOR. WE EXPECT THIS EXPERIMENT TO START AT TWENTY MINUTES AFTER ELEVEN AND RUN FOR FIFTEEN MINUTES.

Looking for Gifted Subjects

IT IS JUST ABOUT TWENTY MINUTES AFTER ELEVEN AND HAL SHOULD BE AT HIS TARGET LOCATION BY NOW.

WHY DON'T YOU TELL ME WHAT KIND OF PICTURES YOU SEE AND WHAT YOU THINK HE MIGHT BE DOING OR EXPERIENCING.

The first thing that came to mind was some sort of a large, square kind of a shape. Like Hal was in front of it. It was a ... not a building or something; it was a square. I don't know if it was a window, but something like that so that the bottom line of it was not at the ground. About where his waist was, at least. That's what it seemed to me. It seems outdoors somehow. Tree.

DOES HAL SEEM TO BE LOOKING AT THAT SQUARE?

I don't know. The first impression was that he wasn't, but I have a sense that whatever it was, it was something one might look at. I don't know if it would be a sign, but something that one might look at.

CAN YOU TELL IF IT IS ON THE GROUND OR VERTICAL?

It seemed vertical.

I don't have a sense that it was part of anything particular. It might be on a building or part of a building, but I don't know. There was a tree outside, but I also got the impression of cement. I don't have the impression of very many people or traffic either. I have the sense that he is sort of walking back and forth. I don't have any more explicit picture than that.

CAN YOU MOVE INTO WHERE HE IS STANDING AND TRY TO SEE WHAT HE IS LOOKING AT?

I picked up ... he was touching something—something rough. Maybe warm and rough. Something possibly like cement.

IT IS TWENTY-FOUR MINUTES AFTER ELEVEN.

CAN YOU CHANGE YOUR POINT OF VIEW AND MOVE ABOVE THE SCENE SO YOU CAN GET A BIGGER PICTURE OF WHAT'S THERE?

I still see some trees and some sort of pavement or something like that. Might be a courtyard. The thing that came to mind was it might be one of the plazas at Stanford campus or something like that, cement. Some kinds of landscaping.

I said Stanford campus when I started to see some things in White Plaza, but I think that is misleading.

I have the sense that he's not moving around too much. That it's in a small area.

I guess I'll go ahead and say it, but I'm afraid I'm just putting on my impressions from Stanford campus. I had the impression of a fountain. There are two in the plaza, and it seemed that Hal was possibly near the ... what they call Mem Claw. [Correct.]

WHAT IS THAT?

It's a fountain that looks rather like a claw. It's a black sculpture. And it has benches around it made of cement.

ARE THERE ANY BUILDINGS AT THE PLACE YOU ARE LOOKING AT?

Mind-Reach

ARE THERE ANY BUILDINGS? YOU DESCRIBED A KIND OF A COURTYARD. USUALLY AT SUCH PLACES THERE SHOULD BE A BUILDING, LARGE OR SMALL, THAT THE COURTYARD IS ABOUT. LOOK AT THE END OR THE SIDES OF THE COURTYARD. IS THERE ANYTHING TO BE SEEN?

I have a sense that there are buildings. It's not solid buildings. I mean there are some around the periphery and I have a sense that none of them are very tall. Maybe mostly one-story, maybe an occasional two-story one.

DO YOU HAVE ANY BETTER IDEA OF WHAT YOUR SQUARE WAS THAT YOU SAW AT THE OUTSET?

No. I could hazard different kinds of guesses.

DOES IT SEEM PART OF THIS SCENE?

It . . . I think it could be. It could almost be a bulletin board or something with notices on it maybe.

Or something that people are expected to look at. Maybe a window with things in it that people were expected to look at.

WHAT KIND OF TREES DO YOU SEE IN THIS PLACE?

I don't know what kind they are. The impression was that they were shade trees and not terribly big. Maybe twelve feet of trunk and then a certain amount of branches above that. So that the branches have maybe a twelve-foot diameter, or something. Not real big trees.

NEW TREES RATHER THAN OLD TREES?

Yeah, maybe five or ten years old, but not real old ones.

IS THERE ANYTHING INTERESTING ABOUT THE PAVEMENT?

No. It seems to be not terribly new or terribly old. Not very interesting. There seems to be some bits of landscaping around. Little patches of grass around the edges and peripheries. Maybe some flowers. But not lush.

YOU SAW SOME BENCHES. DO YOU WANT TO TELL ME ABOUT THEM?

Well, that's my unsure feeling about this fountain. There was some kind of benches of cement. Curved benches, it felt like. They were of rough cement. [Correct.]

WHAT DO YOU THINK HAL IS DOING WHILE HE IS THERE?

I have a sense that he is looking at things, trying to project them. Looking at different things and sort of walking back and forth not covering a whole lot of territory.

Sometimes standing still while he looks around.

I just had the impression of him talking, and I almost sense that it was being recorded or something. I don't know if he has a tape recorder, but if it's not that, then he is saying something because it needed to be remembered.

IT'S ELEVEN THIRTY-THREE. HE'S JUST PROBABLY GETTING READY TO COME BACK.

5
ABOUT TIME
YESTERDAY'S PARADOX, TODAY'S REALITY

In mathematical physics, "anything which is not prohibited is compulsory."

—Gell-Mann's Totalitarian Principle

I (R.T.) almost never tell anyone my dreams. By and large, I don't think that people would be particularly interested. In the three years that Hal and I have been working together, I have asked him to listen to only four of my dreams. I thought all of these had precognitive elements; all four came true in the following day.

For instance, if every morning I tell my spouse my last night's dream, and one should happen to come true, it would hardly be of scientific interest. On the other hand, if I relate only one dream a year and label it precognitive, and that dream shortly comes to pass, that is more remarkable.

Before I inflict a potentially precognitive dream on a friend, I require for myself that it satisfy some subjective criteria. First, it must be free of the previous day's residue of happenings and unfinished business. That is, if I am studying for an exam, and dream about the next day's exam, that does not for me constitute a paranormal occurrence. I also believe that the dream must be free of hopes and aspirations to eliminate the wish fulfillment category.

Also, the dream should contain material that is intrinsically of very high strangeness, i.e., not the sort of thing that is within my usual experience. Finally, I require the dream to be exceptionally clear and lucid.

Now, one can certainly have dreams which don't meet these conditions but nonetheless come true. These four conditions are simply guideposts for me such that, if they are all met, I find that the dream is more likely to have veridical precognitive content.

In the spring of 1975, we had not yet decided what to do with our anecdotal precognitive data. Hal and I were in Florida on our way to an off-the-record meeting with other physicists who had worked with Uri Geller or others claiming to have the ability to bend metal (the so-called Tarrytown Conference). On the last night in Florida and on our first night in Tarrytown, I had two dreams that turned out to have strong precognitive elements.

The first dream was about our forthcoming conference, so at the outset one of my four conditions was violated. But all the others were strongly met. In the dream, I am standing in the back of a room where the conference is about to begin. At the rostrum is the next speaker. The high-strangeness part of the dream is centered around the fact that the speaker is in formal dress, with a tuxedo, ruffled shirt, and a red carnation in his buttonhole. Not only that, he was singing his paper!

The next day at the Tarrytown meeting we saw such a man standing in the middle of our meeting room. Hal said to me, "There's your man." We walked up to him, and I asked him if he was going to be singing tonight. He said, "Not 'til later." It turned out that he was lost. He was a bandleader and singer, and belonged in the next room. He did sing, but it wasn't a physics paper.

The next night I had an equally realistic and detailed dream, which I also described to Hal as potentially precognitive. In this dream, a young woman known to both Hal and me was rather cere- moniously being given a ring. I could see clearly that it was a large silver ring that opened exactly like the rings in a loose-leaf binder. Our friend was opening and closing the ring.

When I told Hal, he said that it was hardly strange for an at- tractive young lady to be given a ring, since it would in fact not be unlikely for her to become engaged. I explained that it wasn't the kind of ring one would wear on a finger.

Three days later, we arrived in New York and had a chance to ask the young woman about the silver ring. It turned out that on the day after my dream, her roommate had indeed with great ceremony given her an exceptionally large chrome-plated binder-type ring to keep her keys on, since she was always losing them.

Cheered on by these firsthand experiences, together with the copious literature describing years of precognition experiments carried out in various other laboratories and in the field,* we decided to see whether a subject could perform a perceptual task that required both spatial and temporal remote viewing.

At the time we decided to perform these experiments, we did not have much money for research, nor did we have much time to devote to such out-of-scope investigation. However, we had just been reading the book by psychologist Jung and physicist Pauli on the subject of synchronicity, and we felt that this would be an appropriate moment to conduct such work.[1] We called Hella Hammid, who had performed so successfully in remote viewing experiments. "It just so happened" that Hella would be in San Francisco the following week and would work with us.

Some Examples of Spontaneous Time Spanning

Man has long been preoccupied with the concept of time. From the subjective experience of *déjà vu* to the objective space age timekeeping of the atomic clock, time has occupied a central role in mankind's affairs. Early observers of time had their water clock and science fiction buffs have their time warp, while the modern physicist finds himself staking claims in both territories.

Here we present observations that, to be frank, we were reluctant to publish for some time because of their striking apparent incompatibility with existing concepts. The motivation for presenting the

---

* See especially *An Experiment in Time*, by J. W. Dunne, in which he describes techniques for inducing precognitive dreams, reported to be successful for anyone who tries.

data in a recent publication[2] was our conviction that theorists trying to develop models for paranormal functioning should be told of all the observable data. Otherwise, their efforts to arrive at a comprehensive and correct description would probably fail.

During the course of our remote viewing experiments, subjects would occasionally volunteer the information that while thinking about their participation in the forthcoming remote viewing experiment, they had had an image come to them about what the target location would be. On these occasions, the information was given only to the experimenter remaining at SRI with the subject. The outbound experimenter didn't learn of it until the experiment had been completed. Two of these subjects' descriptions were among the most accurate turned in during those experiments. Since the target location had not yet been selected when the subject communicated his perceptions about the target, we found the data difficult to deal with. These spontaneous occurrences did not prove anything, of course, but they opened our eyes to the possibility of obtaining information about future events.

In another instance, a highly successful subject working with a four-state random number generator felt that she not only could tell what the target stored in the machine was, but the next target as well. To test her claim in a rigorous fashion, we modified the machine so that it would make its selection one-fifth of a second after she pressed the button to indicate what she thought the machine's selection was going to be. Therefore, at the time the subject made her choice, the machine had not yet made its choice. In an experiment 672 trials long, she successfully guessed the upcoming machine choice more often than expected by chance at odds of 250:1.

These examples fall into the category of paranormal phenomena known as precognition: the perception of a future event that could not be known through rational inference. Precognition, telepathy (mind-to-mind communication), and clairvoyance (perception of an event hidden from the ordinary senses) comprise the three major categories of paranormal perceptual phenomena.

Of these three phenomena, contemporary physicists may find precognition (at least certain forms) the easiest to digest. The reason for this is the following: In physics it is realized that "causality," the apparent generation of future events out of earlier causes, is a fact observed in our lives or in the laboratory, but it is not necessarily a law of the universe. A lead article in *Science* raised the issue in the opening paragraph:

> An old crisis in science is receiving renewed attention.... This crisis manifests itself most clearly when attempts are made to provide answers to such fundamental questions as: Is the origin of [time] irreversibility ... local or cosmological? Is it in the laws or in the boundary conditions? What might be the physical interrelationships underlying the expansion of the universe, information theory, and the electromagnetic, biological and statistical arrows of time? What is the basic nature of the somewhat mysterious time coordinate system in which the very physical laws are embedded?[3]

The conclusion of that author, along with a number of others, is that "time irreversibility," the apparently inexorable flow of events along a single line directed from past to future, but not in reverse, appears to be more "factlike" than "lawlike." This is somewhat like recognizing that our planet happens to be 8,000 miles in diameter: a fact, yes; a law fixing planetary size, no.

Therefore, although information is usually observed to travel from the present to the future, we should not be upset if experiments are devised that show that sometimes information is found to be transmitted in the other direction. Indeed, the equations of physics contain discarded solutions which correspond to just this case, and thus suggest models which may begin to provide a working description of precognition.

Time Travel with Hella Hammid

The experimental protocol for precognitive remote viewing experiments with Hella Hammid was identical to that followed in the remote viewing experiments described in Chapters 2, 3, and 4, with one exception: Hella was required to describe the remote location during a fifteen-minute period beginning twenty minutes *before* the target was selected and thirty-five minutes *before* the outbound experimenter was to arrive at the target location.

On the first day of the new experiment, Hella asked us how she was supposed to "see" a place that had not yet been selected. She correctly pointed out that in all of her previous work she had been directed to find one of us at some remote place at a time when we were actually there.

That was a reasonable question, but we didn't have enough information about paranormal functioning to be reasonable about it.

We found an answer for Hella. It came right out of Jung.

We explained that we would simply assume that these experiments were going to be successful. We even brought in a professional engineering consultant (David Hurt) to independently observe and record the events.

To Hella's final question, "Yes, but what do I *do*?" we answered, "Just relax when Hal leaves. After he has been gone for ten minutes, you just describe whatever you see or experience, even though it is still twenty minutes before Hal is to select his location. If you describe your internal pictures correctly and without editing, that is all you can do. It is then up to Hal and his random number generator to arrive at a location which will match your description. Therefore the burden is his." We thus tried to relieve Hella by making the problem Hal's.

With these words of encouragement, we embarked on what turned out to be one of the most successful series of experiments we have done to date.

As shown in Table 12, each day at ten o'clock, one of the experimenters would leave SRI with a stack of ten sealed envelopes containing traveling instructions. These came from a larger pool which was randomized daily. Targets were, of course, unknown to the two experimenters remaining with the subject. The traveling experimenter was to drive continuously from ten o'clock until ten thirty before selecting his destination with a random number generator. (The motivation for continuous motion was our observation that objects and persons in rapid motion are generally not seen in the remote viewing mode of perception. We wished the traveler to be a

Table 12

Experimental Protocol: Precognitive Remote Viewing

Time Schedule	Experimenter/Subject Activity
10:00	Outbound experimenter leaves with ten envelopes (containing target locations) and random number generator; begins half-hour drive.
10:10	Experimenters remaining with subject in the laboratory elicit from subject a description of where outbound experimenter will be from 10:45–11:00.
10:25	Subject response completed, at which time laboratory part of experiment is over.
10:30	Outbound experimenter obtains random number from a random number generator, counts down to associated envelope, and proceeds to target location indicated.
10:45	Outbound experimenter remains at target location for fifteen minutes (10:45–11:00).

poor target until he reached his target site.) At the end of thirty minutes of driving, the traveling experimenter generated a random digit from 0 to 9 by means of a Texas Instruments SR-51 random number generator. While still in motion, he counted down that number of envelopes and proceeded directly to the target location indicated, so as to arrive there by ten forty-five. The target could not be chosen in advance because of the possibility of telepathic leakage contaminating an otherwise clean experiment. He remained at the target site until eleven o'clock, at which time he returned to the laboratory, showed the target name to a security guard, and entered the experimental room.

Back at the laboratory, we used the following protocol during the same period: At ten-ten, the subject was asked to begin a description of the place to which the outbound experimenter would go thirty-five minutes hence. The subject then tape-recorded a description and made drawings until ten twenty-five. At this time, her part in the experiment was ended. Her description was thus entirely concluded five minutes before the beginning of the target selection procedure.

Four such experiments were carried out. Each of them appeared to be a striking success, and this was later verified in a blind judging without error by three judges.

PALO ALTO YACHT HARBOR. SUBJECT HAMMID (S4) DE-SCRIBED "SOME KIND OF CONGEALING TAR, OR MAYBE AN AREA OF CONDENSED LAVA...THAT HAS OOZED OUT TO FILL UP SOME KIND OF BOUNDARIES"

The first target, the Palo Alto yacht harbor, consisted entirely of mud flats because of an extreme low tide (see photo on page 114). Appropriately, the subject's transcript spoke of "some kind of congealing tar, or maybe an area of condensed lava. It looks like the whole area is covered with some kind of wrinkled elephant skin that has oozed out to fill up some kind of boundaries where Hal is standing." Because of the lack of water, the dock where Hal was standing was, in fact, resting directly on the mud.

Note that Hella had learned not to rush into trying to interpret the nature or purpose of the place. This is a result of our cautioning her based on the observation that such efforts tend to be purely analytical and almost invariably incorrect. If a subject can limit himself to what he sees, he is often then able to describe a scene with sufficient accuracy that an observer can perform the analysis for him and identify the place.

The second place Hal visited was the fountain at one end of a

SUBJECT (S4) DESCRIBED A FORMAL GARDEN "VERY WELL MANI-
CURED" BEHIND A DOUBLE COLONNADE

STANFORD UNIVERSITY HOSPITAL GARDEN

large formal garden at Stanford University Hospital (see photo on page 115). Hella gave a lengthy description of a formal garden behind a wall with a "double colonnade" and "very well manicured." When Hella was later taken to the location, she was in fact shocked to find the double-colonnaded wall leading into the garden just as she had described.

SUBJECT (S4) SAW A "BLACK IRON TRIANGLE THAT HAL HAD SOMEHOW WALKED INTO" AND HEARD A "SQUEAK, SQUEAK, ABOUT ONCE A SECOND"

The third location was a children's swing at a small park about six miles from the laboratory (see photo on page 116). Hella repeated again and again that the main focus of attention at the site was a "black iron triangle that Hal had somehow walked into or was standing on." The triangle was "bigger than a man," and she heard a "squeak, squeak, about once a second." This corresponded with the black metal swing that did squeak.

The final target was the Palo Alto City Hall (see photo on page 117). Hella described a very, very tall structure covered with "Tiffany-like glass." She had located it among city streets and with little cubes at the base. The building is glass-covered, and the little cubes certainly describe the small elevator exit buildings located in the plaza in front of the building.

SUBJECT (S4) DESCRIBED A VERY TALL STRUCTURE LOCATED AMONG CITY STREETS AND COVERED WITH "TIFFANY-LIKE GLASS"

PALO ALTO CITY HALL

Three SRI scientists, not otherwise associated with the experiment, were then asked to blind match the four locations, which they visited, against the unedited, typed manuscripts of the tape-recorded narratives, along with any drawings generated by the remote viewer. The transcripts were presented unlabeled and in random order and were to be used without replacement, that is, once each. A hit required that the transcript of a given experiment be matched with the target of that experiment. The three judges independently matched the targets to the response data without error. Under the null hypothesis—no information channel existing and a random selection of descriptions without replacement—each judge independently obtained a result significant at odds of better than 20:1.

For reasons we do not as yet understand, the four transcripts of the precognition experiments show exceptional coherence and accuracy as evidenced by the fact that the judges were able to match successfully all of the transcripts to the corresponding target locations without difficulty. A long-range experimental program devoted to the clarification of these issues and involving a number of subjects is now under way. The above four experiments are the first four carried out under this program.*

As an interesting sidelight, there are discarded solutions to the equations of physics that do not correspond to information traveling from the future to the present. In the history of physics there is a precedent for the idea that such a discarded solution may in fact describe a real, though at the time unobserved, phenomenon. In the early 1920's, P. A. M. Dirac developed his mathematical description of the relativistic electron. His equations yielded a *pair* of solutions, as is often the case in mathematical physics. One of the solutions described a negatively charged particle which was clearly the electron. There was, however, a second solution which would correspond to a particle similar to the electron but with a positive charge. As this could not be the proton, since the mass was wrong, the solution was thrown out. There it lay until a cloud chamber experiment in 1932 resulted in the discovery of the positron, at which point Dirac's discarded solution took on new meaning.

An encouraging note from the world of physics concerning the possibility of precognition, at least in principle, can be found in the eminent theoretical physicist Gell-Mann's famous dictum quoted at the beginning of the chapter that, with regard to the laws of mathematical physics, "anything which is not prohibited is compulsory." As we have indicated earlier, the laws of physics do not absolutely forbid the transmission of information from the future to the present.

Recognizing this, physicist O. Costa de Beauregard of the Poincare Institute in France has put forward rigorous and detailed arguments that the generally discarded advanced-time solutions in physics correspond to a series of events that converge toward "finality" in a manner symmetrical to the usual divergence of effects due to causality.[4] He goes on to argue that although such events are

---

* This work has now been replicated in a lengthy series carried out by psychologists at Mundelein College, Chicago, with similar good results. (J. Bisaha and B. J. Dunne, private communication.)

generally unobservable on the gross level of everyday life for statistical reasons, the finality principle is expected to be maximally operative in just those situations where consciousness intrudes as an ordering phenomenon. At this point, further discussion of the subtleties of such considerations would take us far afield, so we draw this discussion to a close by simply noting with de Beauregard that the so-called advanced-time solutions, if detectable, could in certain cases act as a carrier of precognitive information. Any difficulties we have in dealing with this problem are therefore more likely to belong to linguistics than to physics.

After this technical discussion, it may be useful to remind ourselves that precognition was not invented in the laboratory, but was found to occur naturally in the field. Precognition and its cousin prophecy have a long history which is well documented in the spontaneous cases collected by Louisa Rhine,[5] and in laboratory experiments by Soal and Bateman.[6]

Currently, we have no precise model of this spatial and temporal remote viewing phenomenon, but we are certainly intrigued by models of the universe involving higher-order synchronicity, such as the one offered to us by the physicist Pauli and the psychologist Carl Jung:

> ACAUSALITY. If natural law [as we normally experience it] were an absolute truth, then of course there could not possibly be any processes that deviate from it. But since causality [as usually understood] is a statistical truth, it holds good only on average and thus leaves room for exceptions which must somehow be experienceable, that is to say, *real*. I try to regard synchronistic events as acausal exceptions of this kind. They prove to be relatively independent of space and time; they relativize space and time insofar as space presents in principle no obstacle to their passage and the sequence of events in time is inverted so that it looks as if an event which has not yet occurred were causing a perception in the present.[7]

Such a description, though poetic, has some basis in modern physical theory.

6

IN ONE BRAIN
AND OUT THE OTHER
THE TWO HEMISPHERES
OF THE BRAIN SEE THE WORLD
IN DIFFERENT WAYS

Our normal waking consciousness, rational consciousness as we
call it, is but one special type of consciousness, whilst all about it,
parted from it by the filmiest of screens, there lie potential forms
of consciousness entirely different.
—William James, *The Varieties of Religious Experience*

Since man first began to pursue knowledge, he has endeavored
to understand the nature of his own existence. And at the heart
of that search has been the quest to unlock the secrets of consciousness.

Each new wave of philosophy, theology, science, and education
has brought with it new theories and speculations about the structure and functioning of human consciousness.

In the nineteenth century, a new kind of investigator joined the
search—the neurophysiologist. Early neurophysiologists observed
that the brain is composed of two almost identical halves or hemispheres, and that specific abilities and functions appear to be associated with localized areas of the brain. Early clinical studies of
right-handers showed that the functions of speech and analysis
were often impaired or destroyed when the left hemisphere of the
brain was damaged, but appeared to be unaffected by damage to

the right hemisphere. This observation led early researchers to conclude that the left hemisphere was all-important, and the right of little significance. As a result, efforts were directed primarily toward understanding the physiology of the brain's left hemisphere, neglecting study of the right. In their enthusiasm for the left hemisphere of the brain and the mapping of its specializations, early researchers overlooked, misassessed, and underestimated the importance of the brain's right hemisphere.

Serious investigation of the capacities of the right hemisphere was relatively slow in making its appearance in the neurophysiological field. In the past decade, however, the tempo of this work has been greatly accelerated by the corroborative evidence from widely diverse scientific sectors. The neurosurgeon, the psychologist, and the neurophysiologist, each with their specialized tools of anatomical study, psychological testing, and electronic measurement, are finally beginning to converse on a coherent picture.

What has emerged is the concept that the two hemispheres of the brain are specialized for different cognitive functions: the left for verbal and analytic thought, the right for intuition and the understanding of patterns. The model of cerebral processing that has evolved indicates that the left hemisphere enables us to function in an analytical and logical manner, in which one proceeds step by step. The right hemisphere is associated with intuitive and holistic processes by which one grasps the relationship between the parts directly, rather than by a sequence of deductions. The left hemisphere analyzes over time; the right synthesizes over space. The left codes memory in linguistic description, the right in images. Tentative links between the right brain and musical and artistic abilities have also emerged.

These two alternative and relatively distinct modes of thinking which are mirrored in the architecture of the brain have been pointed out for thousands of years in literature, philosophy, art, and religion. While the scientist dissected and analyzed, the poet soothed and integrated. The significance of this division of labor has been by and large neglected in our modern technological society. This is because our post-Industrial Revolution standard of living and our scientific achievements have depended primarily on the highly developed analytic methods characteristic of left-brain functioning. Perhaps it is not surprising, then, that the overall scope of right-brain activity still remains largely mysterious and elusive.

Creative functioning depends on an integration of the complementary rational and intuitive modes. A well-developed and mature individual has the ability to operate in or to inhibit either mode, depending upon the task at hand.

Right-brain Function and Psi Activity

What has all this to do with paranormal functioning? The answer to this question came to me (H.P.) first from my wife, Adrienne, a specialist in the application of Gestalt, holistic techniques to the education of elementary-school-age children. In looking over the output produced by our research subjects, she noticed that the elements of form—such as the drawings and the general descriptions of shape, color, and material—tended to be correct more often than the analytic elements of name, function, and size. In the experiments, we had found that it was particularly difficult for subjects to read letters or words, even though they might correctly perceive that there was a sign or other written material at a remote site. Adrienne pointed out that such observations suggest the possibility that the primary method of information-processing might be right-hemispheric in nature.

As we looked back through the data, we found many instances which seemed to support this. Pat Price once incorrectly labeled a swimming pool as a water purification plant, and a drive-in movie theater with speaker posts became a parking lot full of parking meters. Hella Hammid mistook an "august" and "solemn" church for a library, expanded an accurately described bicycle shed into an immense barnlike structure, and labeled a pedestrian overpass "a trough up in the air." Hella also correctly described a video terminal as a black box in the middle of a room, complete with glass porthole and light coming out, but incorrectly labeled it an oven or radiation machine. One of our visitors perceived a "kaleidoscopic picture of triangles, squares, and more triangles," and even "some kind of electrical shielding," but he couldn't identify it as the transmission tower it was. All this points to the idea that remote viewing is primarily an exercise in pattern recognition rather than analysis. In retrospect, perhaps it shouldn't be surprising that ESP is right hemispheric, since the right side of the brain is known to be excellent for bridging gaps and perceiving general patterns, even when some of the pieces are missing.

We consulted with Dr. Robert Ornstein and Dr. Ralph Kiernan, who confirmed our interpretation. When we told them that written material was generally not understood, that verbal identification of correct drawings was often inaccurate, and that the drawings were frequently left-right reversed, they indicated that such characteristics have been seen in patients injured on the left side of the brain. This is not to imply that those with brain damage on the left side are likely to be good subjects. Rather, it is simply that the left-brain-injured patient and the person attempting remote viewing are, for different reasons, both forced into a right-brain mode. In the case of a patient, it is because of damage to the left hemisphere; in the case of a subject, it is because his task is to integrate fragmentary and ambiguous input and therefore must resort to right-brain functioning.

An understanding of the principles we have been discussing gives an idea of the difficulties encountered in trying to make use of paranormal perception. On the one hand are the standard ESP tests in which a subject is asked to name which of five different cards is the target. Such tasks tempt the subject into an analytical matching task, rather than coax him into the more intuitive mode that is required. This is unfortunate for us because the simple matching task is best suited for the statistical analysis favored by the left-brain-oriented scientific method. Right-brain results are much more difficult to pin down.

On the other hand, the stream-of-consciousness psychic who lets flow a continuous torrent without any discrimination is equally disconcerting. The random scrambling of order in time and space makes even good information useless.

Thus in the laboratory what we require in the way of *subjects* are individuals who are capable of processing paranormal inputs using, with equal facility, whichever mode is appropriate to the task. What we require in the way of *experiments* are tasks which provide a blend of unstructured, free response target material susceptible to some form of rigorous analysis.

Our own remote viewing work appears to be a task which meets these requirements, since it provides an opportunity for the subject to respond more or less freely to a given target class, while permitting a rigorous blind matching procedure on the part of the judges.

The same blend is found in Honorton's work at Maimonides Hospital, Brooklyn, New York. In his most recent work, Honorton is providing a carefully controlled environment for a subject who attempts to describe color slides viewed by another person in a remote room. The subject listens to the sound of ocean waves, via earphones, and views a uniform visual field imposed by the use of Ping-Pong ball halves covering his eyes. In this setting, known to parapsychologists as the Ganzfeld technique, subjects are able to give correct and often highly accurate descriptions of the material being viewed by the sender.[1]

In Honorton's work and ours, it apparently has been the departure from the repetitive, forced-choice analytical experiment that has made it possible for ordinary people of diverse backgrounds to demonstrate significant paranormal functioning in the laboratory. Further, we also tell every visitor and subject that we expect him to be successful. We are not out to "test his ESP," but rather to provide an environment in which he can explore his own capabilities.

Electronic Random Target Generator

In our own work, we had an opportunity to make a direct comparison of results obtained with six subjects using a free-response task (remote viewing) and a more analytical forced-choice task (using a random target generator).

To accomplish this comparison, we designed an automated ex-

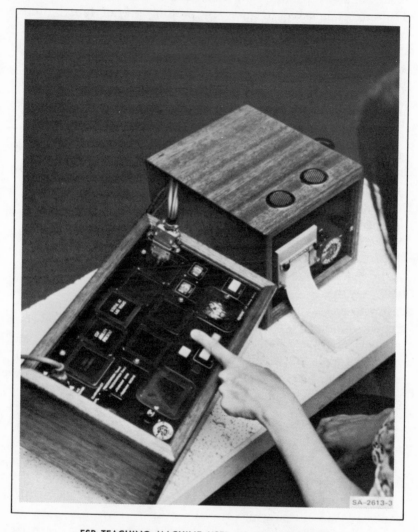

ESP TEACHING MACHINE USED IN THIS EXPERIMENT

TWO OF THE FIVE "ENCOURAGEMENT LIGHTS" AT THE TOP OF THE
MACHINE ARE ILLUMINATED. THE PRINTER AT THE RIGHT OF THE
MACHINE RECORDS DATA ON FANFOLD PAPER TAPE

periment around a four-state electronic random target generator. The subject is asked to guess, by pressing one of four buttons, which of four pictures will be lit up by the machine. The solid-state electronic machine, based on an original design by Russell Targ and David Hurt[2] and manufactured by Aquarius Electronics, Mendocino, California, has no moving parts and provides no sensory cue as to its target.

The machine provides as a target one of four art slides (reproductions of paintings) chosen by an electronic random target generator. The generator does not show its choice until the subject indicates his choice to the machine by pressing a button (yellow, green, blue, or red) associated with each art slide.*

As soon as the subject indicates his choice, the target slide is illuminated to provide visual and auditory (a bell if correct) feedback as to the correctness or incorrectness of the subject's choice. Until that time, both subject and experimenter remain ignorant of the machine's choice, so the experiment is of the double-blind type.

Just to add some spice, five legends at the top of the machine face are illuminated one at a time as the subject makes increasing numbers of correct choices (6, 8, 10 . . .). They read: GOOD BEGINNING, ESP ABILITY PRESENT, USEFUL AT LAS VEGAS, OUTSTANDING ESP ABILITY, and PSYCHIC MEDIUM ORACLE. These words, which we call "encouragement lights," are not intended as a scientific judgment, of course, but are used only to encourage test subjects.

The machine choice, subject choice, cumulative trial number, and cumulative hit number all are printed automatically in groups of twenty-five on a continuous fanfold paper tape that records data from the beginning to the end of a subject's daily session.

One feature of the machine that softens the forced-choice situation is a PASS button which the subject presses when he does not choose to guess. In this case, the machine simply indicates what its choice was, and then goes on to make its next selection, scoring

---

* The machine has four stable internal states. A million-pulse-per-second oscillator sends pulses to an electronic counter which passes through each of its four states—one-two-three-four-one-two . . . —250,000 times per second. The target state is determined by the length of time between subject choices.

neither a hit nor a miss. Thus, the subject does not have to guess at targets when he feels he has no idea which to choose.

Data were collected from our six remote viewing subjects. Each subject was asked to complete 100 twenty-five-trial runs, or 2,500 trials each. Of the six subjects, only one, Elgin, scored significantly above chance. He more than made up for the rest of the group, however, for his score was so good that the probability of obtaining his result by chance was less than one in three million.

As we did with every experiment yielding a positive result, we proceeded to look for any possible way to account for this remarkable result on the basis of other than paranormal means. We examined the tape records to see if there was any possibility in principle of the subject keeping his bad runs and turning in only good runs. The answer was negative: the continuous fanfold paper tapes, which carried a permanent record of every trial, machine state, and trial number, were intact.

Next, the actual statistics of the machine *during the successful experiment* were tabulated to see whether the machine had perhaps gone nonrandom, thereby permitting a strategy to emerge that the subject could turn to his advantage. The results again indicated no significant departures of the machine from chance performance during the successful experiment, and therefore the good result could not be attributed to machine malfunction.

We then investigated the possibility that the subject might have developed an optimum strategy based on slight, even though nonsignificant, machine departures from chance. The most favorable strategy based on actual machine statistics during the successful experiment was determined after the experiment was over, to see if use of such a strategy would be capable in principle of producing a result as significant as that produced by Elgin. It was found that (1) the optimum strategy based on machine statistics was not capable of producing a score as significant as Elgin's; (2) Elgin's selections differed widely from strategies favorable to the production of results based on machine statistics, anyway; and finally, (3) there was no evidence of learning to support the hypothesis that *any* strategy was developed during the experiment, normal or paranormal. Elgin simply began by scoring high at the beginning of the experiment and continued scoring at the same high rate throughout. There was no way we could fault Elgin's success: His excellent result stood.

Elgin agreed to participate in a second study to see if his high scoring rate could be replicated under somewhat modified conditions. This time, in addition to the printer, a teletypewriter recorded his results on punched paper tape that would be fed directly into a computer. His results fell to chance. His subjective impression with regard to the decline was that he found himself under considerably more pressure during the second experiment for two reasons. First, having performed successfully during the first experiment, he was extremely anxious to prove to himself and to us that it was not a "fluke," and this degree of self-expectation was foremost in his mind. Second, the idea of being connected to a computer through a teletypewriter made the task seem much more formidable and impersonal, even though analytically he knew that the target selection procedure was identical (an example of conflict between right- and left-hemispheric evaluations).

We asked Elgin to participate in another replication experiment. This time the mechanical recording equipment was removed altogether, but at the price of being under continuous surveillance by an experimenter who would record the scores after each twenty-five-trial run. Furthermore, Elgin was permitted "freebie" practice runs that would be tallied separately, provided that these runs were so labeled by him *before* the run in question, to prevent after-the-fact selection of good versus poor runs. We knew, of course, that this plan to provide a low-pressure environment for Elgin would require careful reporting. Elgin did regain a high scoring rate during this third experiment, this time significant at odds of greater than 2,000:1—not as good as in the original experiment, but excellent nonetheless. If we include in the statistics the preselected practice runs (which were only slightly better than chance), the study is still significant at odds of 150:1, a very respectable result. The fact that there was a significant difference between the outcome of the preselected "practice" runs and the preselected "real" runs showed that Elgin could before the fact ascertain how well he would do in a given run—an important result in itself.

With regard to this study, one might argue that a weak point in an otherwise successful replication was the fact that scores were recorded by hand, a situation known to invite unconscious errors in the positive direction by an experimenter motivated to obtain a positive result.* In this case, however, the machine still automatically totaled the results for each twenty-five-trial block; the hand recording was therefore minimal, being confined to recording of total scores for each block rather than on a trial-by-trial basis. We therefore concluded from the machine study that of the six remote viewing subjects, one (Elgin) gave a significant and replicable result.**

Returning to the theme responsible for this particular study—the comparison of results obtained on a free-response pattern-recognition task like remote viewing and the more analytical forced-choice machine task—we observe the following: Whereas four of our six subjects produced statistically significant results in remote viewing, only one succeeded in the machine task. Therefore, from a statistical viewpoint, a subject is more likely to describe an actual remote site chosen at random from a hundred-square-mile area than he is to select correctly one of four known, but randomly sequenced, targets.

Our experience with these phenomena leads us to believe that at least part of this difference in task performance may stem from fundamental considerations closely related to the difference in cognitive styles between left- and right-brain functioning.

In detail, the two principal sources of error in paranormal functioning appear to be memory and imagination, both of which can give rise to mental pictures of greater clarity than the target to be perceived. In the random generator task, for example, a subject can

---

* Hand-scoring was used *only* in this third series.
** In a larger study for NASA,[3] devoted specifically to the question of whether learning could take place, 147 subjects were screened using the machine. Of these subjects, 6 showed positive learning significant at odds of 100:1 or better; the probability of this number of successful subjects showing up by chance is itself significant at odds of better than 250:1. At the other extreme, no subjects showed a *decline* significant at odds of 100:1 to counterbalance the learners. The tendency toward learning, or lack of it, for the remaining 141 subjects was normally distributed as expected on the basis of chance.

create out of his own imagination a perfect mental picture of each of the four possible targets. Because of this, he is then tempted to obtain his answer by a mental matching operation which is highly analytical, or left hemispheric, in nature. (The same is true for card-guessing experiments.) On the other hand, a subject in remote viewing is more likely to approach the task with a blank mind as he attempts to perceive pictorial information about which he will in general have no stored mental data—a strategy much more holistic, or right brain, in nature. To our way of thinking, therefore, there is a natural advantage for success in such tasks as remote viewing in contrast to tasks like forced-choice matching among known targets.

Remote Viewing of a Flashing Light

On the basis of such results indicating that paranormal functioning is intimately connected with brain functioning, we thought it should be possible to obtain direct evidence of remote perception by measurement of brain waves.

Well-known researchers in the neurosciences, Dr. Joseph Kamiya, Dr. Karl Pribram, Dr. W. Grey Walter, and others, brought together to discuss physiological methods to detect ESP functioning, have suggested that brain wave EEG (electroencephalogram) responses may be sensitive indicators of parasensory detection of remote stimuli.[4] We therefore undertook such a study.

Related experimentation of this type had been carried out by Douglas Dean at the Newark College of Engineering. In his search for physiological indicators of information transfer, he used a plethysmograph to measure changes in the blood volume in a finger during telepathy experiments. (The plethysmograph is a sensitive indicator of autonomic nervous system functioning.) A sender looked at randomly selected target cards consisting of names known to the subject, together with names unknown to him (selected at random from a telephone book). The names of the known people were contributed by the subject and were to be of emotional significance to him—mother, wife, sweetheart, stockbroker, etc. Dean found significant changes in the chart recording of finger blood volume when the remote sender was looking at those names known to the subject as compared with when he was looking at those names randomly chosen.[5]

Three other experiments using the physiological approach have now been published. The first work by Tart,[6] a later work by Lloyd,[7] and most recently the work by the authors in collaboration with SRI neurophysiologists Dr. Charles Rebert and Dr. Ann Turner,[8] all follow a similar pattern. Basically, a subject is closeted in an electrically shielded room while his EEG is recorded. Meanwhile, in another laboratory, a second person is stimulated according to a random schedule. The time of that stimulus is marked on magnetic tape, along with the recording of the subject's EEG. (The subject does not know, of course, when the remote stimulus periods are.)

In previous work, others had attempted without success to detect changes in a subject's EEG in response to a single flash from a stroboscopic lamp being observed by another subject.[9] In a discussion of that experiment, Kamiya had suggested that because of the unknown characteristics of the information channel with regard to the amount of time required to receive a signal, it might be more appropriate to use a train of light bursts to increase the probability of detecting information transfer.[10] Therefore, in our study, we chose to use a stroboscopic flash train of ten-second duration as the target in a remote viewing experiment.

In the design of the study, we assumed that the remote stimulus would result in responses similar to those obtained under conditions of direct stimulation. For example, when an individual is stimulated with a low-frequency (less than twenty cycles per second) flashing light, the EEG typically shows a decrease in the strength of the resting alpha brain wave pattern and a driving of the brain waves at the frequency of the flashes.[11] We hypothesized that if we stimulated one subject (the sender) in this manner, the EEG of another subject (a receiver) in a room with no flash present might show changes in alpha activity and possibly an EEG driving similar to that of the sender.

We informed our subject, Hella Hammid, that at certain times a light was to be flashed in a sender's eyes in a distant room, and if she perceived that event, consciously or unconsciously, it might be evident from changes in her EEG output. She was seated in a visually opaque, acoustically and electrically shielded double-walled steel room about twenty-five feet from the sender. The experiment consisted of seven runs of thirty-six, ten-second trials each (twelve periods each for no-flash stimuli, for six flash-per-second stimuli, and for sixteen flash-per-second stimuli, randomly intermixed).[12] This experiment proved to be successful: Hella's alpha activity showed a significant reduction in average power (−24 percent) and peak power (−28 percent) during the sixteen flash-per-second condition as compared with periods of no-flash stimulus. (A similar response was observed for the six flash-per-second case [−12 percent in average power, −21 percent in peak power], but the latter results did not reach statistical significance.)

Extensive control procedures were undertaken to determine if these results were produced by system artifacts, electromagnetic pickup, or by subtle cueing; the system and protocols were found to be clean.

There were several interesting occurrences during these experiments. The reduction in alpha brain wave power that we observed when the strobe light came on was not only statistically significant for the seven runs as a whole, but was observed in each of the seven individual runs except one: In that one, we told Hella that there would not be anyone in the remote room looking at the strobe light, and the result did not show up. On a later run, however, just as the experiment was starting, a visitor suggested that we remove the sender from the remote room to see what would happen. In this case, the observed alpha reduction effect was one of the strongest. And this was in spite of the fact that when Hella emerged from the shielded room, and before anyone said anything, she stated, "I didn't feel anyone in that room. Are you sure there was a sender?"

One of the most interesting results, however, and one that we think is of great significance, was the following. As part of the procedure, Hella was asked to indicate with a telegraph key whether the light was flashing, and if it was, at which frequency; analysis showed these guesses to be what one would expect by chance alone. Thus, her response to the remote stimulus as evidenced by significant alpha blocking occurred *only* at the noncognitive level of physiological brain wave response. Hence, the experiment provided direct physiological (EEG) evidence of perception of a remote strobe light *even in the absence of overt conscious response.*

In these experiments, we had attached the EEG lead of interest to the scalp at the midline of the head. Therefore we did not obtain any discrimination between left- and right-hemisphere functioning. When the significance of hemispheric specialization became apparent, we carried out three further experimental runs, this time with separate monitoring of left and right hemispheres. Each of these bilateral experiments consisted of twenty, fifteen-second trials; ten no-flash trials and ten, sixteen flash-per-second trials randomly intermixed. The arousal response indicated by a reduction in alpha activity occurred for the flash cases as in the previous experiments, but they essentially occurred *only* in the right hemisphere (average alpha reduction 16 percent in the right hemisphere, 2 percent in the left). This tends to support the hypothesis that paranormal functioning might involve right-hemispheric specialization, but the sample was too small to provide confirmation without further work, which is now under way.

In our experiments, we used a remote light flash as a stimulus. Tart[13] used an electrical shock to himself as sender in his work, and Lloyd[14] simply told the sender to think of a red triangle each time a red warning light was illuminated within his view. Lloyd observed a consistent evoked potential (a specific brain wave response) in his subjects. In our experiments and in Tart's, a reduction in strength and a desynchronization (spread in frequency) of alpha output was observed (an arousal response—if a subject is resting in an alpha-dominant condition and he is then stimulated in any direct manner, for example by a handclap, there will be an observable decrease and desynchronization in alpha power). We consider that these combined results provide evidence for the existence of noncognitive awareness of remote happenings, and as such, they have a profound implication for paranormal research.

New Possibilities

Much of this discussion has centered on brain function. At this point it is important to indicate also what has *not* been said. In particular, we have not said that the brain (or the right hemisphere) is the organ of paranormal functioning, the "seat of the soul," or anything like that. Rather, it is simply that the output of any paranormal experiment in the laboratory is, in the last analysis, a series of drawings, a string of words, a sequence of button pushes, etc.—all of which have undergone considerable processing in the brain. It would seem that sometimes even that structure gets in the way, for how often have we heard, "Damn it—I knew it was green, but I couldn't help pressing red!" We can speak of consciousness and the locations of its effects, but cannot pin down where the "I" is sitting.

In technical terms, all we can speak of are behaviors and physiological correlates, not causes. Analysis of the perceiver, the knower, the "I," must be found elsewhere than in tape transcripts, button pushes, and meter readings. We can use all the help we can get along the way, and the addition of neurophysiology has provided us with yet another set of tools to probe the universe both without and within. When the new understanding of cerebral functioning is thoroughly translated from the esoteric language of neurophysiology into language that can be applied to day-to-day living, a giant step will have been taken and humankind can participate more dynamically in its own forward evolution.

7
IS CHAOS NECESSARY?
URI GELLER IN THE LABORATORY

There was magic in the world. There was the magic of day and night, of springtime and winter, of buds creaming into bloom, of first grains cleaving their green shoots through the unviolated earth, and of rivers flowing down to the sea. There was the magic of winds and clouds, and of the tides, which were alive and moved at the thunderbidding of unknown gods.

—From the Preface of *Greater Magic*, by
John Northern Hilliard

I (R.T.) was sound asleep on a Sunday morning in September, 1972, when events began to conspire to bring Uri Geller into our lives. It was seven o'clock in the morning, which is a time that I consider all phone calls to be somewhat unwelcome. But especially unwelcome are calls that require me to get out of bed and be elsewhere in half an hour. The caller was an old friend, Jean Mayo, a doctoral candidate with the Humanistic Psychology Institute, who had an extra ticket to an all-day conference on psychic healing. Would I like to come? She would pick me up in thirty minutes if I could be ready.

Although we are willing to consider that some percentage of the patients who go to psychic healers do get the help they are seeking, we have always felt that this area was too complicated for a pair of physicists to get involved in. But since my friend added that Andrija Puharich and Stan Krippner, both well known in the field of parapsychology, had been looking for me on the previous day, I decided that I would pull myself together and go. Even if the lectures were a little murky, I would be very happy to see my friends from New York.

In the morning, we heard papers on Kirlian photography, laying on of hands, and even a paper dealing with our ESP teaching machine. Finally, it was lunchtime—a time that all conference attendees look forward to. We rounded up Andrija Puharich and several of the entourage who seem to accompany him everywhere.

URI GELLER

We all settled down in a comfortably dark restaurant where we divided our attention between some pitchers of beer and Andrija's description of his remarkable discovery, Uri Geller. Andrija had just returned to the United States from Israel, where he had been investigating the apparent psychic ability of Uri. Andrija could not find enough words to praise Uri's "power," believing that Uri could bend rings without touching them and cause objects to move using only his mental powers. According to Andrija, Uri could cause objects to disappear, or dematerialize, from closed containers and reappear elsewhere. There was even something about the disappearance of Andrija's Mercedes from the front of his house in Tel Aviv and its reappearance at the edge of a lake a hundred yards away. Andrija told us more, and it was fascinating.

Although I was skeptical, I have had dealings with Andrija Puharich intermittently since 1965, and I consider him to be an exceptionally intelligent and imaginative scientist and medical researcher. Having kept up to date on his reports and patents, we were also aware of his background in microminiature electronics.

Later that night, Hal, Andrija, and I tried to put it all together. The prospect of working with a "gifted" subject was exciting. Since Uri could "do anything," there should be no problem in designing experiments that could satisfy us. We would do the work at SRI with everything recorded on videotape and film. The principal thing we all wanted to record was Uri bending something without touching it. The objects would be under a bell jar, so that if they disappeared during an experiment we wouldn't have to worry about whether Uri had just palmed them off the table.

Uri did come to SRI. In the course of his six weeks with us, we saw many wild and wonderful things. We shot thirty thousand feet of 16 mm movie film and thirty hours of videotape, although we did not ever photograph what we had set out to observe. But that's getting ahead of the story.

The end of October found us ready for Uri's arrival at SRI. He was to arrive at San Francisco International Airport accompanied by Andrija and Shippi Strang. Shippi remained in California with Uri for his entire stay, while Andrija returned to New York after only two days. Because of past experience, he felt that his mere presence in California would cast doubt on anything Uri might do in the laboratory.

Shippi had been a good friend of Uri's for some time and was a comfortable traveling companion for him. At the time Uri was with us, he was twenty-five, Shippi, nineteen. Because of their youth, we were especially wary. I could remember back to my own activities at nineteen, when I was earning money performing magic myself. We were fully aware of the negative possibilities of the situation.

Hal and I picked up our four visitors in my brand-new station wagon. Uri is a very engaging and perceptive fellow, and we had an upbeat and cheery ride back to Palo Alto.

Uri explained how it was important that we all work together to make the experiments a success. We must have faith in each other. So that we could start off together on the right foot, Uri said he would drive my car the rest of the way home himself—blindfolded!

Now this posed a dilemma for me, since we had had a very hard time convincing Uri to take part in laboratory tests at all. He had told us through Andrija that the entities through whom he gets his power don't want him to get involved in anything as unequivocal as laboratory tests yet. We were never really sure he would show up until we saw him at the airport.

I am very familiar with techniques for blindfold driving, and had every confidence that Uri could do that trick as well as any of the dozens of other magicians who do it. My concern was only that he might misjudge because of the enormous size of my car and have an accident for nonparanormal reasons.

However, at the risk of being a spoilsport, I offered the use of astronaut Edgar Mitchell's rented car as soon as we got to Uri's new home, an apartment in south Palo Alto. So, shortly after arriving at Uri's apartment, we had an exciting blindfold drive at high speed through the streets of residential Palo Alto with Uri calling out the color of passing cars, the color of houses, and the presence of stop signs—all in rapid succession. It was accomplished with flair and style. After this initiation rite, we agreed to meet later that evening for a planning session. During dinner, I briefed my family on the events of the afternoon. My youngest son, Nicholas, who had been listening to our plans for the past several weeks, expressed some worry—not about the driving adventure, since that was obviously a thrill-a-minute opportunity to a seven-year-old, but about the dematerialization.

The question was: "If Uri makes a ball of string disappear, and you are holding onto the end of the string, do you go wherever the ball goes?" That was one of the best questions I had heard in some time. I filed that one away to ask Uri at some later time.

Is Chaos Necessary?

In due course, we assembled at Uri's apartment. Uri, Shippi, and Andrija were just finishing their dinner when Hal and I arrived. Shortly after us came Edgar Mitchell, who had agreed to raise the money to pay for the experiments. With him was Dr. Wilbur Franklin from Kent State University. Dr. Franklin had seen Uri bend and break some metal objects at an earlier meeting in New York. Since he is a metallurgist, he rightly considered any such goings-on to be in his province.

What followed might have been called a sitting in the days of Sir Oliver Lodge, except that there were no spirits present (or so we assume). Since this is the twentieth century, I hardly need to add that the lights remained on. What followed was not considered by us to be an experiment, but rather a happening at a special kind of party.

Hal and I had brought with us some rings which we had cut from metal tubing at SRI. About an inch in diameter and made of fifty mil stock (fifty thousandths of an inch), anywhere from fifty to a hundred pounds of force are required to bend them. It is obviously impossible for most people to bend them at all, but a person does not have to be outside the range of human variation to do so. These rings had been weighed and given stamped serial numbers.

Our plan was to take out one ring, show it to Uri, but not let him hold it. According to many newspaper accounts of Uri's exploits in Europe, that was his standard routine. "A girl takes off her ring, holds it in her fist. She then reports that her hand gets 'all tingly.' She opens her hand and the ring is bent." That is the "effect." In the magic business, there are two parts to every trick. The "effect" is what the observer thinks is happening. It's what he will report as having taken place, even under cross-examination, because this is all he has actually seen. The other part of the trick is aptly called the "secret" and it is this that actually happens to cause the "effect." Such is the analysis from the standpoint of magic.

Magic tricks fall into two general categories which I will call "sleights" and "illusions."

Sleight-of-hand tricks are simply misdirections of the observer's attention by the performer. A magician can take a half-dollar and appear to put it into your hand. As long as you keep your hand closed, you will think you have the coin in your fist. When you open your hand, you will find a rabbit made of sponge, a dime, or any other small object the magician has decided to give you.

In magic, as in psychic research, attention is everything. If you can keep your attention fixed on what is happening, you have a good chance of not being fooled.

However, attention will not help you keep track of the other form of trick, an illusion. I am not as dexterous as most practicing professional magicians, so I make more use of this latter category of tricks. An illusion, which need not be a big stage production, is any trick in which the observer is invited to greatly underestimate the amount of preparation necessary to create the "effect." Even simple-seeming card tricks can have days of preparation and be tailor-made for the particular person who is going to see them. This preparation may have begun the moment the magician learned that on a particular day in the next month he will have a meeting with a given person who just might ask to be shown some magic. And with a month to prepare for a meeting, a magician can do *anything*. A magician will spend that kind of time to prepare a single trick, because that's what he does for a living.

Why all of this attention to magic? Although our critics would have the public believe that we were too naive to consider that such a nice young man as Uri would try to fool us, actually we were cautious to the point of paranoia. After all, we already had a successful project under way and a number of outstanding proposals for tens of thousands of dollars under consideration. Perhaps a potential client had sent not just a masterful magician, but a *Six-Million-Dollar Man* with a *Mission Impossible* backup team to see if our system could be cracked.

To return to Uri: In general, we can give an accurate description of the "effects" we saw that night. But, because these effects were carried out on Uri's terms (unlike our later experiments) we are unable to explain what really happened.

When the time seemed appropriate, Hal took out one of our SRI rings, which happened to be copper. He showed it to Uri, but kept it in his own hand. Uri said, "I need more metal," and we knew that although this was only the beginning, it was also the beginning of the end of anything like a controlled observation.

As bracelets, watches, and other rings were added to the pile, it became apparent that it was not going to be possible to tell what was "really" happening. We no longer had control of the "effect." The unspoken protocol at this informal social event was that if anything bent, we should be grateful and consider it a small miracle. Uri picked up all the metal things and put them into Hal's open hand. He held his hand over Hal's and asked us all to help him. After a period of apparent effort, Uri said that he thought something should have bent. Sure enough, Hal's copper ring was bent into a slightly elliptical shape! This was a cause for much excitement. It was taken as a sign that "they" were willing for Uri to work with us.

We made another attempt at carrying out a reasonably "uncluttered" experiment with only one object at a time. Uri willingly agreed. He picked up Hal's intact heavy silver bracelet, laid it on the table, and stroked it with his finger. The observant reader will notice who is again directing the experiment. Uri kept up a verbal barrage as he concentrated, saying, "It's too heavy" and "I can't do it," etc. When he removed his finger, the bracelet was broken in two places.

We did not conclude from these demonstrations that Uri had paranormal ability. Neither did we conclude that he was attempting to deceive us. Just because a man is found at the scene of the crime with a smoking gun in his hand, the law doesn't say unequivocally that he was the one who did the deed. Uri creates confusion around himself, even when he is not performing. Weeks later, we were able to deal with this problem by obtaining Uri's consent to remain in an electrically shielded, soundproof booth while experiments were in progress outside. That, of course, limited the kind of experiments we could do with him, but scientists have to work with phenomena under controlled conditions.

We were unhappy with our initial encounter and felt that little would be accomplished while sitting around Uri's kitchen table.

I thought nothing could be lost by engaging Uri in a little card magic. I produced a brand-new deck of my own from my pocket and broke the seal on the cellophane wrapper. I made a full fan of the deck and looked at the backs and faces of the cards. All this was recorded on film by Andrija. While casually shuffling the cards overhand, I asked Uri about the partial dematerialization question raised by my son earlier. With a real non sequitur, he asked me for the cards, which he continued to shuffle overhand for about fifteen seconds while we watched him most attentively. He was shuffling rather inelegantly—a ruse perhaps. At that point, he fumbled the cards. They appeared to fall from his hands, hitting the table edge. All this would be of very little interest, except that the cards appeared to penetrate the top of the Formica-covered table. When they fell over, we grabbed the deck immediately. All the cards were there, but five of them had pieces missing. Furthermore, the missing pieces were nowhere to be found.

The reason that the deck looked as though it had penetrated the table was that a slice amounting to about 25 percent of the card was missing from each of the five cards. Since the cards had a large missing diagonal slice, they were able to fall beyond the rest of the cards as they hit the table.

This was the first definitely nonregular event that we had seen during our interaction with Uri. We had just asked Uri about partial dematerialization, and fifteen seconds later he presented a handful of cards with pieces missing.

It wasn't until the next day that we solved that puzzle. We solved it by generating a larger, more global puzzle. A possible explanation is that this deck of cards, which I got on an airplane coming home from Amsterdam and had kept for two months without opening, could have had some of its cards struck twice by the die cutter in the playing-card factory, once the normal way and a second time with the cards slightly rotated. Such a double strike would produce exactly the defect we observed—namely an extra pair of parallel cuts. The missing pieces from the cards were never found, and the simplest explanation is that the cards came from the factory just the way we observed them. We have probably had almost five hundred decks of cards pass through our hands as bridge players and card shufflers, and we have never seen such a fractured deck before. Neither has any of the professional magicians whom we have queried on the point. Nonetheless, we consider this the most likely solution. But it's still a very improbable occurrence for those cards to travel through time and space to find themselves in Uri's hands at just the moment he needed them.

This whole question of coincidences is one that plagues psychic research. For example, if you ask a psychic to tell you the serial number engraved on the inside of your watch, and he correctly gives you the six digits in their proper order, do you conclude that he is psychic or that it was just his lucky day? How many times would you have to see such a one-in-a-million event repeated before you conclude that he is psychic? That is the essence of what we have come to call the "Lucky Day" hypothesis. In the case of Uri and the cards, because of the exactitude of the separation of the parallel cuts, we must conclude that it was coincidence at work.

Arthur Koestler deals with this problem at length in his book *The Roots of Coincidence*. He argues that to ascribe such occurrences to "just coincidence" is to misunderstand this small reminder of a universal order that overlays all activity, even though we have the illusion of complete person/event independence.

By this argument, it might be impossible to work with Uri and not be plagued with these occurrences. Immediately after the discovery of the sliced cards, Uri said that before he could continue with us he would need a sign from "Spectra," which is the code name for his "extraterrestrial intelligence" and claimed source of his power. With the words "I need a sign," Andrija turned on his movie lights and began filming Uri, since if a miracle were about to occur, he didn't want to miss recording it on film. Seconds after he began filming, we heard a clear, loud dingdong from the next room, which was unoccupied except for our ESP testing machine, a four-choice random number generator. As described in Chapter 6, the machine rewards a subject who makes a correct guess with a dingdong from an internal door chime. Although we have never before, or since, heard the chime from the machine for any reason except a correct button push, it is certainly possible that the switched-on movie lights could have produced a transient current flow in the house wiring that caused "the sign." We were unable to cause any further chimes by turning the lights on and off in subsequent attempts. But electrical transients are like that sometimes.

At this point, we found that the copper ring had become further bent. It had gone from a slight ellipse to a definite oval, and later became a definite dumbbell shape. It seemed as though this was all taking place spontaneously, though of course none of us was focused on the little ring while large-scale miracles were seemingly taking place around us!

We drank some coffee, which we stirred with bent spoons, and discussed the work we would try to do in the coming weeks.

As Hal and I walked down Uri's driveway to our car, we observed a stop sign quite logically placed at the end of the driveway, which intersected a busy cross street. What was illogical was the unusual condition of the sign, which had been supported by the usual five-foot iron stand. The sign, however, was now only two feet off the ground. That was because its support had been bent and twisted to form three complete loops around an imaginary center of rotation, as if to form a spiral slide about the right size for a mouse. As there was no possibility that we would have missed such an object as we entered Uri's house, the twisting must have occurred during our eight-to-midnight bending session. It was difficult to imagine how such a neat job could have been done without the use of heavy machinery.

On the first morning with Uri in the laboratory, we had a lot of learning to do. We learned that a large, hyperactive twenty-five-year-old Uri was not going to sit quietly like a piece of laboratory equipment waiting for an experiment to be set up and tested.

One of our first efforts in measuring Uri's ability was to ask him to attempt to change the meter reading on a magnetometer which measured the magnetic field near a sensitive probe taped to a tabletop. We used this same probe to go over Uri's hands and body to make sure he didn't have any magnets hidden away, although an implanted, intermittently powered electromagnet might have escaped detection. This whole operation was both filmed and videotaped. The film clearly shows Uri bringing open hands up to the magnetometer probe, and causing the meter to deflect full-scale several times by an amount about equal to the earth's magnetic field of roughly a half gauss. Toward the end of the experiment, an unfortunate thing occurred. The two delicate ink pens of our strip chart recorder were observed to have bent off the chart paper toward the end of the run, a seemingly inexplicable event since Uri was under continuous filming some distance away and no potential accomplices were present. While in this mutilated condition, the pens were bleeding red ink down the graph, indicating Uri's accomplishment.

At lunch, there was much good fellowship, since Uri felt he had accomplished one of the main goals we had set for our project with him. Using the magnetometer, he had apparently generated a psychokinetic event in the laboratory under controlled conditions. He had not yet bent a ring without touching it, but after all, this was only the first morning. (He never did manage ring bending under controlled conditions in our laboratory, although we didn't then suspect that this event was to evade us for the next six weeks.)

At lunch on that first day, we had a chance to observe an abundance of remarkable occurrences. We had a bent spoon for almost everybody at the table. The spoons didn't exactly bend before our eyes, but that's what it seemed like. Typical was astronaut Mitchell's observation that the spoon in his coffee cup had its bowl bent up at a right angle to its handle, and he was sure that it hadn't been that way when he used it to stir his coffee. We never had a chance to pick up a spoon, look at it and make sure that it hadn't been pre-bent or fatigued by repeated bending, and then have it bend while watched. This was of course our fondest wish, but it never happened.

On another day, on the way toward lunch, Uri saw a group of people working in a nearby laboratory. These engineers were crowded around a television monitor where an ultrasonic visualization system was being tested. (This is a device that allows one to see inside people without the use of X rays. The system uses sound waves and doesn't present the hazard that repeated use of X rays does. It also permits the doctor to observe soft tissues in addition to bones.) Uri stood in the doorway, looking at a picture on the TV screen. He said, "Let me show you what I can do"—a declaration we were to hear many times. He held up his fist like a threatening boxer as he looked at the TV screen fifteen feet away. We were amazed to hear him shout, "Up," "Down," "Up," "Down." We were even more amazed to see that the picture moved up and down, and right off the screen in time to his shouted commands. He then continued on toward lunch, the entire episode having taken a couple of minutes.

To determine whether such observations might occur under more controlled conditions, we arranged for a great performance that afternoon, this time with videotape surveillance. Furthermore, in our continuing paranoia we arranged for an SRI scientist to be stationed at every switch, every piece of electronic equipment. To be certain they recognized the seriousness of our endeavors, they were required to write up affidavits to account for their positions and activities during the replication experiment. The phenomenon repeated itself right on schedule and also on videotape. System failure of this type had never been observed before and has never been observed since. Nonetheless, with such complex equipment what can be said? Psychokinesis? Hidden electronics? In the end, it is an observation and nothing more should be said.

A simpler experiment (and therefore better experiment from our point of view) involved Uri's efforts to affect the weight of a one-gram weight placed on an electrical scale. It was covered by an aluminum can, also on the scale, and then the entire scale with weight was covered by a glass bell jar to eliminate the possibility of deflection by air currents. The entire experiment was filmed. The first part of our protocol involved tapping the bell jar; next tapping the table on which the apparatus rested; then kicking the table; and finally jumping on the floor, with a record made on strip chart of what these artifacts looked like.

In this experiment Geller's efforts resulted in deflections corresponding to weight gains and losses on the order of one gram, well out of the noise level. The signals he produced were single-sided pulses of about one-fifth-second duration, unlike the artifacts, which resulted in two-sided oscillations that slowly died out. In tests following this experimental run, a magnet was brought near the apparatus, static electricity was discharged against the apparatus, and controlled runs of day-long operation were obtained. In no case were artifacts obtained that resembled the effects that occurred during Geller's efforts, nor could anyone else duplicate the effects. We have no ready hypothesis on how these signals might have been produced.

Although the focus of our work with Uri was on his psycho-kinetic ability, there was another aspect which is somehow always left unsaid in discussions of Uri's achievements: his telepathic talent. Every morning before we would begin our day's scheduled adventures, Uri would suggest that we start with some kind of telepathy experiment. Not really an experiment, just something to warm up and develop a little good feeling. In the beginning, Uri would ask us to draw something. It took us only one day to counter the old "watching the top of the pencil trick" by showing up with predrawn targets made at home and carried to work in a com-bination-locked briefcase, to be withdrawn only at warm-up time. Much to our surprise, this gambit did not dampen his near-perfect (greater than 90 percent) ability to reproduce simple line drawings. In order to remove the burden of this observation from our shoul-ders alone, we encouraged other skeptical SRI laboratory personnel to show up from time to time with predrawn targets not to be re-moved from their pockets—and still success continued unabated.

On many days, our cameraman and constant companion, Zev Pressman, would bring in a little something from home for Uri to identify telepathically. Zev would select some unlikely object, like a chess knight or a Mexican peso, and put it in his pants pocket or inside jacket pocket. Uri would try to describe what Zev had. Uri never failed to do this correctly when he made a guess, although he would pass (that is, decline to guess) about 20 percent of the time. One day we all found particularly remark-able. Zev asked Uri to try to guess what he had brought in. Uri saw sets of concentric semicircles on a thin strip. None of us could imagine what that represented. It turned out the object was a collar stay that Zev had made from an old credit card cut into thin strips; the semicircles had been part of the design of the Master Charge card.

Why, you might reasonably ask, if Uri could daily demonstrate almost perfect telepathy, did we not pursue that line of investiga-tion and leave the elusive psychokinesis for another time? That is what we eventually did, although Uri resisted this, maintaining that "anyone can do telepathy." He argued that what makes him special is his psychokinetic ability.

We spent the next several weeks attempting to film or videotape any sort of metal bending under controlled laboratory conditions. One of Geller's main attributes that had been reported to us was that he was able to bend metal from a distance without touching it. In the laboratory we did not find him able to do so. When he was permitted to touch the metal, bending did occur. However, even though the bending was observed under continuous filming, it was never clear whether the spoon or other object was being bent because he had extraordinarily strong fingers and good control of micromanipulatory movements, or whether in fact the spoons "turned to plastic" in his hands as he claimed. Simple photo interpretation was not sufficient to determine whether the metal was bent by normal or paranormal means, and time restrictions prevented us from pursuing it further.

In this fashion, we spent the main part of our initial six weeks with Uri trying to verify his metal bending claims. Although we were not able to do this, we certainly observed a great number of unusual occurrences. One day in the middle of filming Uri's attempt to bend some wire rings inside a plastic box, we heard a strange noise coming from inside the movie camera. One of the small pulley wheels had disappeared from the film magazine, and four hundred feet of 16 mm film was being crammed into the body of the camera, an event our cameraman considered impossible under the conditions for film loading in use. We have no good explanation for the disappearance of this wheel, although it turned up a day later on the enlarging easel in a neighboring darkroom.

An almost limitless list of equipment failures was associated with our attempts to observe Uri's paranormal ability. On one of our last days with him, we set up a very elegant experiment in which Uri was to try to deflect a laser beam whose position was accurately monitored by an array of photo detectors. As always, the ultimate record was kept by a chart recorder whose pens make a continuous record on a moving strip of paper.

We explained to Uri that if he moved the light beam even a

fraction of a millimeter, he would get a large deflection of the pen on the chart recorder. He said, "Oh, I understand; you want me to move that little pen," and holding his fist about two feet over the chart recorder, he shouted "Move!" The pen moved all the way across the paper and never moved again. For reasons never determined, the sensitive preamplifiers of both channels of the recorder burned out and had to be replaced.

On one of our last attempts to observe psychokinesis in the lab, a large ball bearing was placed under a bell jar on a glass-topped table. The table was carefully balanced so that the ball bearing would not roll, even when we jumped on the floor next to it. Of course, if one kicked the table, the ball would roll from one side of the inverted bell jar to the other. The table was set up so that the entire experiment could be observed by our video camera, while the movie camera would watch just the ball and the inverted bell jar.

Uri came in early that day. Zev and I had just finished setting up the experiment and getting it balanced. He said that it was a terrific experiment and was sure he could move the ball. He tried and tried, and he huffed and he puffed. The little ball wouldn't move. Finally, in despair, Uri turned his eyes heavenward and in a true psychic's prayer said, "Dear God, help me move this shit." Uri placed his fist over the bell jar and the ball jiggled back and forth and then rolled across the table.

Unfortunately, in our excitement at having Uri arrive just at the moment when the apparatus was set up, none of the recording instruments was turned on. But the story has a happy ending. An hour later when the rest of the experimenters arrived, Zev was able to observe the ball through the cross hairs of his camera. The video recorder was able to watch the whole table and the rest of the room, and I was able to watch Uri, who said, "Let's pray that this thing works again." Hal and Uri put their hands over the top of the bell jar and waited quietly. The ball, as before, started a little jiggling dance and then rolled across the table, recorded by film and videotape.

Although the rolling of a steel ball and the deflection of the TV picture clearly seemed to us evidence of paranormal activity, they fell into a general category of funny things that happened in the laboratory, rather than into the much preferred category of controlled experiments.

The basic problem is perhaps best illustrated by the following example. The task was to deflect a compass needle, which indeed Geller did. Before and after the experiment he was gone over with a magnetometer probe, and his hands were continuously filmed from above and below as he worked over a compass resting on a special glass-topped experimental table. As a result of these precautions we were certain there were no obvious pieces of metal or magnets in his possession. However, according to our protocol, if we could in any way debunk the experiment and produce the effect by any other means, then that experiment was considered null and void even if there were no indications that anything untoward had happened. In this case, we found later that these types of deflections could be produced by a small piece of metal, so small in fact that it could not be detected by the magnetometer. Therefore, even though we had no evidence of this, we still considered the experiment inconclusive and an unsatisfactory type of experiment altogether.

The line we are drawing is one that gives us no pleasure, and it provides a lot of discomfort. It is our impression that Uri possibly did perform a number of genuine psychokinetic feats in the laboratory, but in the world of science no one at all cares what we think possibly may have happened. "Possibly" is not good enough. And it never happened under good experimental conditions.

For that reason, we continued to look for an area in which Geller felt he had ability, and in which we felt that a systematic investigation could be carried out. The eventual answer came through our looking at Geller's most pervasive ability—telepathy.

We had satisfied ourselves that Geller had a good functioning telepathic ability. Our job was to conduct experiments in such a manner that we could learn something about the information rate, or about how much detail he could pick up, and how fast. A more important consideration, of course, was that the experiments be carried out under thoroughly controlled laboratory conditions.

The first requirement for having a well-controlled experiment was to get Uri out of the way. To accomplish this we made use of a special isolation chamber in another building at SRI. The room was designed for recording brain waves and was ideally suited as a temporary home for our charismatic subject fitted as it was with a comfortable reclining chair. The double walls were made of metal separated from each other by four inches of acoustic insulation which provided electrical shielding and soundproofing. The room also had an inner and an outer door, both of which fastened with a type of locking mechanism found on large walk-in refrigerators. The object was to have Uri safely tucked away inside with a pencil and paper while we (in another room) made drawings for him to receive telepathically and reproduce. The shielded room is shown below.

SHIELDED ROOM USED FOR GELLER EXPERIMENTS

The formal protocol for these experiments is very simple to describe. First, since even the best shielded room will pass electromagnetic waves at extremely low and extremely high frequencies, and recalling Puharich's expertise in microminiature electronics, we permitted no one in the target area so as to eliminate the possibility of a confederate radioing information. In particular, Uri's friend Shippi was never in a position to observe the target picture before or during an experiment. Second, silence was maintained in the target area so that even if all the rooms had been bugged, there would have been nothing to overhear.

The authors had the assistance of doctoral candidate Jean Mayo in several of the experiments because of her ability as a professional artist. The experiments were conducted as follows: Uri was locked in the shielded room while one of the experimenters watched the door on the outside. The other two experimenters would then go to a large 1,700-page college dictionary and choose a page by inserting a file card at random. The dictionary would then be opened and the first item in the first column that could be drawn was selected as the target picture.

If, for instance, the dictionary was opened to "taciturn," it would not be possible to draw this adjective. However, the next entry on the page would be "tack," and this object could be drawn. When we finally published the results of these experiments in *Nature*,[1] some referees felt that this method of target selection might not be sufficiently random, a spurious argument in our estimation. Here we will merely describe some of these individual drawings to give a feeling of how the experiments were conducted.

In this series, the target pictures were drawn and then hung up on the wall in a neighboring room down the hall or in a room in another building. We communicated with Uri through an intercom that operated with a push-to-talk switch so that we could hear him at all times, but he could hear us only when we depressed the switch. During the first experiment, moments after we told him that we were ready, he announced that he saw "a cylinder with noise coming out of it." That could be taken to have something to do with a firecracker—"fuse" was the target word and Jean had, in fact, drawn a firecracker—but the drawings he made speak for themselves (see Figure 22). During the experiments when he said he had drawn as much as he felt he could, one of the experimenters would open the door and obtain the drawings from Uri before showing him the target.

To determine if Uri was indeed perceiving the target picture,

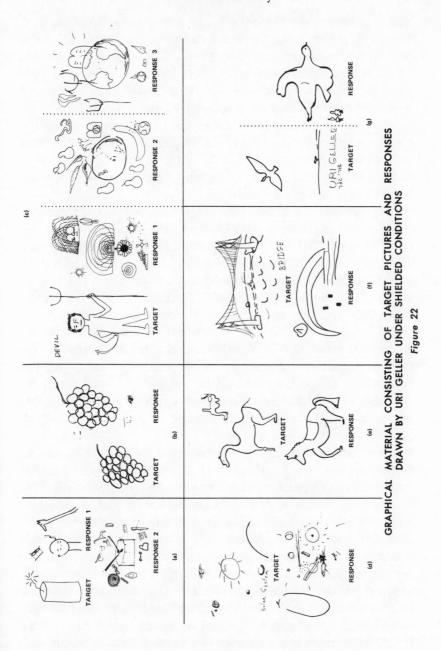

GRAPHICAL MATERIAL CONSISTING OF TARGET PICTURES AND RESPONSES
DRAWN BY URI GELLER UNDER SHIELDED CONDITIONS

Figure 22

and to eliminate the charge of biased interpretations on our part, we would, at the end of the series, enlist the aid of two SRI scientists who, as independent judges, had nothing otherwise to do with the experiments. Everything that Uri drew in response to a given picture was stapled together. A judge was then confronted with ten sets of Uri's drawings in one pile, and ten target drawings, randomized, in another. The task of the judges was to match the corresponding pairs of target and response drawings. The two judges were able to match correctly all ten of the drawing pairs, at odds of greater than 1,000,000:1 against such an event happening by chance for either judge alone.

Although reasonable men may differ over whether Uri's response to "fuse" has anything to do with the target picture, almost everyone will agree that his second attempt produced a good match. The target word from the dictionary was "bunch" and Jean drew a bunch of grapes. After some incoherent mumbling from Uri, he said he "saw some purple circles." (Since the grapes, and all the other drawings, were made with black felt pen on white paper, it would appear that either it is information content, not literal anatomical detail, that is carried by the channel of interest, or else there is significant internal processing before the image reaches awareness.) When Uri said that he was finished, we opened his door and received a drawing that very much seemed to resemble Jean's. In fact, Uri's drawing of "purple circles" had the twenty-four grapes of the target picture.

The third drawing made under these ground rules involved two of the investigators, Jean and I (R.T.) going into the shielded room with the dictionary and leaving Hal on the outside with Uri. This surprise switch on Uri was in many ways a more satisfactory arrangement, since it allowed an experimenter to watch Uri as he made his drawing. The intercom was of course turned off for this experiment. This time the target obtained with the random dictionary technique was "solar system," which Jean drew within the crowded confines of the shielded room. Uri then spent almost a half hour puzzling over what to draw, all under the watchful eyes of Hal, who was of course ignorant of the target selection. After struggling to capture a feeling of vast space, he made his drawing of the solar system and submitted it to Hal, who then knocked on the door to signal the end of the experiment. Uri's drawing greatly resembles the one drawn in the shielded room, except that the center is full of a variety of space trash including the *2001: A Space Odyssey* monolith and an angel thrown in for good measure.

It was evident that some sort of communication channel existed. We therefore decided to move our artist from the life sciences building, where the shielded room was located, to the engineering building a quarter of a mile away. Uri was put safely back in his shielded room, while Jean and I returned with the dictionary to my office in the engineering building, leaving Hal to guard Uri.

The target selection proceeded as before. This time the dictionary yielded "farmer," which in the drawing looked more like a devil than the Grant Wood farmer of American Gothic. I called Hal to tell him that Uri could begin, but of course did not say what the target picture was. After twenty minutes, Hal called back to say that Uri had finished, although Uri was very unhappy about the target. I asked Hal to collect Uri's pictures and said we would come over with the target picture, still not telling Hal what the target was. In the comparison that took place when we arrived, we saw that Uri had drawn the tablets of the ten commandments, a worm coming out of an apple, and symbolic representations of God, but he said he couldn't figure out what the target was supposed to be. Upon seeing that the target was the devil, Uri became extremely agitated, complaining that in an Israeli household mention of the devil was taboo.

Thirteen experiments of this type were carried out. Uri always had the opportunity to pass, that is, to refuse to submit drawings, if he felt that he didn't have any idea what the target was. The decision had to be made before the target was made known, of course. We feel that it is the mark of an individual with well-developed psychic functioning to be able to know when all he is seeing is his own self-generated images of memory and imagination and not the external target. We always encourage subjects not to guess if they don't have an answer that feels right to them. The three times that Uri exercised the pass option special circumstances were involved. In one case, the possibility of a telepathic link was eliminated by arranging for a drawing unknown to the experimenters with Uri to be placed inside the shielded room; then he was brought to the room and asked to draw the picture hidden there. Uri said that he got no clear impression and did not submit a drawing. In the other two cases, we attempted to record Uri's EEG with a maze of electrodes during his efforts to perceive the target pictures. He found it difficult to hold adequately still for good EEG records, said that he experienced difficulty in getting impressions of the targets, and again submitted no drawings.

In the final three experiments of this series, Uri was closeted in a different shielded room on the second floor of the engineering building, which houses a number of large digital computers. The purpose of these experiments was to determine if Uri could obtain pictorial information from the face of a TV tube or from a computer memory instead of from a conventional drawing. The shielded room in this case was about a hundred yards down a hall and around a corner from the computer room.

The target pictures were selected and drawn by three computer scientists who were not otherwise associated with either our experimentation or Geller, and who agreed to help us with the research. They first used a light pen to draw a kite on the face of the video terminal of their PDP-11 computer graphics system. Uri seemed very interested in the idea of getting information from a computer. In this first case, the kite was displayed on a TV display screen at the computer location. Uri felt very confident that he had the kite drawing correct and even signed his name over it. In the remaining two experiments, there was no visible picture. One picture was typed directly into the computer's memory and existed only as a set of program instructions, while a second was displayed on the TV screen with zero intensity; in both cases there was no visible display. Uri felt less confident about these two, which were nonetheless successfully matched by our judges. The computer targets along with Geller's responses are shown in Figure 23.

In the above experiments no experimenter in contact with Geller knew what the target was, so it was possible to conclude that the information came from the target area. The question then arose as to whether it was necessary for anyone at the target end to be aware of

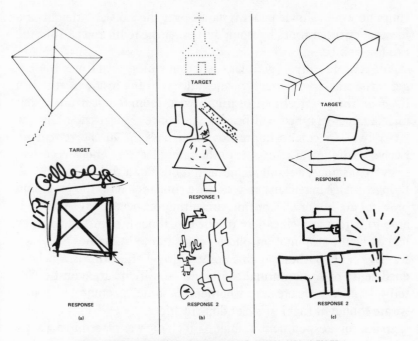

TARGET

TARGET

TARGET

RESPONSE 1

RESPONSE 1

RESPONSE

RESPONSE 2

RESPONSE 2

(a)

(b)

(c)

COMPUTER DRAWING EXPERIMENTS WITH URI GELLER
(A) PICTURE STORED ON VIDEO DISPLAY
(B) PICTURE STORED IN COMPUTER MEMORY ONLY
(C) PICTURE STORED ON VIDEO DISPLAY WITH ZERO INTENSITY

Figure 23

the target. That is, was it necessary to have a potential telepathic link, or could Uri obtain the information directly from the target itself, that is, clairvoyantly?

One experiment carried out to clarify this issue went as follows. An individual not otherwise associated with our research entered the laboratory, placed a small object in one of ten aluminum film cans, screwed on numbered steel lids at random, lined them up at random, and then left the area. We would then enter the lab with Uri, with none of us knowing which can contained the object. Geller's task now was to identify the target can, which he must do without touching the cans or table upon which the cans rest. (Should he touch a can or the table accidentally, that would count as an automatic miss.) The experiments were observed by a number of researchers besides ourselves, and some of them were filmed. Sometimes he would slowly pass his hands over the cans at a height of a few inches; other times he would just enter the room and call out the can-top number.

We repeated this experiment fourteen times. Five times the target was a small permanent magnet affixed to the inside of the steel lid, five times a steel ball bearing, twice room-temperature water, once a paper-wrapped ball bearing, and once a sugar cube. On the latter two Uri got no impression and passed. On the remaining twelve he did make a guess as to the target location and was correct in every instance, a result significant at odds of a trillion to one. Although a stage magician can produce a similar effect if the props and protocol are under his control, consulting magicians have not been able to detect any chicanery in our experiment, even though they had available stop-motion photography frame by frame. Although we have no hypothesis at this point as to whether this is a heightened sense of some normal sense (i.e., sensitivity to acoustic patterns, temperature, etc.), or whether it is some "paranormal" sense, we are confident that it was not done by trickery.

In a second experiment a single ¾-inch die was placed in a 3 x 4 x 5-inch steel file box; both box and die, the latter stamped with a serial number, were supplied by SRI. The box was then vigorously shaken by one of the experimenters and placed on a table, a technique found in control runs to produce a distribution of die faces differing nonsignificantly from chance. Geller's task was then to write down which die face was uppermost, the answer at that point being unknown to all involved in the experiment. This experiment was performed ten times, with Uri passing twice and giving a response eight times, each experiment taking about thirty seconds. In the eight times he gave a response, he was correct each time. The probability of this occurring by chance is about one in a million. (Contrary to what some critics have suggested, at no time did Uri have an opportunity to "peek" into the box, nor were there additional unreported throws of the die: these ten trials were the only ten, and were not selected out of a longer run.) Thus it appeared that it was not necessary for someone to know an answer in order for Uri to get it. A possible alternative to clairvoyance, of course, is precognition, since in these cases Uri found out when the box was opened just what the answer was. To settle this issue would require more extensive testing.

To summarize our work with Uri, in the total time that we spent working with him, we must have seen dozens of objects move, bend, and break. It often looked as though they were bent by paranormal means. However, our job was to separate the wheat from the chaff, and we summarily rejected any data obtained under circumstances which might *in principle* permit a nonparanormal hypothesis, even in those cases in which there was no evidence for the proposed alternative. Critics of our work often overlook the fact that as physicists we are the ones who have the greatest motivation to insure that we do not waste the next ten years of our lives writing equations for possibly nonexistent phenomena. Thus we consider only those data we observed under controlled conditions where there was no known possibility for error.

The experiments conducted under rigid conditions left no doubt as to Uri's paranormal perceptual ability. We are not saying that he doesn't have psychokinetic ability also; we simply were not able to establish it to our satisfaction. The response to our reported results is about evenly divided between those who are upset with us for finding Uri has any paranormal ability and those who are upset with us for not finding more.

It is worth repeating that Uri feels that his telepathic ability is the least of his gifts and that anyone can exercise telepathy to some degree, which our combined data would indicate is probably right.

Thus far in our psychic research, we have worked with more than a dozen individuals in addition to Uri Geller. All exhibited psychic functioning in the remote viewing perceptual task described earlier. From our present viewpoint, we would have been surprised if Uri Geller was so unique as to be the only one lacking such ability.

The particular ability that Geller demonstrates is not unusual in the field of paranormal functioning. Picture drawing experiments are the traditional test offered to anyone who claims to have telepathic ability. The experiments we carried out with Geller are neither the first nor the most successful of this genre; they are not even the best publicized. It is important not to lose perspective with regard to the antecedents to this work.

159

The following are two extensive series of experiments giving results very similar to the results we obtained with Geller. We are presenting this material in order to indicate the generality of this ability and thereby place Geller's work in perspective.

In 1930, the well-known author Upton Sinclair published a book entitled *Mental Radio*.[2] In it he presented more than a hundred picture drawing experiments he and others had carried out with his wife, Mary Craig. In the book she describes in very convincing fashion her technique for picking up the mental images. Figure 24 shows eight picture pairs selected from more than one hundred fifty such line drawings in the book.

We were especially interested in the general analytic confusion about the *meaning* of the pictures, in contrast to the correctly perceived patterns. This greatly resembles what we see regularly in our own experiments, both in picture drawing and in remote viewing.

Sinclair lived in Princeton, New Jersey, at the time, and was a friend of Albert Einstein, who observed some of the experiments. In fact, Sinclair's book has a preface written by Einstein in which he says:

> The results of the telepathic experiments carefully and plainly set forth in this book stand surely far beyond those which a nature investigator holds to be thinkable. On the other hand, it is out of the question in the case of so conscientious an observer and writer as Upton Sinclair that he is carrying on a conscious deception of the reading world; his good faith and dependability are not to be questioned.

Why then has this treasure trove of a book been neglected for the past forty-five years? Precisely because we do not have a comfortable physical model to describe the mechanism responsible for such phenomena. As soon as we can explain telepathy in terms that we use to explain other phenomena we feel we understand, the Sinclair work and others will no doubt be rediscovered.

A second more recent example is the research work of Musso and Granero published in the March, 1973, *Journal of Parapsychology*.[3] The two authors are both psychology professors at the Na-

HERE IS THE FLAG, MADE SIMPLER—
"E PLURIBUS UNUM!"

HERE IS A LOVE STORY THAT SEEMS
TO GO WRONG, THE HEARTS BEING
TURNED TO OPPOSITION

IN THE FOLLOWING CASE I DREW
SIXTEEN STARS, AND YOU MAY
COUNT AND SEE THAT CRAIG GOT
TWELVE OF THEM, AND MADE UP
THE DIFFERENCE WITH A MOON!

HER COMMENT WAS: "I FEEL THAT
IT IS A SNAKE CRAWLING OUT OF
SOMETHING—VIVID FEELING OF
SNAKE, BUT IT LOOKS LIKE A CAT'S
TAIL"

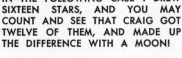

NOR THIS WINDMILL BECAUSE THE
SAILS ARE LEFT OFF

AND THESE THREE CIRCLES, WITH
COMMENT "FEEL SURE IT IS" WRIT-
TEN ABOVE THE DRAWING

TELEGRAPH WIRES, APPARENTLY SEEN
AS WAVES

THIS ALPINE HAT WITH FEATHER
SEEMS TO ME NO LESS OF A SUC-
CESS BECAUSE IT IS CALLED "CHAF-
ING DISH"

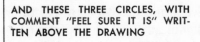

THESE DRAWINGS ARE SELECTED
FROM MORE THAN A HUNDRED SUCH
SAMPLES IN UPTON SINCLAIR'S BOOK
MENTAL RADIO, DESCRIBING TELEPA-
THY EXPERIMENTS CARRIED OUT BE-
TWEEN HIMSELF AND HIS WIFE, MARY
CRAIG KIMBROUGH

Figure 24

tional University of Rosario in Argentina. They had observed certain coincidences and had heard anecdotes about one of their colleagues, Dr. José Muratti, a practicing psychiatrist, that led them to consider carrying out some informal telepathy tests with him to see if he really had any unusual perceptual ability of the type suggested by his stories.

On the basis of informal observations, Dr. Muratti appeared to be a remarkable subject, and a formal series of experiments was initiated. In these experiments, the subject and sender were at all times in different rooms. The ninety experiments were divided into three randomly intermixed groups. One group consisted of pure clairvoyance trials in which no one knew the contents of a target envelope chosen at random from a previously prepared set. In a second group, the sender in a room across the hall would draw the target picture at the same time as Dr. Muratti was trying to perceive it in his room with the second experimenter. In the third group, the sender held a picture previously drawn by himself, chosen at random from a set, and looked at it while Dr. Muratti, still across the hall, tried to perceive it and make a copy. All three modes of perception were highly significant, and no important difference among the three was found. That is, it didn't matter whether or not anyone knew the contents of the target envelope, nor did it matter whether the target picture was being drawn during the experiment or had been drawn previously. Figure 25 shows the experimenters' selection from each of the three experimental modes used in their work.

With the inspiration of these two excellent studies, we would encourage the reader to try some simple experiments for himself. A good beginning guide to entering the proper frame of mind is provided by Sinclair's wife, Mary Craig:

> You have to inhibit the impulse to think things about the object, to examine it, or appraise it, or to allow memory trains to attach themselves to it. The average person has never heard of such a form of concentration and so has to learn how to do it. Simultaneously, we must learn how to relax, for strangely enough a part of concentration is complete relaxation.

Is Chaos Necessary?

Condition C₁ — Target 46, Response 46, Target 55, Response 55, Target 60, Response 60

Condition C₂ — Target 2, Response 2, Target 5, Response 5, Target 87, Response 87

Condition C₃ — Target 36, Response 36, Target 39, Response 39, Target 58, Response 58

THESE DRAWINGS ARE FROM A PAPER ENTITLED "AN ESP EXPERIMENT WITH A HIGH-SCORING SUBJECT" BY J. R. MUSSO AND M. GRANERO, BOTH OF WHOM ARE PSYCHOLOGY PROFESSORS AT THE NATIONAL UNIVERSITY IN ARGENTINA. THEIR HIGH-SCORING SUBJECT WAS DR. JOSE MURATTI, WHO IS A PRACTICING PSYCHIATRIST

Figure 25

The Coincidence Factor

Since our Geller experiments, we have talked with many other scientists who have worked with Uri. One of the threads which seems to run through experiments with Uri is the strange chain of coincidences that appear to follow him around. The incident of the fractional cards described at the beginning of this chapter is certainly remarkable and fortuitous. However, we recently had a series of events take place around us that we found just as striking.

One night in April, 1975, we met with an East Coast colleague who was collecting information about the different scientists who had worked with Uri. We met with him just after our plane landed in Washington, D.C., and our meeting began around eleven-thirty in our hotel room.

Our friend asked our opinion about some unexplained "Uri phenomenon" at another laboratory where Uri had been investigated. Some photographs had been taken of Uri trying to cause an iron rod to bend—a familiar task. The photo, however, seemed to show an additional arm suspended over Uri's head. "What," we were asked, "do you make of that?" Since we are accustomed to people calling us at least once a week with private information about the "end of the world" and the like, we answered somewhat facetiously that "the arm was probably just a helping hand for Uri." Our colleague was not amused. He told us that this was a serious matter because the photographer who took the picture had recently been awakened from his sleep to see an apparition of just such an arm floating above his bed in the middle of the night. "The arm," we were told, "was totally real-looking, covered with plain gray cloth, and was rotating with a hook at the hand end. What about that?" That sounded more sinister to me, but Hal said lightheartedly, "That's the sort of thing that you could expect from a three-dimensional hologram projected by a second-class extraterrestrial civilization who wanted to scare a man in bed."

By this time, it was almost midnight and we were all feeling a little silly from the jet lag and late hour. At that point, we heard a rattle at the door. Somebody had just put a key into the lock and was opening our hotel room door. After a half hour of ghost stories, we were frozen in an instant. The door continued to swing open, and a man walked into our room—a man who wore a plain gray suit and had only one arm.

The explanation was simple, of course. He was only looking for his suitcase which had been moved elsewhere when the hotel had shifted his room to make a place for us. The hotel had unfortunately neglected to tell him of the move. We assumed our colleague had set us up. He assumed we had set him up. Neither of us could find evidence to support our respective hypotheses. Of such coincidences are the lives of psychical researchers made.

What does that have to do with Uri Geller? We don't know the whole answer to that either, but we find that working with him not only allows one to observe unusual events but also to experience them.

As though our experiences with Geller will never end, the single Xerox copy of this chapter turned into dusty gray pages without a trace of print while safely stored away in our files. We presume this dematerialization was caused by a faulty Xerox machine. . . .

8
THE LOYAL OPPOSITION
WHAT ARE THEY THEY LOYAL TO?

Just because you're paranoid doesn't mean they're not out to get you.

—Contemporary Poster

Now we deal with such unsavory matters as charlatans and dupes, hoaxes and conspiracies, terms not unfamiliar in the field of parapsychology. Such epithets are often thrown at those who would affirm or even investigate the existence of paranormal functioning.

We assume that critics can be taken at face value, that is, that they are individuals who, in good faith, genuinely believe in the nonexistence of paranormal functioning, and as a corollary, genuinely believe that those who entertain the possibility of paranormal functioning must be mistaken, misguided, or worse.

The reason we are interested in examining the statements of the Loyal Opposition is that they provide a sociological commentary on man's difficulty in facing up to those aspects of reality which have not yet been fully integrated into the social fabric at the level of underlying beliefs. The Loyal Opposition is not monolithic, however, but is more like a mosaic, each piece representing a different form of resistance, and it is necessary to look at each piece separately.

"It is the province of natural science to investigate nature, impartially and without prejudice."[1] This is a statement that even the Loyal Opposition agrees with, at least in principle. In practice, however, nowhere in scientific inquiry has this dictum met as great a challenge as in the area of so-called paranormal functioning.

Such phenomena, although under scientific consideration for over a century, have historically been fraught with unreliability and controversy, and validation of the phenomena by accepted scientific methodology has been slow in coming. Even so, a recent survey conducted by Christopher Evans and published in the British magazine *New Scientist* revealed some interesting results. Evans found that 67 percent of the nearly 1,500 responding readers (the majority of whom are working scientists and technologists) considered ESP to be an established fact or a likely possibility, and 88 percent held the investigation of ESP to be a legitimate scientific undertaking.[2] What, then, are the problems in the scientific community? The answer lies on many levels.

The most severe criticism is that leveled by the well-known British parapsychology critic C. E. M. Hansel.[3] He began his examination of the ESP hypothesis with the stated assumption, "In view of the a priori arguments against it *we know in advance* that telepathy, etc. cannot occur." Therefore, Hansel's examination of the literature centered primarily on a search for possible fraud, by subjects or investigators. He reviewed in depth four experiments that he regarded as providing the best evidence of ESP: the Pearce-Pratt distance series,[4] and the Pratt-Woodruff series,[5] both conducted at Duke; Soal's work with Mrs. Stewart and Basil Shackleton;[6] and a more recent series by Soal and Bowden.[7] Hansel showed how fraud *could* have been committed (by the experimenters in the Pratt-Woodruff and Soal-Bateman series, or by the subjects in the Pearce-Pratt and Soal-Bateman experiments). He gave no evidence that fraud *was* in fact committed in these experiments, but said, "If the results could have arisen through a trick, the experiment must be considered unsatisfactory proof of ESP, *whether or not it is finally* decided that such a trick was in fact used."[8] As discussed by Honorton in a review of the field,[9] Hansel's conclusion after 241 pages of careful scrutiny was that these experiments were not "fraud proof" and therefore could not in principle serve as conclusive proof of ESP.

As damning as the above argument may seem, it could be applied equally well to any other scientific endeavor. It is therefore the a priori assumption of the nonexistence of paranormal functioning that makes this argument appear damaging, and not anything in the argument itself.

Although a review of the literature reveals that experiments by reputable researchers yielding positive results were begun over a century ago, many consider that there is not yet any clear evidence for paranormal functioning.

One reason for this is that no satisfactory theoretical framework has been advanced to correlate data or to predict new experimental outcomes. Consequently, the area in question has remained for a long time in the observational stage reminiscent of electricity when all we had to go on were spontaneous lightning strokes and the static effects produced by rubbing silk on glass.

The difficulty in accepting, or even thinking about, phenomena that do not fit into an accepted hierarchy of scientific beliefs has been discussed at length by Gunther Stent in a *Scientific American* article entitled "Prematurity and Uniqueness in Scientific Discovery."[10] Reflecting on what it means to say a discovery is "ahead of its time," Stent argues that any discovery which does not arise in a logically connected fashion from the already existing body of generally accepted knowledge will necessarily constitute a premature discovery. Although writing as a molecular geneticist on premature discovery in the field of DNA research, he cites ESP as an example of here-and-now prematurity. He points out that "until it is possible to connect ESP with canonical knowledge of, say, electromagnetic radiation and neurophysiology, no demonstration of its occurrence can be appreciated."

Stent goes on to ask:

> Is this lack of appreciation of premature discoveries merely attributable to the intellectual shortcomings or innate conservatism of scientists who, if they were only more perceptive

or more open-minded, would give immediate recognition to any well documented scientific proposition?

[Scientist-philosopher Michael] Polanyi is not of this opinion. He declared, "... There must be at all times a predominantly accepted scientific view of the nature of things, in the light of which, research is jointly conducted by members of a community of scientists. A strong presumption that any evidence which contradicts this view is invalid, must prevail. Such evidence must be disregarded, even if it cannot be accounted for, in the hope that it will eventually turn out to be false or irrelevant."

This view of the operation of science is rather different from the one commonly held, under which acceptance of authority is seen as something to be avoided at all costs. The good scientist is seen as an unprejudiced man with an open mind who is ready to embrace any new idea that is supported by facts. The history of science shows, however, that its practitioners do not appear to act according to that popular view.

To put the problem in its clearest perspective, we were recently told by a journal editor to whom we had submitted a paper that an individual consulted by the editor said, "This is the kind of thing that I would not believe in even if it existed."[11]

However, there is still hope for a rational consideration of paranormal functioning, since many contemporary physicists are now of the opinion that these phenomena are not at all inconsistent with the framework of modern physics: the often-held view that observations of this type are incompatible with known laws is not only outdated but false, being based on the naive realism prevalent before the development of modern physics. Since the early days of psychical research, information theory, quantum theory, and neurophysiological research have developed considerably, and these disciplines have begun to provide powerful conceptual tools that appear to bear directly on the issues of interest. In the emerging view, it is accepted that research in the area of the paranormal can be conducted so as to uncover not just a catalog of interesting events, but rather patterns of cause-effect relationships. These patterns would then lend themselves to analysis and hypothesis in the forms with which we are familiar in the physical and psychological sciences.

For example, one hypothesis for remote viewing is that information is carried by extremely low frequency (ELF) electromagnetic waves, a proposal that does not at the outset seem to be ruled out by any obvious physical or biological facts. As discussed in Chapter 2, this is the hypothesis favored by Kogan of the USSR and by Persinger of Canada.[12] Experimental support is claimed on the basis of (1) little if any observable decrease in accuracy with increases in distance, (2) the apparent ineffectiveness of ordinary electromagnetic shielding, and (3) the observed low data rate—all factors in common between ELF and ESP. A paper by the authors may be referred to for a discussion of the pros and cons of this hypothesis.[13]

An alternative viewpoint held by many physicists (including the authors) is that the reconciliation of observed data with modern theory may take place at a more fundamental level—namely, at the level of the foundations of quantum theory. There is a continuing dialogue, for example, on the proper interpretation of the effect of an observer (consciousness) on experimental measurement.[14] There is also considerable current scientific interest in the implications for our world view, brought on by the recent experimental observation of "quantum interconnectedness,"[15] an apparent connection between distant events.[16] This Quantum Connection is codified in a theorem of great elegance known as Bell's Theorem.[17] This theorem emphasizes that "no theory of reality compatible with quantum theory can require spatially separated events to be independent."[18] Rather it must permit physically separated events to interact with each other in a manner that is contrary to ordinary experience.[19] This aspect of modern theory, which has been experimentally tested and confirmed,[20] reveals that parts of the universe apparently separated from each other can nonetheless act together as parts of a larger whole, a statement perhaps more expected to be found in mystical writing than in a theory of physics.

With arguments such as these being put forward and examined, rejection of the possibility of paranormal functioning by the scientific community is fading rapidly. Physics seminars on the possible mechanisms involved in paranormal functioning are becoming part of the current scene.

As an example, we attended an international conference on quantum physics and parapsychology held in Geneva, Switzerland, in August, 1974. We presented papers on remote viewing,[21] and on our magnetometer work and its implications for physics.[22] The conference brought together papers by such internationally known scientists as Gerald Feinberg of Columbia University, O. Costa de Beauregard of the Poincare Institute in Paris, and C. T. K. Chari of Madras Christian College in India to discuss possible models for paranormal functioning.[23] The Loyal Opposition thus numbers fewer and fewer scientists among its ranks; the physicists by and large are leaving first, the psychologists last.

On the basis of the above, one might think that the Loyal Opposition would crumble, but such is not the case. There is always a cultural lag between the generation of new ideas by those on the forefront, and their acceptance by those further removed from where the action is. This should be expected, since those not directly involved in day-to-day research find themselves forced to struggle just to get on top of yesterday's paradigm, let alone today's. This is not necessarily a completely negative factor, however. In fact, in the light of Polanyi's analysis referred to earlier, it is healthy for this second echelon to resist innovation, and to require that the burden of proof lie with the innovator who would seemingly bring chaos into the previously established order. Nonetheless, it can be trying at the personal level, as is shown in the following events that have occurred in connection with our own work. Although some of the events may seem incredible, it is useful to keep in mind that members of the Loyal Opposition see their role as saving science from our form of heresy, and therefore from their viewpoint high stakes ride on the outcome.

The Loyal Opposition in Action

One of the first indications that our work would be met by other than straightforward scientific interest came when we wrote a *per-*

sonal letter ("... hope you will treat this letter as confidential and personal ...") to Gerald Piel, publisher of *Scientific American,* in December, 1972. In that letter we inquired whether his publication would in principle be interested in receiving a survey paper on the field of ESP, pointing out that the previous article on this subject published by them was in July, 1934.[24] Since that time, a great many additional investigations had been conducted. In support of our desire to submit such a paper, we cited some of our own preliminary results which indicated to us that this was an important area of research. We stressed that our goal in research was to explore the relationship between ESP functioning and the physical and psychological variables with which we are familiar.

Unfortunately, we found that "premature discovery" can lead to "premature publicity." The letter was leaked to Leon Jaroff of *Time* magazine, who soon after cited its contents in a March, 1973, *Time* article critical of our doing research with Uri Geller even though we had not yet published or described our results.[25]

The *Time* article was of necessity based on hearsay, since we were maintaining a sealed-lips policy until ready to publish our findings in an appropriate scientific forum. One of the major sources of hearsay for the *Time* article was yet another leak, this time, incredibly, as a result of a privileged, confidential visit requested by George Lawrence, at that time a projects manager for the Department of Defense's Advanced Research Projects Agency (ARPA). Lawrence had visited SRI accompanied by two of his consultants, Ray Hyman, a psychology professor from the University of Oregon, and Robert Van de Castle, a University of Virginia psychologist. Their stated aim was to determine whether anything in our study would be of interest to ARPA.

As they arrived during the time of Geller's stay at SRI, they requested an opportunity to see an experiment in progress. We denied their request for two reasons. First, we had had several such requests per week and had previously concluded that it would be impossible to carry out controlled experimentation under such conditions, and our time with Geller was running out. Second, we were at that time still suspicious that Geller might have been sent to try through trickery to crack the protocols of our ongoing program, and we did not want to provide an opportunity for any collusion to take place. (This was before the controlled experiments that were eventually published in *Nature*.)

As an alternative to watching one of our experiments, we suggested that they conduct some experiments of their own with Geller. That way, whatever they observed could not be laid at our door. They then spent an engaging couple of hours with Geller in which they observed the informal coffee-table type of demonstration that Uri favors. They tried a number of their own, and from our standpoint largely uncontrolled, experiments (which we have on videotape). Van de Castle did, however, carry out one experiment under good control in which Geller reproduced a drawing made by Van de Castle himself and sealed in double envelopes, out of Geller's sight. From that, Van de Castle concluded that Geller was "an interesting subject for further study." Hyman and Lawrence were not impressed by the results obtained in their experiments, however, which were not as controlled as Van de Castle's, and left feeling that Geller was probably simply a clever magician; not an altogether unreasonable conclusion given what they saw and the informal manner in which they chose to interact with Geller.

Nonetheless, we were amazed when a *Time* article came out with quotes from a letter by Hyman in which he wrote that the SRI tests of Geller were performed with "incredible sloppiness." First of all, we could hardly believe the lack of professional responsibility that would permit a straight line between a privileged visit to a laboratory involved in sensitive and controversial work, not yet published, and the pages of a popular newsweekly. Beyond that, however, the only tests of Geller observed by Hyman at SRI were those conducted by himself and his colleagues, which, whatever he thought of them, could hardly be our responsibility. Not yet understanding the deep emotional reactions to be touched off by this area of research, we could only wonder at the turn of events. We eventually obtained a copy of Hyman's letter describing his visit to SRI, and it was clear that the encounter had impacted him strongly at the emotional level; in fact, to such a degree that although he had interacted face to face with Geller for a number of hours, he came away from the interaction describing Geller's eyes as blue (they are dark brown).

We were to find that our initial negative experience with *Time* was only a taste of what was to come. The most perfidious series of interactions with a representative of the news media that we have so far encountered began innocently enough with a request for a visit to our laboratory by science reporter Joe Hanlon of the British weekly science magazine *New Scientist*. He knew that we had done work with Geller and that we were preparing a lengthy publication on our findings. Assuring us that he was not coming as a reporter, he presented himself as a member of a *New Scientist* panel that had been set up to investigate Geller in a series of their own experiments,[26] a series Geller had reportedly agreed to.

Since we had just completed a series of experiments with Geller that were partially successful, but not yet published, we welcomed the opportunity to cooperate with such a panel, for we realized that an independent investigation would in all probability yield results similar to ours.

Hanlon arrived at SRI in January, 1974. After some preliminary discussion, he suggested that we might consider publishing our results with Geller in the *New Scientist* and asked to see an advance copy of whatever we had written up. We let him see a copy, but declined the invitation, indicating that we had put together a technical paper of journal quality and planned to submit it to *Nature*. (*Nature* had run an editorial challenging us to publish our results, which we took as an invitation.)[27]

Since there was a possibility that Hanlon would work directly with Geller, we got right to the heart of the matter, passing on to him the strategies and precautions that magicians and other consultants had cautioned us to employ. These included the necessity of generating target drawings out of sight; the requirement that no one in Geller's presence before or during an experiment should have knowledge of the target (to avoid the possibility of subliminal cueing by body language, subvocalization, etc.); the elimination of potential confederates from the target area (to prevent radio reception by means of an implanted receiver); the necessity of maintaining silence in the target area (to foil "bugging" of the target area, a potentially useful strategy on the part of a subject should he have an implanted receiver); the necessity in die-in-the-box experiments to use one's own die and box, marked and continually checked by the experimenter; the absolute requirement that target responses be obtained from Geller on paper and be in the experimenter's physical possession before the target was revealed to Geller (to prevent post hoc alteration of the data); etc., etc., etc. During Hanlon's two-day visit, he watched the videotapes that we made available to him, took copious notes, including notes on the paper to be submitted to *Nature*, expressed his thanks, and left.

The next we heard of Hanlon was a few months later when *New Scientist* published as its cover story a long (fifteen-page), impassioned negative article on Geller[28] (which was timed for release on the *day before* our *Nature* publication). The long article was put together by Hanlon on the basis of the interviews he had had with those who had seen or worked with Geller. On the one hand, we felt betrayed, given Hanlon's expressed purpose for the SRI visit; on the other hand, we felt he had a right to express his opinion.

As we scanned the issue, it looked at first glance like a reasonable effort on the part of a member of the Loyal Opposition to place in perspective some of the exaggerations in the press, which, especially in England, seemed bent on sensationalizing the whole area of the paranormal. ("We are hurt more by our would-be friends than by our enemies" is a popular saying among researchers in our field.)

The material discussed by Hanlon was anecdotal in nature, since Geller had not shown up for testing by the *New Scientist* panel. The descriptions therefore consisted primarily of what happened on this television show, what happened at that press conference, etc., written with a view of how Geller could have cheated here, gotten cues there, and so on.

From a scientific standpoint, of course, anecdotal material is not very helpful. If a researcher tried to use material obtained under uncontrolled conditions as proof of paranormal functioning, he would be considered derelict in his scientific responsibility. From the standpoint of a serious researcher or accurate journalist, that sword is double-edged. Anecdotal material, no matter how circumstantial, must be handled with the same caution and restraint with regard to *refuting* a phenomenon as with regard to *validating* it.

When we got to Hanlon's remarks on the SRI work, however, we began to realize that there might be more to the article than met the eye. The SRI work was substantially distorted, and in ways that were difficult to account for on the basis of simple skepticism.

To begin with, Hanlon repeated the *Time* version of the Lawrence-Hyman story, even though it had already been corrected in a previous issue of *New Scientist* itself,[29] and he had heard our rebuttal in person. (We could have shown him the videotapes of the Lawrence visit had he expressed any doubts about our version of the story.) But that was a minor point in comparison with what followed. The article went on to say that Puharich, or Geller's friend Shippi, had probably acted as a confederate in our picture-drawing experiments, even though Hanlon knew from our conversation that Puharich was in New York at the time of the tests, and we had discussed at length the elaborate precautions we had taken to prevent access to the target area by Shippi or any other potential confederate. In the article, he justified his allegation on the basis that Ed Mitchell (who also was not present at the Geller tests reported in *Nature*) told him that one problem in doing anything with Geller was that Shippi is generally underfoot (true). Hanlon altered this a bit to say that Shippi was underfoot at SRI *during the* Nature *tests* (false).

The denouement of the article, however, was an elaborate description of how Geller might have used a receiver implanted in his tooth (including a reproduction of Puharich's patent), *but with no mention of the fact that Hanlon knew that we had been aware of that possibility and had taken specific precautions against it*! He went on to say that shielded rooms are not perfect with regard to foiling radio transmission, but will permit electromagnetic radiation to penetrate at extremely high and extremely low frequencies. That is of course true, but clearly the implication of his long description was that we might not know it, *even though we had made our knowledge of this obvious in the very* Nature *paper he was criticizing* by publishing the frequency characteristics of the Faraday cage shield, showing the pass and stop bands! The security lay in the protocols, not the rooms, and Hanlon knew it. Geller could have had a mouth full of receivers and it wouldn't have helped him.*

We decided to confront the issue head-on. We were of course not at all interested in defending Geller with regard to what he does under uncontrolled conditions; we could, however, speak for what he did at SRI under the conditions we imposed. Our letter to the editor of *New Scientist* read in part, "In view of the above we take great exception to the allegations that we were heedless of these possibilities, and we consider such reporting to be a substantial and deliberate misrepresentation of the facts."

As the letters to the editor began to pour in, it became obvious that we were not the only ones who felt this way. Other labs and individuals found themselves in the same position.[30] One of the letters that did not get published, but which we have on file, was from Brendan O'Regan, now research director of the Institute of Noetic Sciences, the organization set up by Astronaut Mitchell to fund frontier research. In his letter, setting aside minor distortions, O'Regan cited no less than forty-two major errors in the *New Scientist* article that he was personally aware of.

As the dust has settled and time has passed, the article has become somewhat of an embarrassment in science reporting, even for members of the Loyal Opposition. Many of them excuse Hanlon's excesses with a shrug, and say simply, "Well, the passions and excitements of the time were high."

The real answer is, however, more involved than that. At first, we spun paranoid theories with Cold War overtones. Perhaps there really was a developing ESP gap as implied by the Ostrander-Schroeder book *Psychic Discoveries Behind the Iron Curtain.*[31] Perhaps United States efforts in the study of the paranormal were the target of a deliberate program of disinformation, with the press the unwitting accomplice.

---

* A New York City dentist who examined Geller in 1974 attested that Geller not only had no foreign objects implanted, but had had no prior dental restorations whatsoever. See *The Geller Papers*, Charles Panati, ed. (Boston: Houghton Mifflin Co., 1976), p. 18.

The Psychology of the Loyal Opposition

As titillating as such theories are, however, the deep-rooted distrust of apparent paranormal functioning precedes the Cold War struggle by at least a century. No, the opposition to even the possibility of paranormal functioning is probably more psychological than sociological.

Critics suggest that those inclined to accept the possibility of paranormal functioning do so more out of psychological need than out of sound observation, even maintaining that such individuals have a strong, almost religious, commitment to promote a belief structure that includes the possibility of paranormal functioning.

When we look more closely, however, we find that such statements apply more accurately to the hardened skeptic than to the parapsychological researcher. It is the skeptic, not the researcher, who is short on rigorous observation and long on theory. It is the hardened skeptic who betrays a strong emotional commitment to an a priori belief structure, being motivated as he is to go out of his way to criticize a field of research about which he has little firsthand data. Furthermore, in these days of gravitational waves, ELF propagation, and "quantum interconnectedness," the burden of proof with regard to excluding the possibility of paranormal functioning now lies with the skeptics.

A detailed study carried out under the direction of Dr. Leon Festinger of the New School for Social Research in New York City summarizes the dynamics of the more vehement members of the Loyal Opposition quite succinctly. The study, reported by Emenegger,[32] dealt in part with how a confirmed skeptic about some given phenomenon could be expected to respond to escalating proof that the phenomenon in question is, in fact, true. (In the study, the target phenomenon was the hypothesized existence of extraterrestrial intelligence rather than the hypothesized existence of paranormal functioning, but the principles are the same.) The sequence of responses given is for a "hard case," that is, one who does not change his opinion, regardless of the facts which confront him, and

178

of course not all members of the Loyal Opposition fall into this class by any means.

First, our apocryphal skeptic, upon hearing of a new report of paranormal functioning, will, according to Festinger, simply assert that it is not true. The individual involved is, it is asserted, gullible at best, perpetrating a hoax at worst. If pressed that the conditions are such that these interpretations are unlikely, our skeptic will react by quoting an authority, such as Hansel, who showed that even under conditions that seemed unlikely to permit error or fraud, there was always at least the possibility of such in principle; therefore the new data probably falls into this category and, as a result, cannot be considered definitive. Should it then be shown that the data as reported are apparently authoritative enough to withstand even this criticism, then our superskeptic must denigrate and dispose of this new authority directly (they are lying for some purpose, or it is an elaborate plot, etc.). Under this pressure, the skeptic will seek out those who think as he does, and seek to convince others that his original position was correct.

The evidence underlying this reasoning stems largely from the theory of cognitive dissonance.[33] If an event occurs that is compatible with one's belief structure or prior commitments, one feels happy and affirmed. If, on the other hand, events occur that run counter to the person's beliefs and commitments, he experiences cognitive dissonance and strives to reduce that dissonance. One way to reduce the dissonance is to deny the fact that the event in question actually occurred, constructing a plausible explanation for the apparent occurrence that is consistent with the primary belief. One must then bolster that explanation by seeking out the company of those who believe the same way, and by trying to convince others as well.

A case in point, almost classically textbook in nature, is provided by one of the staunchest members of the Loyal Opposition, Martin Gardner, author of *In the Name of Science*,[34] and staff writer for *Scientific American* ("Mathematical Games" column). He began with a long series of letters to various members of the SRI management, asserting that SRI was becoming a laughingstock because of our work, and culminated his efforts in a critical review of our ESP teaching machine (random target generator) project in his column.[35] In his eighth and final letter (this one to the director of SRI public relations), he made one last plea that Mr. Charles Anderson, president of SRI, should reconsider where his loyalty lay after reading the column.

Gardner's a priori belief structure is expressed best in his own words. His chapter on ESP research begins, "There is obviously an enormous irrational prejudice on the part of most American psychologists—much greater than in England, for example—against even the possibility of extrasensory mental power. It is a prejudice which I myself, to a certain degree, share."[35]

Gardner's first assumption upon hearing of possible success in the teaching machine project was that it was not true, and his early letters accuse SRI of suppressing the final report to NASA because our results were probably negative. ("An attempt to suppress the report because of its negative results would be far more damaging to SRI, from a public relations standpoint, than to allow its continued distribution.")

In fact, the results were not negative, and we were endeavoring to publish them. Six of the 147 volunteer subjects had learning performances significant at the 0.01 (odds of 100:1) level or better; the probability of this occurring by chance is less than 1 in 250. At the other extreme, no subject had a negative learning experience of equal significance. In our report, we took these findings to indicate that "there is evidence for paranormal functioning from our work with the ESP teaching machine." The evidence included our work with Elgin, who achieved scores significant at odds of better than 1,000,000:1.

Upon being confronted with the report that indicated that in fact positive results had been obtained, Gardner must then move to position two, that of constructing a plausible explanation, consistent with his primary belief, for the apparent occurrence of paranormal functioning. The explanation offered in his article is fraud on the part of subjects, who, he suggests, probably turned in the good runs and threw away the bad (impossible because of automatic recording on the continuous fanfold paper tape). The movement into position three, the need to convince others, speaks for itself with the publication of his article.

As stated in our letter of rebuttal to *Scientific American*:

> Gardner's major criticism of the experiments is based on an error in fact, namely his misconception of the manner in which data were collected. Subjects made runs of 25 trials. These trials were automatically printed on continuous fanfold paper tape, which carries a permanent record of every trial, machine state, and trial number from 1 to 25 for each run. After a series of eight to ten runs, the subject would bring the continuous fanfold tape to one of the experimenters for entry into the experimental log. The tapes were always delivered to us intact with all runs recorded. They were never torn into "disconnected bits and pieces" as Gardner asserts (implying that an individual could, post hoc, select which runs he turned in). Since we were interested in evidence of learning within each day's session, it was of particular importance to us to have the complete intact tape.[36]

In response to this, Gardner says simply that someone told him that the tapes were turned in in bits and pieces. So we have a major U.S. science publication presumably exposing the inadequacies of a major research effort on the basis of a piece of erroneous hearsay, anonymously authored!

Of course, the greatest disappointment to researchers like ourselves is not that a Gardner or anyone else would write a negative article per se, but that few members of the Loyal Opposition are really up to the task of significant scientific criticism. After all, the accepted scientific approach is the carrying out of experiments, the analysis of data, and the reporting of results. What we looked for in Gardner's criticism was perhaps a discussion of a scientifically controlled effort at replication with negative results, or at least an independent analysis of statistics (he had all the data) which in principle might be capable of showing error. Instead, we were disappointed to find the usual misstatement of experimental protocols, allegations of fraud and incompetence, etc. Thus Gardner fell back on the "believerism" approach, the taking of a position on the basis of an a priori belief, in this case a belief in the nonexistence of paranormal functioning. All this is not very encouraging to researchers like ourselves who dream of a world in which observations count, not belief structure.

Extreme Members of the Loyal Opposition

On the far extreme of the Loyal Opposition are those who do not even pretend to maintain a stance of objectivity with regard to the possibility of paranormal functioning. These are individuals who, by and large, earn their livelihood playing the role of Professional Skeptic. They are usually not a serious factor as far as the scientific issues are concerned, but their potential for spreading misinformation among the public is inordinately large. This is due in part to the fact that they are not burdened with the necessity of spending long hours of experimentation in the laboratory to decide an issue on the basis of observation. The basic issues are already settled in their mind, so their energies can be turned almost entirely toward espousing their views before the public, on talk shows and in books and articles. It is this relatively easy access to the media which often makes their position appear quite strong to an uninformed public.

An individual in this category who has been making the rounds denigrating Uri Geller and his claims to the paranormal is a magician who calls himself the Amazing Randi. In his recent book, *The Magic of Uri Geller*, and on talk shows, Randi purports to explain how it is all done by trickery. His knowledge of the art of magicianship stands him in good stead, and indeed he performs a valuable service in demonstrating to those unfamiliar with the art of conjuring how chicanery can be used to duplicate effects often taken to be paranormal by an unsuspecting observer.

To observe a good magician creating effects under conditions he controls can be quite an education on the limitations of the powers of observation. The only conclusion that can be reached, and a correct one it is, is that essentially anything can be done by a magician *if the conditions are under his control.*

Now of course it is a logical fallacy to say that *if* it could have been done by magic, it *was* done by magic. Nonetheless, the only appropriate attitude in a case like this is "buyer beware."

So far, so good. Where the reasoning of a Randi goes awry is the generalization to a laboratory situation where the conditions are under the control of the experimenters. The difficulty with a Randi lies in the fact that his guesses as to how a particular experiment in the laboratory was foiled by trickery are made with great authority, find their way to print, and finally become part of the public lore. And all this, even though the particular hypothesis put forward might have been anticipated and countermeasured from the beginning. What could have been dialog has now become polemic. As Randi expressed to me in a letter recently, "I've been told that you are very 'hard-nosed.' Dr. Puthoff, you don't know noses until you've known mine."

Two examples from Randi's book and our fact-sheet rebuttal will illustrate the problem.

RANDI: And finally, as if there were not enough doubts about the procedure used to conduct this "test" [die-in-the-box test], *Time*'s Wilhelm has reported that the set of tries with the die actually consisted of MANY HUNDREDS OF THROWS, the object being to get a run of consecutive wins.

FACT: There was no selection of a good run out of "hundreds of throws." There were ten throws only, as reported in the *Nature* paper, eight of which were correctly guessed by Geller, two of which were passed. All throws were reported.

RANDI: Few of the Geller experiments, especially the famous tests at SRI in which Geller performed apparent miracles of ESP, include in their reports the fact that one Shippi Strang was present. [This is followed by descriptions of how Shippi might have acted as a confederate.]

FACT: During the SRI experimentation, neither Shippi nor any other potential confederate was permitted in the target area, a precondition for experimentation adopted on the basis of advice by project consulting magicians.

And so on. When pressed in a KPFA radio interview with regard to Shippi's alleged presence to say either we were lying, or else admit that in fact he didn't know what happened at SRI in this regard, Randi admitted he didn't know.

As bad as such misinformation is with regard to muddying up the issues in the public, as researchers we are in fact encouraged when we read Randi's book, or listen to his arguments on talk shows, for we find that Randi, in his efforts to fault the SRI experiments with Geller, is in every instance driven to hypothesize the existence of a loophole condition that did not in fact exist.

The way one can assess for oneself what is fact and what is fantasy is simply by tracing to its source any statement which, on the face of it, sounds unlikely. Example (a true one): One reads a review in *Scientific American* by a respected scientist, Philip Morrison.[37] The review is of a book written by a magician, the Amazing Randi, which purports to indicate that ESP experiments carried out at a major research laboratory, SRI, were flawed because a confederate passed the answer to the subject through a hole in the wall while the experimenters were watching. Even for a hardened skeptic, such a statement sounds unlikely. One looks in the book, where he finds a reference to a statement made by science reporter Joe Hanlon in a *New Scientist* magazine article. In the article, one finds the statement that Shippi, friend and companion to subject Geller, was underfoot at SRI during the *Nature* series of tests. The statement is ascribed to one of the project sponsors, Ed Mitchell. One contacts Mitchell, only to find that the statement was a generality taken out of context, not at all meant to apply to the series of controlled experiments in question. The mystery is solved! A general statement, which is true, is altered and expanded into an article, picked up and expanded into a book, and finally given the stamp of scientific respectability by a positive review in a semitechnical publication. And nowhere on the track could the train of runaway skepticism be braked.

I summed up our position in a letter to Randi this way:

... To give you more perspective on our work with Geller, I should point out some additional salient points. First, when we were contacted to investigate Geller's abilities, rather than being naive with regard to the possibility of chicanery, quite the opposite was the case. Since we had a lot at stake with regard to a program that had already been going on for some time in this area on a low profile basis, we were concerned that he might be a highly trained magician being sent by potential sponsors of our work to try to crack our protocols. Therefore, before we began our work with him we talked to people from Israel who had observed him, looked over Puharich's latest work, consulted with magicians, etc., resulting in our emphasis on strict protocols, multiple surveillance techniques, etc. In particular, we were encouraged to see that in your book in every case you hypothesized a loophole condition that did not in fact exist, simply because we thought of the same possibilities *before* experimentation (along with others requiring more technology) and were thus able to take appropriate safeguard measures. What perhaps you don't appreciate is that we are more highly motivated than anyone to ensure that we don't waste the next ten years of our lives writing equations for phenomena that don't exist. Given the lack of viable alternative hypotheses under the conditions we instituted, we continue to stand by our modest and very measured response with regard to Geller's abilities; the nature of honesty in scientific work is that what is observed, and the conditions under which it was observed, should be reported no matter how unpopular it might be. . . .

Concerning our work with Geller, I am of course not at all interested in defending him with regard to what he does under uncontrolled conditions; I can only speak for what he did at SRI under conditions we imposed. From our published work and interviews it should be clear that, rather than providing a blanket endorsement *or* condemnation of Geller's abilities, we simply found him unable to perform satisfactorily in some areas of claimed abilities (e.g., metal bending), but possessing some ability in an area that is not unusual in the field of so-called paranormal functioning, picture drawing (see enclosed paper)[38] or Upton Sinclair's book *Mental Radio* with foreword by Einstein.[39] . . . We shall, of course, continue to be interested in entertaining any further hypotheses you and others might have with regard to how Geller might have cheated. However, although Geller has become a "cause célèbre" for you, his interaction with us constitutes only 3 percent of our overall program effort in so-called paranormal functioning, and, therefore, in the absence of viable criticism applicable to the conditions under which we investigated his abilities, we shall continue to go forward with other research in this field which is of far more interest. . . .

> (signed)
> H. E. Puthoff, Ph.D.
> Electronics and Bioengineering Lab.

Who Cares About the Loyal Opposition?

And what is the response of the subjects to all this criticism? In general, they take it in good stride for the simple reason that they have a unique advantage over their critics—*they* know they didn't cheat. Confident in their abilities, they look on those who criticize their efforts as would a sighted person in the land of the blind. With a mixture of compassion and frustration, they listen with incredulity to the arguments that it's impossible, and that if some can do it, why can't everybody? In fact, gifted individuals sometimes feel that it is *they* who are the effect of some giant hoax, having committed a social faux pas in admitting to seeing the emperor without his clothes. When the heat is truly hot and heavy, they will remark, with a trace of bitterness, that it is at least some consolation to know that those who are the most critical will be the last to develop their own paranormal abilities. It is a hollow victory, though, for it reminds them of the gulf that separates them from many of their contemporaries.

In the last analysis, what can be said with regard to accusations of fraud and incompetence that are hurled at researchers who find evidence in the laboratory for paranormal functioning? Is it simply that in each generation a new researcher must take his place on the stage and deliver again the speech of Sir William Crookes?

> Will not my critics give me credit for some amount of common sense? Do they not imagine that the obvious precautions, which occur to them as soon as they sit down to pick holes in my experiments, have occurred to me also in the course of my prolonged and patient investigation? The answer to this, as to all other objections is, prove it to be an error, by showing where the error lies, or if a trick, by showing how the trick is performed. Try the experiment fully and fairly. If then fraud be found, expose it; if it be a truth, proclaim it. This is the only scientific procedure, and it is that I propose steadily to pursue.[40]

As eloquent as the above may be, the answer to the spurious accusations of fraud and incompetence (as opposed to legitimate scientific criticism) must lie elsewhere, for until paranormal functioning is an integral part of our world view, the accusations will continue, and it is clear that the eloquence of neither the detractors nor the defenders is capable of resolving the controversy. No, the eventual rejection of the accusations will come not from the researchers, but rather from a new quarter, an informed and sophisticated public, aided by the press, who by and large deal fairly with this area of research.

Paranormal functioning is a sensitive and controversial topic. The facts of the matter are very subtle and complex. Every piece of false data places an obstacle in the way of nurturing such functioning by an individual who must overcome each and every piece of false data on a one-by-one basis as he struggles up through the layers of mass conditioning in his efforts to be an autonomous human being. That is the reason it behooves all who would comment on this field, researcher and critic alike, to take care with their every statement to avoid betraying the public trust. We take this edict to be one of the most serious requirements of our work.

9
THE PEACEFUL
USE OF
PSYCHIC ENERGY

To any person prepared to enter with respect into the realm of his great and universal ignorance, the secrets of being will eventually unfold, and they will do so in a measure according to his freedom from natural and indoctrinated shame in respect of their revelation.

In the face of the strong and indeed violent social pressure against it, few people have been prepared to take this simple and satisfying course towards sanity.

—G. Spencer Brown, *Laws of Form*

In this chapter we expand beyond the boundaries of our scientifically verified statistical data into the psychological and sociological realms of personal and interpersonal experience. Though often anecdotal in nature, such experiences should not, in our estimation, be discounted out of hand. As imprecise as they may be, as described to us by subjects and others, they are often straightforward extrapolations of abilities that *have* withstood the rigors of laboratory investigation. Personal anecdotal experience therefore provides a useful benchmark to define the boundaries and limitations of the paranormal spectrum.

In our laboratory experiments, the evidence showing that a person in the proper frame of mind can perceive and experience events distant in both space and time continues to mount. The observable situation is perhaps summarized most easily in terms that our colleague Pat Price used. In a phrase, Pat considered himself to be "potentially omniscient in space and time." And we are forced by our data to conclude that such a statement is not as great an exaggeration as it might seem.

The remote connection being described is not necessarily limited to the passive perception of remote scenes, however. Magnetometer studies also indicate that a person can interact with a remote physical system toward which he has his attention directed. This suggests a continuum of paranormal interaction—a continuum ranging from the relatively passive remote viewing mode at one end of the spectrum to the other extreme, where one not only views a remote system, but interacts with it physically as well.

For example, when Swann or Price "put their attention" on the remote magnetometer, the instrument gave evidence of their act. Apparently this is yet another example of a principle that pervades many disciplines, as with the Heisenberg Uncertainty Principle in physics, or the Hawthorne Effect in sociology. The principle states that a phenomenon or system is in some way perturbed by the act of observing it.

The easiest and least involving paranormal activity is apparently simple remote viewing. In this process, a person focuses on a person or place in order to gather information. Technically, this generalized form of ESP would, in standard nomenclature, be considered a mixture of telepathy and clairvoyance. As mentioned earlier, we have never encountered a person who couldn't perform to some degree satisfactory to himself once he has agreed that he was willing to do so. Furthermore, in the course of over a hundred such experiments, none of our subjects has ever had a "bad experience" as a result of remote viewing of the type we have been describing.

The next step along the continuum is the so-called out-of-body experience (OOBE), surveyed in a number of books ranging from the classic Sylvan Muldoon treatise *The Case for Astral Projection*[1] to the detailed descriptions that Robert A. Monroe provides in *Journeys Out of the Body*.[2] Monroe and other practitioners of the

OOBE would seem to get more out of their experiences, subjectively, than those involved in simple remote viewing, perhaps because they put more into it.

In Monroe's technique, for example, which involves launching from the platform of sleep, a seemingly more profound separation of body and consciousness is made than in remote viewing. In remote viewing, a person may be smoking a cigar or drinking a cup of coffee while accurately describing a scene. His consciousness and body cannot be said to be separated from each other any more than are a spectator's when he is focused on a play. Individuals like Monroe, on the other hand, have seemingly made a greater commitment to the experience in terms of overall attention. They take with them to the remote place their perceptions, their emotionality, and their sexuality.

In an OOBE, it is not uncommon for the person being visited to be reminded of, or in some other way to experience, the presence of the traveler, which brings us to our third step along the continuum: the possibility that the person or system at the destination may register the presence of the traveler. We do not know, of course, if this is a "simple telepathic" contact, or if it is some physical manifestation. Whatever it is, it can be a quite profound subjective experience for the individuals involved, as in the following example from a paper in the *Proceedings of the Society for Psychical Research* in London:

Mr. S. R. Wilmot, a manufacturer of Bridgeport, Connecticut, sailed on October 3rd, 1863, from Liverpool for New York, on the steamer *City of Limerick*, of the Inman line, Captain Jones commanding. The night following a severe nine-day storm he had the first refreshing sleep since leaving port. "Toward morning I dreamed that I saw my wife, whom I had left in the United States, come to the door of my stateroom, clad in her nightdress," he reports. "At the door she seemed to discover that I was not the only occupant of the room, hesitated a little, then advanced to my side, stooped down and kissed me, and after gently caressing me for a few moments, quietly withdrew.

"Upon waking I was surprised to see my fellow-passenger, whose berth was above mine, but not directly over it—owing to the fact that our room was at the stern of the vessel—leaning upon his elbow, and looking fixedly at me. 'You're a pretty fellow,' said he at length, 'to have a lady come and visit you in this way.' I pressed him for an explanation, which he at first declined to give, but at length related what he had seen while wide-awake, lying in his berth. It exactly corresponded with my dream."

This gentleman was William J. Tait, a sedate fifty-year-old man who was not in the habit of practical joking. From the testimony of Mr. Wilmot's sister, Miss Eliza E. Wilmot, who was also on board ship, he was impressed by what he had seen. She says: "In regard to my brother's strange experience on our homeward voyage in the *Limerick*, I remember Mr. Tait's asking me one morning (when assisting me to the breakfast table, for the cyclone was raging fearfully) if I had been in last night to see my brother; and my astonishment at the question, as he shared the same stateroom. At my, 'No, why?' he said he saw *some* woman, in white, who went up to my brother." Miss Wilmot said her brother then told her of his dream.

Mr. Wilmot continues: "The day after landing I went by rail to Watertown, Connecticut, where my children and my wife had been for some time, visiting her parents. Almost her first question when we were alone together was, 'Did you receive a visit from me a week ago Tuesday?' 'A visit from you?' said I. 'We were more than a thousand miles at sea.' 'I know it,' she replied, 'but it seemed to me that I visited you.' 'It would be impossible,' said I. 'Tell me what makes you think so.'"

His wife then told him that on account of the severity of the weather she had been extremely anxious about him. On the night in question she had lain awake for a long time thinking of him, and about four o'clock in the morning it seemed to her that she went out to seek him. Crossing the wide and stormy sea, she came at length to a low, black steamship, whose side she went up, and then descending into the cabin, passed through it to the stern until she came to his stateroom.

"Tell me," she said, "do they ever have staterooms like the one I saw, where the upper berth extends further back than the under one? A man was in the upper berth, looking right at me, and for a moment I was afraid to go in, but soon I went up to the side of your berth, bent down and kissed you, and embraced you, and then went away."

The description given by Mrs. Wilmot of the steamship was correct in all particulars, though she had never seen it. Mrs. Wilmot states that she thinks she told her mother the next morning about her dream; and "I know that I had a very vivid sense all day of having visited my husband; the impression was so strong that I felt unusually happy and refreshed, to my surprise."[3]

Although the story is anecdotal, there is in fact rigorous laboratory evidence that travelers are detected at the destination. In a series of cleverly designed experiments at the Psychical Research Foundation in Durham, North Carolina, a cat was used to detect the presence of its owner during research on out-of-body experience.[4] The cat was placed on a large grid system which provided an objective measure of its activity (number of boundary crossings per unit time). The experiment was carried out in a double-blind fashion so that no cues, subliminal or otherwise, were available to the cat. It was found that the animal became very inactive during the time intervals corresponding to the OOBE visits of its owner, and the experiment was statistically significant at odds of better than 100:1.

Again, it is difficult to separate an alleged out-of-body experience from some other form of psi experience such as telepathy. Indeed, with regard to certain criteria such distinctions are recognized as being arbitrary and untestable. As one subject put it to us, "As I sit here and talk to you, I am having one of my rare *in*-the-body experiences."

After subjects first suggested that it was possible to interact with a distant person, we became increasingly aware that there was an abundance of references to such experiences in the literature. There appear to be as many descriptions of the phenomenon as there are people to ask.

Where the experiences have been of a sexual nature, there are strong indications that these were more than simple fantasy or dreaming. In several cases it has been possible to obtain independent verification from both parties. Monroe describes such an encounter with another free spirit during the course of an out-of-the-body flight:

> Here is the closest possible analogy to the second state experience [of sexuality] of which physical sexuality is merely a shadow. If opposite charged poles of electrostatics could "feel," as the unlike ends approach one another, they would "need" to come together. There is no barrier that can restrain it. The need increases progressively with nearness. At a given point of nearness the need is compelling; very close, it is all encompassing; beyond a given point of nearness the attraction-need exerts a tremendous pull and the two unlikes rush together and envelop one another. In the immediate moment there is a mind (soul?)-shaking interflow of electrons, one to the other, unbalanced charges become equalized. Balance is restored and each is revitalized.

Mackinlay Kantor wrote a popular novel, *Don't Touch Me*, with this subject as its theme.[5] Kantor, who flew with the Air Corps in World War II, told the story of a couple who were separated during the war. The man, a pilot, would periodically visit his stateside sweetheart, who resisted these disembodied, yet physical visitations. Her problem was that her ghostly lover would sometimes catch her driving to work, or at other inopportune moments.

As we have become aware of this type of remote physical interaction, we have been shocked, not by its apparent existence, but rather by the great number of people who believe themselves to have had such experiences.

The preceding descriptions, ranging from simple viewing to more intense interaction, represent a consensus derived from interviews with a number of otherwise respectable, intelligent, clear-thinking people. Because of the personal nature of such experiences, it is difficult in principle to determine whether such assertions are in fact true. We therefore must offer these not as hard data, but only as anecdotal evidence for what appears to be a profound and perhaps archetypal experience. Like much of the material in this book (for which we *do* present hard evidence), we are aware that this data will be found difficult to believe in some quarters. Fortunately, *belief* does not seem to be a necessary prerequisite for *experiencing* the phenomena, and we feel we have provided enough information to allow one to be a participant, should he so desire. The question of the existence of remote viewing or of remote interaction phenomena can therefore become a matter of observation, rather than belief. And it can be fun.

Although fun and profit are undoubtedly among the most powerful elements that motivate lives, the profit motive is the one that has seemingly eluded the individual who tries to make use of his paranormal abilities to make a killing in the stock market, or win at the casino. There are strong indications that this also is changing.

From what has been said previously about the nonanalytic nature of psychic functioning, it would seem that only under the most unusual conditions could a gifted psychic walk into a casino and accurately predict which of the thirty-six numbers is going to come up next; neither would we expect him to accurately guess which stock was going to go up in the next day's trading at the stock exchange. However, there is evidence that he can fool his psychic ability into giving him the information he needs to be successful in such ventures.

As discussed in an earlier chapter, it is possible in principle to amplify a small amount of psychic ability into a usable result by repeating the message over and over, in which case the noise washes out and the signal emerges, as in the computer processing of signals from space probes. The details of the technique, which is a very general one, have been published by the authors.[6] Casino exploits have, in fact, stood up to scientific investigation and have resulted in published papers.

In the spring of 1970, a pair of articles were published in the *Journal of Parapsychology*,[7] a scholarly journal devoted to studies in the general field of psychic research that is published quarterly by the Foundation for Research on the Nature of Man. The articles—"Psi Application, Part I—A Preliminary Attempt" and "Psi Application, Part II—The Majority Vote Technique— Analysis and Observations"—described a successful strategy for casino gambling using paranormal techniques. The authors were an ideal pair to be working on applications of psychic functioning to casino gambling. Robert Brier is a scholar, philosopher of science, and well-known psychical researcher, while Walter Tyminski is president of Rouge et Noir, a corporation that publishes and disseminates information relevant to the world of casino gaming.

Survival

Pleasure and profit are apparently not the only, or even the primary, motivating factors in eliciting paranormal functioning, however. An examination of spontaneous cases shows that the common denominator is *survival*. It is primarily in life-threatening situations that exceptional spontaneous paranormal functioning seems to occur, alongside exceptional strength and courage.

During a recent discussion of these matters with a visiting government scientist who was familiar with our work, he related the following incident to us. He had gone to a senior official to discuss our work, and the latter interrupted to say, "If you had come in here with that story a couple of years ago, I would have thrown you out. But something has happened in my own house since then.

"Some time back we had a son in Vietnam who was a helicopter mechanic. One night my wife sat bolt upright in bed and said, 'Oh, my God, our son has been shot down in a helicopter flight behind enemy lines!' I tried to calm her down, telling her that our son was a repair mechanic and never went on missions, so there was no way that he could have been involved in a helicopter crash under those circumstances. I told her she had just had a bad dream. She was not easily convinced, but finally my logic won out. Not long after that we received a letter from our son which was full of the usual news, but there was no mention of any helicopter crash, so that pretty well settled it for both of us.

"After our son returned to the States, I happened to mention his mother's bad dream, and I thought he was going to fall right over on the spot. It turned out that just such an event had occurred. One night his buddies had invited him along on a mission, saying there wasn't any chance of combat where they were going. Unfortunately, they were spotted, their helicopter was disabled by enemy fire, and they crashed behind enemy lines. Fortunately, no one was hurt, and they all made it back safely that night through the jungle on foot. Since our son was not supposed to have been on that mission, the crew agreed among themselves not to tell anyone. We worked out the date and time, and as close as we could tell, it corresponded pretty well with the time of my wife's dream. So what can I say—maybe there is something to it after all."

A number of people have related similar stories to us, many of which we have been able to verify.

Survival events involving paranormal functioning are not always so dramatic, and also not as clear-cut. Probably everyone has experienced what may be a more mundane form which is often not thought to be paranormal because it can always be rationalized away. Following is one such example that involved one of the authors (R.T.) and our colleague David Hurt who works with us on many experimental projects. On this particular occasion, David provided Russell with an object lesson in "sympathetic magic," which he had never encountered before. Russell explains:

"Shortly before my wife and I moved to our present house, David brought us a Tarot card and a drawing recently shown to him by a neighbor. The previous night, the neighbors, a husband and wife, had been meditating on the meaning of a Tarot card as some people do on a summer evening in northern California. About ten o'clock their seven-year-old came into the living room from a distant part of the house with a crayon drawing. The drawing happened to be an excellent rendition of the card called the Tower, which was the one that the parents had been studying for the previous several minutes. The drawing had a brown tower, with an orange sun and blue water. It would have been matched by any of the judges in our experiments, and the parents were shocked by what their child had done. Knowing of David's interest in such things, they brought the card and drawing to his house, and told him the whole story. Of course, we know that all of the above is anecdotal and would never stand up in a court of psychic law, but the balance of the story involves witnesses who can still be produced.

"The next day David brought the Tower card and the drawing to my house so that I could see the remarkable resemblance. I looked at them and was also struck by the good match. I remember that David told me that the parents had been drawn to the Tarot as a means of achieving a better relationship with each other, and there were emotional overtones to the episode. My reaction to the incident, which occurred in the midst of our work with Uri Geller, was that it looked like a case of simple telepathy of the sort that we see in the laboratory every day. I thanked David very much for the card and drawing and put them away somewhere.

"About a year later, the mother of the child who drew the picture decided that one of the most meaningful things in her life at that moment was that drawing, and she would like to have it back. David delivered this message to me. I searched the entire house thoroughly with no luck—no drawing, no card. Since we had moved our household in the meantime, I didn't hold out much promise for finding them.

"That was not a satisfactory result for David, to whom these now precious relics had been entrusted.

"One Sunday night about midnight (the hour when David does his best work) he arrived at my house. He explained that we were going to find the card NOW by using sympathetic magic, and I would find it all very simple.

"Once upstairs, he showed me a complete deck of Tarot cards exactly like the one containing the card I had lost. The purpose of the exercise was for me to locate the Tower card in the new deck and use it to locate the missing identical card. It was to be like searching for a resonance with a tuning fork. I went through the new deck and quickly located the Tower card. But when David told me that I was to use this card to find the other I replied that I was just too tired to try any ESP experiments at such a late hour. I put the cards together, and put them back into their box. At that moment I suddenly knew where to look for the missing card! The two of us tumbled downstairs from the loft in which we had been working.

"I headed for my wife's desk where she has a basket of special papers that are too important to throw out and too old to look at. With great excitement I dumped everything out on the dining room table, and shuffled through the papers. No card was there.

"As I looked across the room to where the basket had been, I saw a remaining sheet of paper folded in thirds, standing on edge. The paper had been held on edge between the basket and a stack of books. In the paper was the missing card and the drawing!

"My impression is that I had not seen the card since I had moved into the new house. There is no doubt that David's sympathetic magic achieved exactly the purpose he had intended. I realized I would never know if the adventure was one of remote viewing or something more mundane, such as stimulated subliminal recall."

Sometimes the drive for survival can take on humorous overtones. The following case of applied ESP does not admit to any such handwaving dismissal as stimulated subliminal recall, for it is one involving completely nonverbal and what would appear to be psychic communication. Russell's account is as follows:

"We have a large, attractive mixed breed cat named Mushroom. She has luxurious long fur, which is a uniform beige in color, hence the name. We call her Mush for short.

"For some unknown reason, this affectionate cat began to piddle on the living room rug, instead of outdoors as was her usual custom since she was a kitten. As time went on, she became more and more bold and would even urinate with the whole family in the room. Needless to say, such activity was vigorously discouraged. A whole research program was mounted to try to find a way to get the damn cat to quit peeing in the house. Nothing succeeded.

"Finally my wife and I decided that the cat had to go. Joan called the animal shelter, and arranged to have the cat received, and probably "put to sleep" the next afternoon. On the morning of the appointed day, Joan spied the cat curled up on a chair sleeping in the morning sun. She wished that she could find a way to tell the cat that it was really important that she mend her ways. But at that point it was too late; only a miracle could save her. However, with one's life hanging in the balance, miracles are seemingly not so hard to come by.

"As the children were dressing for school, we heard a shout of excitement. Joan and I came to see what the commotion was about. The source of the wonderment was the cat, who was standing on the toilet seat, urinating into the toilet.

"One can only conclude that she got the message.

"Six months have gone by and she has never gone back to her old life-threatening ways. It is interesting to note that even if she had happened to go outdoors on that fateful morning, that would not have saved her. It required something really momentous."

Now if all the peaceful uses of psychic energy were limited to personal experiences of this type, paranormal functioning would be more of a personal art form than a technology. However, there apparently are no such limitations.

Executive ESP

One area where paranormal functioning has found practical application has been in the decision-making area of business. Although it usually passes under the guise of intuition and hunch, many businessmen are now publicly admitting that it goes beyond that.

A case in point is provided by the remarkable December, 1974, issue of *Psychic* magazine.[8] Having been frustrated by the number of stories that people in high places will confide on a one-to-one basis, but do not generally make public, editor and publisher James Bolen went with his associate publisher David Hammond to a number of executives armed with "Will you tell if he does?" Eventually a number of executives agreed to be candid. The result was an issue devoted to interviews of, among others, Alexander M. Poniatoff, founder and chairman of the board, emeritus, of Ampex Corporation; William W. Keeler, recently retired board chairman of Phillips Petroleum; John L. Tishman, board member and executive vice-president of Tishman Realty and Construction; John E. Fetzer, chairman of Fetzer Broadcasting Company and owner of the Detroit Tigers; and Eleanor Friede, editor-publisher whose intuition led to the publication of best sellers *Jonathan Livingston Seagull* and *You Can Profit from a Monetary Crisis*. The theme of the interviews was to determine the role of hunch, intuition, and ESP as factors in decision-making.

On the face of it, it would be difficult to draw a line between the usual interpretation of intuition as unconscious processing of known data versus an interpretation which would include the integration of paranormal inputs. Fortunately, however, the paranormal interpretation of "Executive ESP" has been put to the test under rigorous conditions, as described in a book of the same name.[9] In studies of corporation presidents attending business conferences, John Mihalasky and E. Douglas Dean of the Newark College of Engineering, New Jersey, found statistically significant correlations between profits over a five-year period and the ability of the executives to score above chance in a 100-number precognition experiment. Perhaps the executives' own views on ESP are more telling. In questionnaires handed out at the conferences, the ratio of those corporation presidents who considered ESP to be a fact to those who felt otherwise was typically in the range of three-to-one to five-to-one, well above the national average of the 53 percent belief in ESP reported in a recent Roper poll, a belief which is strongly correlated with increasing levels of education and income.[10]

Indeed, the attitude among many businessmen is typified by a remark made to me by a corporation president as I described some of our latest laboratory results to him. "You know, when I bring up your work to my friends on the golf links, they just say, 'It's about time those scientists caught up!' " It would seem that perhaps the existence of ESP may simply be one of the better-kept secrets in our culture.

Futurist Prediction

The laboratory observations of precognition discussed in Chapter 6 indicate the possibility of the prediction of future economic, social, and political trends by a process of analysis, extrapolation, and psychic integration in which the lines between "normal" and "paranormal" become blurred and indistinct. In this case, the goal is the important thing; and hair-splitting as to which components may be paranormal becomes of little interest.

When Ingo Swann was in residence at SRI, he and Dr. Willis W. Harman of SRI's Educational Policy Research Center evolved a pilot study of this nature. The center is deeply involved in Futurist trend-prediction studies based on more conventional analysis techniques, and Dr. Harman was curious as to whether there was any potential contribution to be made by paranormal predictive techniques.

Therefore, in May, 1973, it was agreed that Ingo and two other similarly gifted individuals would independently address those areas of societal concern indicated by Dr. Harman as being of pressing interest. The goal was to determine if it was possible to obtain a consensus as to which of the many possible futures would be most likely to occur.

Dr. Harman's challenge, which he incorporated in a memo to Ingo and the other two subjects, read as follows:

> Present trends (expanding technology, increasing affluence, increasing urbanization, automation and cybernation of white-collar work, lengthening lifespan and earlier retirement age) continue to increase the severity of assorted societal problems— depletion of natural resources, particularly minerals and fossil fuels; impact of growing energy demands on the environment (strip mining, air pollution, radioactive waste, etc.); technological disemployment, unemployment, and underemployment; growing welfare and social security load; increasing technological impact on the environment, rights of privacy and liberty, quality of life. Increased costs of producing goods and services, arising partly from labor demands for higher real income and improved working environment, and partly from environmentalist, consumer, and civil rights pressures for greater corporate responsibility, are reducing the relative com-

petitiveness of American industry. Possible consequences of this may include further automation and cybernation, leading to further disemployment, and further exodus of multinational production to other countries. The scramble for resources, and the increasing gap between have and have-not nations, made more visible by worldwide communications, will continue to threaten world peace.

In view of these factors, what is likely to be the state of the nation and of the world with regard to unemployment, welfare costs, economic and monetary crises, role of multinational corporations, environmental and ecological crises, perceived legitimacy of business and governmental institutions, citizen morale and sense of national purpose, etc., in 1975? In 1980? In 1985? In 1990?

What actions or significant events might alter these predictions, and in what way?

It looked like a tall order, even for one omniscient in time and space! The three attacked the problem with gusto, although cautioning that their attempt at prediction should be considered only as a research endeavor.

All participants indicated that it was extremely difficult emotionally as well as psychically to involve their sensitivities in the direction of prophecy suggested by the guidelines because of the apparent negative characteristics of the immediate future. One participant indicated that he had not wanted to see and feel what came to him, and another experienced similar apprehension. The third felt overwhelmed at his view of the swift negative changes he perceived.

The protocol was such that the participants did not discuss the guidelines among themselves prior to submitting their renderings, and did not have the opportunity to compare notes. Nonetheless, their results were essentially the same.

First, the participants decided that "the major concern would revolve around economic considerations and disappointments." In fact, a major economic slump was seen in the immediate future, beginning in the fall of 1973, and becoming worse in 1974. (This was in May–July, 1973.) It was also indicated that "prior to 1975 several government institutions will come under increasing governmental attack."

The 1975–1980 period was seen as "characterized by neo-spiritual and parapsychological as well as new energy developments." It was also seen as "characterized by politico/religious restructuring which cannot be without repercussions on all strata of society. The vast change will sponsor dramatic emergences of personalities who will tend to lead masses in different directions both in personal as well as in social awareness. Behind the scenes, this socio/religio manifestation will be utilized by various political and economic interests to curtail or influence popular thought." Nonetheless, individuals would emerge "who possess a potential for a new kind of practical spiritual and yet non-religious leadership to which the masses can respond and thus help stabilize their emotions in a time of great crisis." At the same time, however, "religion, as man has known it . . . and dogmatism and structure are on the way out."

Although the guidelines asked for prophetic responses beyond 1980, it was increasingly difficult for the participants to use their sensitivities concretely beyond 1985. One participant indicated that it seemed to him as if a split in society was to occur, "like a giving up of all technology and a returning to nature in one segment, and a highly structured scientific space age in the other." Another participant felt that "around 1985 something would happen in relation to human potential that would bring current concepts of man to an end." For those interested in the details, the entire report is reproduced in Swann's book detailing his participation in paranormal research, *To Kiss Earth Goodbye*.[11]

The important part of this study probably was not what was found, but simply that it was tried. The material itself is of course extremely difficult if not impossible to evaluate. Should even a major part of the predictions turn out to be accurate, it would be difficult to determine what percentage was essentially enlightened extrapolation from known factors, and what percentage could be laid to paranormal functioning; and the participants would be the first to agree with this. Nonetheless, we should keep in mind that this was a pilot effort, and future research is bound to uncover additional knowledge. Such discovery can be expected to lead to an increased understanding of how to discriminate between the true and the false in predictive paranormal functioning. Since by any standard of Futurist trend prediction we are entering a time of survival-threatening acceleration, we cannot afford to ignore the possibility that paranormal functioning may have something to contribute to the survival of humankind.

Medical Diagnosis

Another potentially useful application of enhanced paranormal capacity is in the area of medical diagnosis, and perhaps healing as well. With regard to diagnosis, a number of excellent examples are given in Dr. Shafica Karagulla's book *Breakthrough to Creativity*.[12] Dr. Karagulla received her early education at the American University of Beirut, Lebanon, receiving her degree of Doctor of Medicine and Surgery from the medical school of this university in 1940. She then traveled to Edinburgh, Scotland, to obtain her training in psychiatry under the well-known psychiatrist Professor Sir David K. Henderson, at the Royal Edinburgh Hospital for Mental and Nervous Disorders. In 1950 she passed the examination to become a member of the Royal College of Physicians of Edinburgh, the highest medical qualification in Britain. She crossed the Atlantic in 1952 to Canada to study the effect of electrical stimulation to the brain of conscious patients during neurosurgery. At this time, she worked as consultant psychiatrist in association with the world-famous neurosurgeon Dr. Wilder Penfield at McGill University. She then came to the United States in 1956, and in 1957 she became assistant professor at the State University of New York, in the Department of Psychiatry. Just after being offered an associate professorship at another medical school, she read of the work of Edgar Cayce, famed for his psychic diagnosis, and began exploring the medical evidence for such phenomena on a rigorous basis.

The technique employed by Dr. Karagulla was to have her subject, a person apparently gifted in psychic diagnosis, accompany her to a waiting room of a medical center. There the subject was asked to diagnose a patient selected at random by Dr. Karagulla. The patient's condition at that time was not known to either of them. After obtaining from her subject the information needed, Dr. Karagulla would then check the medical records to make a comparison.

Day after day, correct and detailed medical diagnoses were rendered. Following is an example taken from Dr. Karagulla's records.

One of the early cases was a patient with Paget's disease. Neither Diane nor myself knew anything about the patient's condition at the time we made the observations. I simply selected one of the patients sitting in the waiting room a little over twelve feet away from us. Diane's report on the patient, as was customary, included a description of the general energy body, the vortices of force and then the actual physical condition. . . .

When she observed [clairvoyantly] the physical body of the patient she said that the thyroid appeared "dead looking." Quite a bit of it was not there. The energy of the parathyroids was "flickering," and she was sure the person had a disease of the parathyroids. The trouble was more on the right side than the left. When she looked at the patient's head, the skull on the right side, which I identified as the parietal region, appeared thinned out. The same characteristic showed to a less extent at the back of the head. As she looked at the rest of the body, the bones of the legs and spine looked "crummy" to her. She explained that normal bones looked harder and thicker. She came back to the right side of the head, somewhat puzzled to explain what she saw. She said, "Not enough bone is present. It does not seem to be complete. It is thinner and granular."

She found the liver slow in function and the adrenals were working too fast. The right kidney was hardly functioning at all and had the same "crummy stuff" in it. She described the left kidney as functioning only fairly well, and it seemed to have some kind of "soft stones" in it. She saw the same "crummy stuff" in the wall of the gut, and she said that the intestines were slow in their function.

The medical report on this patient gave Paget's disease as the clinical diagnosis. X rays showed thinness of the skull on the right side of the parietal region and at the back of the head. Part of the thyroid had been removed and the right parathyroid. The left parathyroid was still present. The right kidney was hardly functioning at all, and the X rays indicated what appeared to be stones in the left kidney. There was a mass the size of a fist in the colon. The patient complained of general weakness and pain in the bones of the spine and legs. Diane's observations, although they were in layman's language, correlated very accurately with the medical diagnosis.[13]

Dr. Karagulla is continuing to investigate what she prefers to call "higher sense perception" in a Beverly Hills research foundation, of which she is president and director of research. Her view of individuals with developed paranormal abilities is that, from a clinical viewpoint, they should be classified as "supersane."

The Exploration of Space

Perhaps one of the most exciting possibilities, and one that we had a chance to observe, is the application of remote viewing to the exploration of space. As far-fetched as this may seem, we have excellent statistical data that this phenomenon works around the globe, so that the possibility of extending its functioning to regions away from the earth cannot be discounted.

On the other hand, we have to admit that when Ingo Swann proposed such a study we resisted for the simple reason that, as a laboratory experiment, the resulting descriptions would by and large be impossible to verify, and those that we could verify by available data would not constitute proof of anything. Unlike our earthbound experiments, we were not likely to send a panel of judges to the target destination for some time.

Ingo held his ground, however, indicating that he and the noted sensitive Harold Sherman, of Mountain View, Arkansas, had already arranged to remote view Jupiter before the upcoming Pioneer 10 flyby in the hopes that they might beat supertechnology to some discovery. We compromised and agreed to record the experiment at SRI as a personal exercise and not an official project. Although we could already hear the arguments that would be raised by those observing our every step, we were nonetheless curious. We had confidence in Ingo's ability, at least over short range, on the basis of our laboratory experiments; Sherman was well known for his experiments in which he targeted on the Arctic explorer Sir Hubert Wilkins at the North Pole, an experiment the two of them set up in advance and carefully documented throughout.[14]

It was arranged that Ingo and the authors would meet at the lab on the night of April 27, 1973. Ingo began his probe at 6:00 P.M Pacific Standard Time, and it had been agreed previously that Sherman would carry out his probe simultaneously (8:00 P.M. Central Standard Time) in Mountain View, Arkansas.

The transcript began:

No big sharp noises for the next half hour, please.

6:03:25 [three seconds fast] There's a planet with stripes.

6:04:13 I hope it's Jupiter.

I think that it must have an extremely large hydrogen mantle. If a space probe made contact with that, it would be maybe 80,000–120,000 miles out from the planet surface.

6:06 So I'm approaching it on the tangent where I can see it's a half moon; in other words, half lit, half dark. If I move around to the lit side, it's distinctly yellow to the right.

6:06:20 Very high in the atmosphere there are crystals—they glitter—maybe the stripes are like bands of crystals, maybe like rings of Saturn, though not far out like that; very close within the atmosphere. I bet you they'll reflect radio probes. Is that possible if you had a cloud of crystals that were assaulted by different radio waves? [That's right: H.P.]

6:08:00 Now I'll go down through. It feels really good there [laughs].

> Inside those cloud layers, those crystal layers, they look beautiful from the outside—from the inside they look like roiling gas clouds—eerie yellow light, rainbows.
>
> 6:10:20 I get the impression . . .

And so it went for a half hour. What we heard was certainly aesthetic, in addition to being intriguing. Perhaps along with scientists we should send artists in our ordinary nuts and bolts spacecrafts. Sherman's description was quite similar to that of Swann, as can be seen in the table below.

Sherman	**Swann**
1. Atmosphere:	
. . . gases, giving off a golden glow and crystal-like diamond sparkles.	. . . there are crystals—they glitter—maybe the stripes are like bands of crystals . . .
. . . giving off a golden glow . . .	. . . distinctly yellow . . .
It is a gaseous mass of myriad colors—yellow, red, ultraviolet, some greens—like a giant fireworks display.	Inside those cloud layers . . . they look beautiful from the outside—from the inside they look like roiling gas clouds—eerie yellow light, rainbows.
The enormous cloud cover . . .	Then I came through the cloud cover . . .
The enormous cloud cover must be miles deep.	The atmosphere of Jupiter is very thick.
2. Surface:	
. . . a reddish-brown formation extending in a curved line as far as my mind's eye can see.	. . . the horizon looks orangish or rose-colored . . . the whole thing seems enormously flat.

There appear to be huge volcanic peaks, great cones rising some miles . . .

There is an enormous mountain range about thirty-one thousand feet high . . . those mountains are huge.

It looks almost metallic—molten and sparks red-hot.

. . . the surface of Jupiter will give a high infrared count.

3. Other surface characteristics:

. . . ice crystals . . . I am wondering if they are not icy cold.

. . . a band of crystals . . . kind of bluish. It's colder here . . .

. . . swirling vortices of increasing velocity . . .

I see something that looks like a tornado.

. . . powerful magnetic forces . . .

I seem to be stuck, not moving.

. . . winds of terrific velocity . . .

Tremendous winds . . .

There must be water.

I feel that there is liquid somewhere . . . liquid, like water.

The atmosphere seems unusually dense on some levels and extremely rarified on others.

. . . in the atmosphere are crystals . . . they'll reflect radio probes . . . another layer farther down like our clouds.

The descriptions sounded reasonable; nothing was particularly at variance with any known facts. Of course, from a strictly scientific viewpoint it was not definitive either. However, we knew that would be the case so our expectations were not in that direction, and we valued the experience for what it was: an opportunity to explore the subjective factors involved in an extension of a phenomenon we were confident of to an uncharted new realm.

A further problem in comparing the above results with those provided by the Pioneer 10 flyby was that the NASA probe was not instrumented to bring back the visual detail provided by our more ethereal travelers. In post-experiment discussions with astronomers, the consensus was that the results of our experiment were not at odds with either what was already known or what additional data were radioed back by the flyby, but no definitive evaluation could be made either. We considered that to be a satisfactory result for the level of effort the observation was intended to be.

A year later, after Swann had returned to New York, he and Sherman carried out a similar experiment to probe Mercury before the Mariner 10 flyby. This experiment provided a better opportunity for verifying the remote viewing in an objective way, since less was known about Mercury than about Jupiter beforehand. The experiment was carried out on the evening of March 11, 1974, 9:00 P.M. Eastern Standard Time, with Swann in New York and Sherman in Arkansas viewing simultaneously. The experiment was monitored and recorded by Janet Mitchell, a parapsychologist at the American Society for Psychical Research and research associate to Dr. Gertrude Schmeidler at City College of New York. The impressions were recorded, transcribed, notarized, and deposited by noon March 13 with various interested parties, including the Central Premonitions Registry in New York.

The responses in this case, recorded in detail in Swann's book, contained several pieces of data later verified by the Mariner 10 probe and that were contrary to the predictions of the astronomers. These included observation of a thin atmosphere, the existence of a small magnetic field, and the existence of a helium tail streaming out from Mercury in a direction away from the sun, shaped by the magnetic field.

Again, from a strictly scientific standpoint, one could argue that even though these features were essentially unexpected by scientists, a layman might reasonably guess that they were there on the basis of uninformed extrapolation from what is known about other planets. Nonetheless, the results were again intriguing, and in this case the results couldn't be attributed to prior knowledge gained from reading. Further, once a given subject has provided excellent results in local remote viewing experiments, there is resistance to rejecting these more speculative results without cause, regardless of what critics may say. In any case, the experiment had moved in the direction of greater objectivity and has therefore provided additional incentive for future, even better-controlled, experimentation along these lines. Perhaps we have seen human evolution come full circle whereby explorations of outer space and inner space come together.

The Cultural Reemergence of Man's Psychic Nature

Like gravity and other natural phenomena, the phenomenon we have been rediscovering and exploring in the laboratory has been around since the dawn of humankind's recorded search. And this in spite of what the self-styled arbiters of the local culture might say.

When man first began modeling the universe around him, paranormal functioning was gracefully accepted as one of the phenomena to be accounted for, and therefore occupied an important place in religion and philosophy. However, as models of the universe were built to explain certain mechanical aspects of our environment, the phenomenon of paranormal functioning was found difficult to assimilate into the mainstream exploration. It therefore became suspect, a symbol of the anxiety humankind felt about the inadequacy of its model-building efforts. The tension culminated in the materialistically oriented concepts of early mechanistic science whose claim to fame was its apparent independence from subjective factors.

Now that our modern scientific paradigm has strong roots in our culture, and it is recognized that the inclusion of observable subjective factors will not result in the destruction of all that has been gained, it would appear that the model-builders of our time are secure enough to begin confronting again this important part of the observable universe, paranormal functioning. Rather than seeing such a shift as a sign of regression to primitive concepts, we see it rather as a sign that science has matured.

Perhaps our place in the universe is now secure enough that we can begin to take another look at a piece of ourselves that we have long attempted to ignore. Perhaps humankind has matured.

NOTES

PREFACE

1. H. E. Puthoff and R. Targ, "A Perceptual Channel for Information Transfer over Kilometer Distances: Historical Perspective and Recent Research," in *Proceedings of the IEEE*, LXIV (March, 1976), no. 3, 329–354.
2. R. Targ and H. E. Puthoff, "Information Transmission Under Conditions of Sensory Shielding," in *Nature*, CCLII (October, 1974), 602–607.

CHAPTER 1

1. T. S. Kuhn, *The Structure of Scientific Revolutions* (Chicago: University of Chicago Press, 1962).

CHAPTER 2

1. H. E. Puthoff, "Toward a Quantum Theory of Life Process," unpublished proposal (Stanford Research Institute, 1972).

2. E. P. Wigner, "The problem of measurement," in *American Journal of Physics*, XXXI (1963), no. 1, 6; E. H. Walker, "Foundations of paraphysical and parapsychological phenomena," *Proc. Conf. Quantum Physics and Parapsychology* (Geneva, Switzerland); (New York: Parapsychology Foundation, 1975); O. Costa de Beauregard, "Time symmetry and interpretation of quantum mechanics," *Foundations of Physics* (Lecture delivered at Boston Preprint Colloquium for Philosophy of Science, February, 1974).

3. K. Osis, *ASPR Newsletter* (1972), no. 14; J. Mitchell, "Out of the Body Vision," in *Psychic* (March/April, 1973).

4. B. Julesz, *Foundations of Cyclopean Perception* (Chicago: University of Chicago Press, 1971).

5. R. L. Morris, "An exact method for evaluating preferentially matched free-response material," in *J. Amer. Soc. Psychical Res.*, LXVI (October, 1972), 401.

6. H. E. Puthoff and R. Targ, "A Perceptual Channel for Information Transfer over Kilometer Distances: Historical Perspective and Recent Research," in *Proceedings of the IEEE*, LXIV (March, 1976), no. 3, 329–354.

7. I. Swann, *To Kiss Earth Goodbye* (New York: Hawthorn, 1975).

8. I. Swann, "Scientological Techniques: A Modern Paradigm for the Exploration of Consciousness and Psychic Integration," in *Proceedings of the First International Conference on Psychotronic Research* (Virginia: U.S. Joint Publications Research Service, September 6, 1974), Document No. JPRS L/5022-1.

9. M. Ryzl, "A model for parapsychological communication," in *J. Parapsychol.*, XXX (March, 1966), 18–31.

10. L. L. Vasiliev, *Experiments in Distant Influence* (New York: E. P. Dutton & Co., Inc., 1976).

11. I. M. Kogan, "Is telepathy possible?," in *Radio Eng.*, XXI (January, 1966), 75.
    I. M. Kogan, "Telepathy, hypotheses and observations," in *Radio Eng.*, XXII (January, 1967), 141.
    I. M. Kogan, "Information theory analysis of telepathic com-

munication experiments," in *Radio Eng.*, XXIII (March, 1968), 122.

I. M. Kogan, "The information theory aspect of telepathy," (California: Rand Publ., July, 1969), P-4145.

12. A. S. Presman, *Electromagnetic Fields and Life* (New York: Plenum, 1970).

Y. A. Kholodov, ed., *Influence of Magnetic Fields on Biological Objects* (Virginia: September 24, 1974), JPRS 63038, NTIS.

13. Y. A. Kholodov, "Investigation of the direct effect of magnetic fields on the central nervous system," in *Proc. 1st Conf. Psychotronic Res.* (September 6, 1974), JPRS L/5022-1 and 2.

14. D. Mennie, "Consumer electronics," in *IEEE Spectrum*, XII (March, 1975), 34–35.

15. W. P. Zinchenko, A. N. Leontiev, B. M. Lomov, and A. R. Luria, "Parapsychology: Fiction or Reality?," in *Questions of Philosophy*, IX (Moscow, 1973), 128–136.

CHAPTER 3

1. R. Targ and H. E. Puthoff, "Information Transfer under Conditions of Sensory Shielding," in *Nature*, CCLII, 602–607 (October 18, 1974).

2. H. E. Puthoff and R. Targ, "Physics, Entropy and Psychokinesis," in *Proc. Conf. Quantum Physics and Parapsychology* (Geneva, Switzerland); (New York: Parapsychology Foundation, 1975).

3. E. P. Wigner, "The problem of measurement," in *Amer. J. Phys.*, XXXI (1963), no. 1, 6.

4. E. H. Walker, "Foundations of paraphysical and parapsychological phenomena," in *Proc. Conf. Quantum Physics and Parapsychology* (Geneva, Switzerland); (New York: Parapsychology Foundation, 1975).

O. Costa de Beauregard, "Time symmetry and interpretation of quantum mechanics," in *Foundations of Physics* (Lecture delivered at Boston Colloquium for Philosophy of Science, February, 1974).

CHAPTER 4

1. W. Scherer, "Spontaneity as a factor in ESP," in *J. Amer. Soc. Psychical Res.*, XII (1948), 126–147.

2. Interview with Richard Bach, *Psychic* (October, 1974).

3. R. Ornstein, *The Nature of Human Consciousness* (San Francisco: Freeman, 1973), ch. 7 and 8.
R. W. Sperry, "Cerebral organization and behavior," in *Science*, CXXXIII (1961), 1749–1961.

CHAPTER 5

1. W. Pauli and C. G. Jung, eds., *The Interpretation of Nature and the Psyche* (Bollingen Ser. LI); (New Jersey: Princeton University Press, 1955).

2. H. E. Puthoff and R. Targ, "A Perceptual Channel for Information Transfer over Kilometer Distances; Historical Perspective and Recent Research," in *Proceedings of the IEEE*, LXIV (March, 1976), no. 3, 329–354.

3. B. Gal-or, "The Crisis About the Origin of Irreversibility and Time Anisotropy," in *Science* (April 7, 1972).

4. O. Costa de Beauregard, "Time symmetry and interpretation of quantum mechanics," in *Foundations of Physics* (Lecture delivered at Boston Colloquium for Philosophy of Science, February, 1974).

5. L. Rhine, *Hidden Channels of the Mind* (Clifton, N.J.: Sloane Associates, 1961).

6. S. G. Soal and F. Bateman, *Modern Experiments in Telepathy* (London, England: Faber and Faber, 1954).

7. Pauli and Jung, *The Interpretation of Nature and the Psyche*, (1955).

CHAPTER 6

1. C. Honorton, "State of awareness factors in psi activation," in *J. Amer. Soc. Psychical Res.*, LCVIII (1974), 246–257.
2. R. Targ and D. Hurt, "Learning Clairvoyance and Precognition with an ESP Teaching Machine," in *Parapsychology Review* (July–August, 1972) 9–11.
3. R. Targ, P. Cole, and H. E. Puthoff, "Techniques to Enhance Man/Machine Communication" (Stanford Research Institute, July, 1974), Final Report on NASA Project NAS 7-100.
4. R. Cavanna, ed., *Proc. Int. Conf. Methodology in PSI Research* (New York: Parapsychology Foundation, 1970).
5. E. D. Dean, "Plethysmograph recordings as ESP responses," in *Int. J. Neuropsychiatry*, II (September, 1966).
6. C. Tart, "Physiological correlates of psi cognition," in *Int. J. Parapsychol.* (1963), no. 4, vol. 5.
7. D. H. Lloyd, "Objective events in the brain correlating with psychic phenomena," in *New Horizons*, I (Summer, 1973), no. 2, 69–75.
8. R. Targ and H. E. Puthoff, "Information Transfer under Conditions of Sensory Shielding," in *Nature*, CCLII (October 18, 1974), 602–607; C. Rebert and T. Turner, "EEG Spectrum Analysis Techniques Applied to the Problem of Psi Phenomena," in *Physician's Drug Manual* (January–December, 1974), vol. 5, Numbers 9–12, vol. 6, Numbers 1–8, pp. 82–88.
9. J. Silverman and M. S. Buchsbaum, "Perceptual correlates of consciousness; A conceptual model and its technical implications for psi research," in *Psi Favorable States of Consciousness*, R. Cavanna, ed. (New York: Parapsychology Foundation, 1970), pp. 143–169.
10. J. Kamiya, "Comment to Silverman and Buchsbaum," *ibid.*, pp. 158–159.
11. D. Hill and G. Parr, *Electroencephalography. A Symposium on Its Various Aspects* (New York: Macmillan, 1963).

12. R. Targ and H. E. Puthoff, "Information Transfer under Conditions of Sensory Shielding," in *Nature*, CCLII (October 18, 1974), 602–607; C. Rebert and T. Turner, "EEG Spectrum Analysis Techniques Applied to the Problem of Psi Phenomena," in *Physician's Drug Manual* (January–December, 1974), vol. 5, Numbers 9–12, vol. 6, Numbers 1–8, pp. 82–88.
13. C. Tart, "Physiological correlates of psi cognition," in *Int. J. Parapsychol.* (1963), vol. 5, no. 4, 375–386.
14. D. H. Lloyd, "Objective events in the brain correlating with psychic phenomena," in *New Horizons*, I (Summer, 1973), no. 2.

CHAPTER 7

1. R. Targ and H. E. Puthoff, "Information transmission under conditions of sensory shielding," in *Nature*, CCLII (October, 1974), 602–607.
2. Upton Sinclair, *Mental Radio* (New York: Macmillan, 1971).
3. J. R. Musso and M. Granero, *Journal of Parapsychology* (March, 1973), vol. 37, 13–37.

CHAPTER 8

1. J. R. Smythies, ed., *Science and ESP* (London, England: Routledge, 1967).
2. C. Evans, "Parapsychology—What the questionnaire revealed," in *New Scientist* (January 25, 1973), 209.
3. C. E. M. Hansel, *ESP: A Scientific Evaluation* (New York: Scribners, 1966).
4. J. B. Rhine and J. G. Pratt, "A review of the Pearce-Pratt distance series of ESP tests," in *J. Parapsychol.*, XVIII (1954), 165–177.
5. J. G. Pratt and J. L. Woodruff, "Size of stimulus symbols in

extrasensory perception," in *J. Parapsychol.*, III (1939), 121–158.

6. S. G. Soal and F. Bateman, *Modern Experiments in Telepathy* (London, England: Faber and Faber, 1954).

7. S. G. Soal and H. T. Bowden, *The Mind Readers: Recent Experiments in Telepathy* (New Haven: Yale University Press, 1954).

8. C. E. M. Hansel, *ESP: A Scientific Evaluation* (New York: Scribners, 1966), p. 18.

9. C. Honorton, "Error some place!," *J. Commun.*, XXV (*Annenberg School of Commun.*: Winter, 1975), no. 1.

10. G. Stent, "Prematurity and Uniqueness in Scientific Discovery," in *Scientific American* (December, 1972), 84–93.

11. Editorial, "Scanning the Issue," in *Proceedings of the IEEE*, LXIV (March, 1976), no. 3, 291.

12. I. M. Kogan, "Information theory analysis of telepathic communication experiments," in *Radio Eng.*, XXIII (March, 1968), 122; M. A. Persinger, "The Paranormal P. II: Mechanisms and models" (New York: M.S.S. Information Corp., 1974).

13. H. E. Puthoff and R. Targ, "A Perceptual Channel for Information Transfer over Kilometer Distances: Historical Perspective and Recent Research," in *Proceedings of the IEEE*, LXIV (March, 1976), no. 3, 329–354.

14. E. P. Wigner, "The problem of measurement," in *Am. J. Physics*, XXXI (1963), no. 1, 6.

15. J. J. Freedman and J. F. Clauser, "Experimental test of local hidden variable theories," in *Phys. Rev. Letters*, XXVIII (April 3, 1972), no. 14, 938; J. F. Clauser and M. A. Horne, "Experimental consequences of objective local theories," in *Phys. Rev. D.*, X (July 15, 1974), no. 2, 526.

16. D. Bohm and B. Hiley, "On the intuitive understanding of non-locality as implied by quantum theory," Preprint (London, England: Birkbeck College, February, 1974).

17. J. S. Bell, "On the problem of hidden variables in quantum theory," in *Rev. Modern Physics*, XXXVIII (July, 1966), no. 3, 447.

18. H. Stapp, "Theory of reality" (Berkeley, California: University of California, April, 1975), Lawrence-Berkeley Laboratory Report No. LBL-3837.

19. A. Einstein, B. Podolsky, and N. Rosen, "Can quantum-mechanical description of physical reality be considered complete?," in *Phys. Rev.*, XLVII (May 15, 1935), 777; R. H. Dicke and J. P. Wittke, *Introduction to quantum mechanics* (Reading, Mass: Addison-Wesley Publishing Co., Inc., 1960), ch. 7.

20. E. H. Walker, "Foundations of paraphysical and parapsychological phenomena," in *Proc. Conf. on Quantum Physics and Parapsychology* (Geneva, Switzerland); (New York: Parapsychology Foundation, 1975); O. Costa de Beauregard, "Time symmetry and interpretation of quantum mechanics," in *Foundations of Physics* (Lecture delivered at Boston Colloquium for Philosophy of Science, February, 1974).

21. R. Targ and H. E. Puthoff, "Remote Viewing of Natural Targets," in *Proc. Conf. on Quantum Physics and Parapsychology* (Geneva, Switzerland); (New York: Parapsychology Foundation, 1975).

22. *Ibid.*

23. *Ibid.*

24. W. F. Prince, "Extra Sensory Perception," in *Scientific American* (July, 1934).

25. "The Magician and the Think Tank," in *Time* (March 12, 1973).

26. "Uri Geller and Science," Editorial, in *New Scientist* (November 29, 1973).

27. "Challenge to Scientists," Editorial, in *Nature*, CCXLVI (December 7, 1973).

28. "Uri Geller and Science," Ed. in *New Scientist* (October 17, 1974).

29. "Geller Experimenters Reply," Letters, in *New Scientist* (November 7, 1974).

30. See, for example, "The Geller Correspondence," in *New Scientist*, LXIV (October 31, 1974); Letters, *New Scientist* (November 7, 1974).

31. S. Ostrander and L. Schroeder, *Psychic Discoveries Behind the Iron Curtain* (Englewood Cliffs, N.J.: Prentice-Hall, 1970).
32. R. Emenegger, *UFO's Past, Present and Future* (New York: Ballantine Books, 1974).
33. L. Festinger, *A Theory of Cognitive Dissonance* (Evanston, Ill.: Row, Peterson, 1957).
34. M. Gardner, *In the Name of Science* (New York: G. P. Putnam's Sons, 1952).
35. M. Gardner, "Mathematical Games," *Scientific American* (October, 1975).
36. R. Targ and H. E. Puthoff, Letters, *Scientific American* (January, 1976).
37. P. Morrison, Book Reviews, *Scientific American* (February, 1976).
38. J. R. Musso and M. Granero, *J. Parapsychology* (1973), vol. 37, 13–37.
39. Upton Sinclair, *Mental Radio* (New York: Collier, 1971).
40. A. Gauld, *The Founders of Psychical Research* (New York: Schocken Books, 1968).

CHAPTER 9

1. S. Muldoon, *The Case for Astral Projection* (New Jersey: Wehman, 1969).
2. R. A. Monroe, *Journeys Out of the Body* (New York: Doubleday, 1971).
3. *Proceedings of the Society for Psychical Research* (London, 1891–92), vol. VII, p. 41.
4. R. L. Morris, "The Use of Detectors for Out-of-Body Experiences," *Research in Parapsychology 1973* (New Jersey: Scarecrow Press, 1974), p. 114; W. G. Roll, R. L. Morris, B. Harary, R. Wells, and J. Hartwell, "Further OOBE Experiments with a Cat as Detector," *Research in Parapsychology 1974* (New Jersey: Scarecrow Press, 1975), p. 55.
5. M. Kantor, *Don't Touch Me* (New York: Random House, 1951).

6. H. E. Puthoff and R. Targ, "A Perceptual Channel for Information Transfer Over Kilometer Distances: Historical Perspective and Recent Research," *Proceedings of the IEEE* (March, 1976), vol. 64, no. 3.

7. R. Brier and W. Tyminski, "PSI Application, Part I—A Preliminary Attempt," *Journal of Parapsychology* (1970); R. Brier and W. Tyminski, "PSI Application, Part II—The Majority Vote Technique—Analysis and Observations," *Journal of Parapsychology* (1970).

8. Editors of *Psychic*, "Executive ESP," *Psychic* (December, 1974).

9. L. Schroeder, *Executive ESP* (New York: Prentice-Hall, Inc., 1974).

10. Roper Poll, *National Enquirer* (November 26, 1974).

11. I. Swann, *To Kiss Earth Goodbye* (New York: Hawthorn, 1975, Delta, 1977).

12. S. Karagulla, *Breakthrough to Creativity* (California: DeVorss and Co., Inc., 1967).

13. *Ibid.*

14. Sir Hubert Wilkins and Harold M. Sherman, *Thoughts Through Space* (Greenwich, Connecticut: Fawcett Publications, Inc., 1973).

INDEX

Index

Laying on of hands, 136. *See also* Healing

Learners *see* Subjects

Learning, 129n

Lee, Martin, 20

Left hemisphere *see* Hemispheric specialization

Leningrad Institute for Brain Research, 43

Lloyd, D.H., 131, 133

Lodge, Oliver, 14, 139

"Lucky Day" hypothesis, 143

Lysenko, xvii

Madras Christian College (India), 171

Magic and magicians, xix, 139, 182–83, 185; general trick categories, 139–40; sympathetic, 198–99

Magic of Uri Geller, The (Randi), 182

Magnetometer: Geller's experiments with, 144–45; PK experiments with, 19, 20–25, 58–60, 144–45, 190

Maimonides Hospital (Brooklyn), 124

Mariner 10, 211

Mathematical physics, 107, 118

Mayo, Jean (Millay), 135, 152, 154

McGill University (Canada), 205

Medicine, 82; psychic diagnosis, 205–7

Memory, 129

Mental Radio (Sinclair), 160, 186

Mercury: remote viewing of, 211

Metal bending *see* Geller, Uri, *and* Psychokinesis (PK)

Microwaves, effects of, 44

Mihalasky, John, 201

Mitchell, Edgar, 138, 139, 145, 176, 177, 184

Mitchell, Janet, 211

Monroe, Robert A.: *Journeys Out of the Body*, 190–91, 194

Morris, Robert L., 37

Morrison, Philip, 184

Muldoon, Sylvan: *The Case for Astral Projection*, 190

Mundelein College (Chicago), 118n

Muratti, José, 162

Musso, J.R., 160–62

National Aeronautics and Space Administration (NASA), 210; forced-choice tests for, 129n; SRI study for, 180–81

National University of Rosario (Argentina), 160, 162

Nature (magazine), x, 48, 91, 152, 173, 174, 175, 176, 183, 184

Netherlands: view of psychic functioning in, 16

Neurophysiology, 120–21, 131, 134, 169

Neurosciences, x, 130

Newark College of Engineering (New Jersey), 130, 201

New Scientist (magazine), 167, 184; article on Geller, 174–77

News media, 172–77

Newton, Isaac, 17

O'Regan, Brendan, 177

Oregon, University of, 172

Ornstein, Robert, 102, 123

Ostrander, Sheila, 177

Outline of Science (Thomson), 13

Out-of-body experience (OOBE), 5–6, 90, 190–94; compared to remote viewing, 191; of a sexual nature, 194

Paget's disease, 206

Palo Alto Medical Clinic (California), 70

Panati, Charles: *The Geller Papers*, 177n

Paranormal perceptual phenomena: anecdotal evidence, 189–212; "decline effect," 11; defined, xi; executives' use of, 200–1; individuality of, 5; Ink Fish (Octopus) Effect, 6; interaction continuum of, 190–91; major categories of, 110; principal sources of error, 129; for profit, 195–96; related to physics, 16–17, 18–19,

226

Index

Soviet Union: paranormal research in, 43–45, 170

Space exploration, 43, 207–12

Stanford Research Institute (SRI) psychic research programs: brainwave studies, 130–33; demonstration experiments, 6–10, 88–90, 91; electronic random target generator, 124–30; free-response vs. forced-choice experiments, 124–30; Geller studies, 144–59; media distortion of, 171–88; methodology and protocols of, xv–xvi, xx, 6–10, 11–13, 30–31, 33, 34–35, 49, 50, 54–56, 74–76, 94–98, 111–14, 123–24, 144, 146, 149–54, 155–58; origins of, 18–34; precognition studies, 107–19, 201–5; primary achievement, ix; psychokinesis experiments, 20–25, 56–62, 144–50; remote viewing, 1–4, 11–14, 26–40, 63–68, 207–12; results summarized, ix–x; subject studies, 69–106; telepathy experiments, 150–58

State University of New York, 205

Stent, Gunther, 168–69

Stepanek, Pavel, 43

Stewart, Gloria, 167

Strang, Shippi, 137, 139, 152, 176, 183–84

Subjects, xv, 69–106; experienced, 70, 79–83; individual response patterns, 101; learners, 70, 73–79, 84–87, 104–6; medical profile on, 70, 71; neuropsychological profiles on, 70, 72; preparation of, 111, 124, 126; psychiatric tests, 70, 72; requirements for, 123–24; response to criticism, 186–88; right-mode functioning of, 123; unselected, 87–90

Subliminal recall, 199

Survival: paranormal functioning and, 196–200

Swann, Ingo, 1–4, 10, 19–34, 37–40, 47, 56, 69, 70, 73, 190; approach to research of, 40–43, 45; autobiography, 42; futurist project of, 202–5; PK experiments, 19, 20–25, 58; remote viewing experiments, 1–4, 26–34, 37–42, 80, 81, 83; remote viewing in space, 207–12; response patterns, 101

Synchronicity, 109, 119

Tait, William J., 192

Targ, Nicholas, 138, 142

Targ, Russell, xx, xxiii, 7, 26, 38–39, 63, 126, 197–200; dream theories, 107–9. *See also* Stanford Research Institute (SRI)

Tarot cards, 197–99

Tarrytown Conference, 108

Tart, Charles, 11, 90, 131, 133

Telepathy, 190, 194, 198; Argentine tests, 160–62; blood volume changes in, 130; defined, 110; frame of mind for, 162; Geller's abilities, 147, 150–56, 159; Sinclair's techniques, 160; Soviet research, 43–45. *See also* Paranormal perceptual phenomena

Tempter (Weiner), xvii

Texas Instruments SR-51 random number generator, 113

Thomson, J. Arthur: *Outline of Science*, 13–14

Time (magazine), 183; authors' experience with, 172–74, 176

Time irreversibility, 111, 118

Time spanning: spontaneous, 109–11, 119. *See also* Precognition

Tishman, John L., 200

Tishman Realty and Construction, 201

To Kiss Earth Goodbye (Swann), 42, 204

Turner, Ann, 131

Tyminski, Walter, 196

Ultrasonic visualization system: Geller's influence on, 145–46

U.S. Army, 60

USSR *see* Soviet Union

Van de Castle, Robert, 172–73

Varieties of Religious Experience, The (James), 120

229

Index

Vasiliev, L.L.: *Experiments in Distant Influence*, 43
Virginia, University of, 172

Walker, Evan Harris, 60
Walter, W. Grey, 130
Wiener, Norbert: *Tempter*, xvii
Wilhelm, John, 183

Wilkins, Hubert, 208
Wilmot, Eliza E., 192
Wilmot, S.R., 191–93

X rays, 145

You Can Profit from a Monetary Crisis (Browne), 201